Public Planet Books

A series edited by Dilip Gaonkar, Jane Kramer,
Benjamin Lee, and Michael Warner

Public Planet Books is a series designed by writers in and outside the
academy—writers working on what could be called narratives of public culture—to explore questions that urgently concern us all. It is
an attempt to open the scholarly discourse on contemporary public
culture, both local and international, and to illuminate that discourse
with the kinds of narrative that will challenge sophisticated readers,
make them think, and especially make them question. It is, most importantly, an experiment in strategies of discourse, combining report-
age and critical reflection on unfolding issues and events—one, we
hope, that will provide a running narrative of our societies at this particular fin de siècle. Public Planet Books is part of the Public Works
publication project of the Center for Transcultural Studies, which also
includes the journal *Public Culture* and the Public Worlds book series.

public planet books

Bilingual Aesthetics

A New Sentimental Education

Doris Sommer

DUKE UNIVERSITY PRESS   Durham and London 2004

© 2004 Duke University Press

All rights reserved

Printed in the United States of

America on acid-free paper ♾

Typeset by Tseng Information

Systems, Inc. in Berthold Bodoni

Library of Congress Cataloging-

in-Publication Data appear on the

last printed page of this book.

Contents

Thanks

Bilingual Aesthetics began as an adventure when a few graduate students and I designed a course and then took it. The
theme had been suggesting itself through studying a "rhetoric
of particularism," which issued in a book called *Proceed with
Caution, When Engaged by Minority Writing in the Americas.*
And though the sequel fixed on a specific range of gatekeeping tropes (to syncopate communication and to signal social
discontinuities), bilingual moves opened onto the broadest and
most thrilling range of inquiry we could imagine. I am grateful
to all my first collaborators for their fearlessness and stamina,
especially to José Luis Falconí, companion from beginning to
end, Miguel Segovia, and Joaquín Terrones, along with Carmen
Oquendo, Carolina Recio, Jane Almeida, Esther Whitfield, and
Wanda Rivera.

At the School for Criticism and Theory during the summer
of 2002, I graduated to a veritable United Nations of interlocutors interpellated by a call unfamiliar to aesthetics but commonplace in each of their fascinating lives. Josiane Peltier, for
example, writes about detective fiction in her native French
and elegant English when she is not reading in Spanish and
Chinese literatures; historian Olga Dror's original Russian and

acquired Hebrew added Vietnamese, Latin, and Chinese to study popular religion in Vietnam; Laura Ceia-Minjares reveals Tristan Tzara's private Romanian reveries between his public antics in French. I thank them and all the equally creative participants from Europe, Asia, and the Americas: Constance Anderson, John Barnes, Alexandra Chang, Tanya Gonzalez, Andres Lema-Hincapie, Krystyna Mazur, Marilyn Miller, Mario Moroni, Jeannine Murray-Roman, Cathrine Orkelbog, Hector Perez, Jason Phlaum, Alexander Regier, Carrie Sheffield, Paul Tenngart, Bonnie Wasserman, Yasemin Yildiz, and Gang Zhou. Mostly I thank Seyla Benhabib and Dominick La Capra for the opportunity to offer the seminar.

viii   The result of these explorations is a range of friendly provocations about the benefits of bilingualism. They will be selfevident to some readers, but others will prefer informed arguments. I could not have presumed to argue the points without the guidance, and blessings, of the experts. Many gave me detailed written comments with a generosity that I humbly acknowledge: Benedict Anderson, Peter Elbow, Juan Flores, Eugene Gendlin, Neil Herz, Ernesto Laclau, David Lloyd, Richard Rosa, Greta Slobin, Diana Sorensen, Henry Staten, David Suchoff, Diana Taylor, and Jay Winter. Other colleagues offered much needed general advice and support: Henry Abelove, Homi Bhabha, Judith Butler, Luis Carcamo Huechante, David Carrasco, Arnaldo Cruz Malavé, Roberto G. Fernández, Juan Gelpí, Sander Gilman, Stephen Greenblatt, David Theo Goldberg, Warren Goldfarb, Juan Carlos Godenzzi, Paul Guyer, Michael Holquist, Yunte Huang, Claudio Lomnitz, J. Lorand Matory, José Antonio Mazzotti, Sylvia Molloy, Alejandro Portes, Mary Louise Pratt, Rubén Ríos Avila, Marcelo Suárez-Orozco, Guadalupe Valdés, Kathryn Woolard, and Ana Celia Zentella. Also, my gratitude goes to the David Rockefeller Center for Latin American Studies at Harvard, which supported the writing process of this book. Throughout the writing, my most vigilant reader was Ken Wissoker, who knows that a light touch can carry weighty themes. To him and to all my instructors and companions, I offer my most heartfelt thanks.

Invitation

Come play bilingual games with me. Maybe you already play them, either actively or just by listening for surprises as one language interrupts another. In that case, the invitation is to think together about why the games are good for you and good for the country. For both veteran and rookie players, time out can go toward reflection about what we win. If you haven't yet been wondering about the ways that bilingualism can improve a range of private and public moves—in aesthetics, politics, and philosophy (not to mention business and commerce)—let's take some time out together. What if I said that an extra language, beyond a coordinating lingua franca, promotes personal development, fair procedure, and effective education, while one-way assimilation derails progress on all counts? Would you be curious about the arguments and perhaps willing to change your mind if bilingualism had seemed irrelevant or even damaging? I hope you are willing, and I offer this book as an invitation to consider the cultural conditions for fair and fulfilling contemporary life.

This book is about added value, not about remediation. More than one language is a supplement, not a deficiency. It is a dangerous supplement to monolingualism, whether the addition amounts to two languages or to many. Bilingualism over-loads mono systems, and multilingualism does it more. But in principle bi- and multilingualism make similar mischief with meaning. The underlying goal of thinking about these over-loads as intellectual, artistic, and ethical enhancements will be to open public debates beyond the failing standard of monolingual assimilation. Throughout the following chapters I address the enhancements in the most theoretically sophisticated terms I can muster, but in plain language. Partly the gambit is to demonstrate that theory is practically second nature to bilinguals, who normally abstract expression from meaning, and partly the range of refinements that follow from the "open sesame" of bilingual readings means to persuade some readers that bilingualism is intellectually advantageous. Others will know that already.

Whether or not you have much of a second language yet, the opportunities to play bilingual games are hard to miss. Now that mass migrations take home languages to host settings, the sound of alternative languages interrupts the single standard that modern states had demanded and thereby refreshes regional variants that modernity had banished.[1] Even embarrassing mistakes shouldn't stop you. Most of us make them and they're part of bilingual fun. Mistakes can brighten speech with a rise of laughter (a *sun-risa*)[2] or give the pleasure of a found poem. Always, they mark communication with a cut or a tear that comes close to producing an aesthetic effect. The risk and thrill of speaking or writing anything can sting, every time language fails us. But don't imagine that other more dignified language games are more important. Because knowing how language can fail makes success feel like a small miracle.

Bilingualism, you can already tell, is serious fun, because democracy depends on constructing those miraculous and precarious points of contact from mismatches among codes and peoples. If there were no mismatches, if contact were easy, democracy might cramp from lack of exercise. The exercise needs an almost tragicomic taste for the interrupted communication that requires humility and that begs debate and negotiation. Part of bilingual gamesmanship is to train a predisposition toward feeling funny, or on edge, about language, the way that artists, activists, and philosophers are on edge about familiar or conventional uses.

Can we count on good trainers of an edgy sense of play? No. Not yet, or not enough. My invitation to play bilingual games holds out a hope that you might also consider coaching a taste for edginess. It is modest work, compared to the challenges of world peace, or economic justice, or national security. But today these serious goals require enabling yet unfamiliar predispositions toward doubt and irritation. One incentive to do the training is simply that the work is available to many of us, unlike other interventions that require, say, technical training or economic power. The coaching work might attract administrators, managers, civil servants, lawyers, counselors. But it practically beckons to teachers of literary arts and other performance media whose jobs include fine-tuning the senses to appreciate the small miracles of human creativity.

The kind of aesthetic education of hearts and minds that will promote democracy develops through free play, even some embarrassing antics. Abraham Lincoln, for one, wasn't worried about playing the fool once in a while. Instead he worried about people who refused to lighten up.[3] Lincoln knew that jokes interrupt single-minded zeal and intolerance. Expanding our sense of humor can make us better citizens. Seriously, folks. When imperfectly learned languages play jokes with you by unhinging meaning from intention, don't writhe with embarrassment. Most of the time, you're not even the butt of the joke but only a participant observer who can join the laughter if you choose to. In language games, as in other contact sports, a good sport means one who loses gracefully. Losing also helps to learn the (philosophical, political, aesthetic) lesson: language, including your own, plays hit-and-miss games with the world. This lesson was the centerpiece of the modern university designed by Wilhelm von Humboldt, because "in the study of foreign tongues students best learned the humility that comes from never forgetting . . . to negotiate the otherness of the world."[4]

Learning to anticipate the interruptions and the mistakes that make you feel funny leads to wariness about what you say, and what you hear. And wariness is a reminder that linguistic constructions, including politics, are precarious arrangements in need of periodic adjustment. Thoughtful people also know this in one language, but living in more than one refreshes that sense of caution and responsibility with each missed communication. When freshness is the goal of the game, it's hard to know who are the more privileged players. The poor can play as well as the rich, because bilingual games often level the ground with moves of inclusion and exclusion that don't depend on power. Educated monolinguals may maneuver among more linguistic registers than unschooled counterparts, but even illiterate bilinguals can slip from one language to another to circumvent power and win points. So bilingualism is good for a democratic country, for reasons beyond the obvious economic and security advantages. No kidding.

Think about the challenges to democratic society in times of globalization. Both industrial and developing nations are adjusting to the internal pressures of mass migrations and to the external constraints of international agencies and networks (everything from courts and banks to terrorist grids). The most obvious challenges are probably to balance political processes between national cohesion and personal rights, and to educate people in ways that make the most of personal opportunities without making a mess of social conditions. Maybe you already intuit the benefits of your existing or potential bilingualism and can use the book to back up the position. If, on the other hand, you're not curious enough to hear and to heed arguments, the inertia may itself be a symptom of the debilitating mono system of language and culture. We inherited that single-minded system from an early and outmoded project for national consolidation.

In today's readjustments to global dynamics, mono is a malady of adolescent societies. The world has outgrown a one-to-one identity between a language and a people. Individual people have also added one identity to another in ways that strain against the very concept of identity. Growing pains can't be avoided in the process of maturing toward tolerance for complicated times. How can we avoid pain, while people and languages rub and irritate one another? But surely there are ways to mitigate the danger of irritation and even derive pleasure from the rub. One way is to recognize multiplicity as a medicine for the monolithic condition, instead of dismissing multilingualism as confusion and then wondering how we lost the ability to listen to reason. The point is not to "disidentify" as some theorists prescribe in order to mitigate identity politics and patriotic violence.[5] It is to supplement one identity with others. Human beings are normally complex rather than seamless abstractions. Should we try to purge conflicting identities, as Charles Taylor urges?[6] The very effort would vilify parts of the self and breed the self-hatred that purging claims to cure. If, instead, we learned to tolerate the normally melancholic overload of language and identity, we would train ourselves toward a humane acknowledgment of a world haunted by damaging efforts to cleanse and to conquer.

English as the shared language of the United States is an

indisputable anchor for U.S. civil society, but citizens should know at least one more language (not the same one, please, or we'll sound redundant and predictable) to put English here, and other hegemonic languages elsewhere, on edge and push or pull the anchor toward some wiggle room. Being on edge sharpens the wits, flexes democratic systems, and generally goads creativity. This is obvious to many bilinguals (and to African American code switchers).[7] Monolinguals may not see the advantage if they don't feel the effects. Why, they can ask, would anyone want to make English nervous and play games that risk rights and resources?[8] Better to be efficient and call *el pan pan, y el agua agua.*

Efficiency is the sticking point for most debates about language in the United States: which policies promote English language learning and which are wasteful. The main concern is education, though legal rights come in second place. Aesthetic and intellectual stimulation have hardly mattered yet. What's the best (most cost-effective and quickest) way to integrate immigrants into the rights and obligations they came to exercise? The easy (efficient) answer is to teach them Standard English (or American, if you have real attitude about foreignness).[9] Significantly, business theorists are far more likely to appreciate the creativity that comes from thinking in diverse codes than are policy makers.[10] English-only immersion programs follow from facile, not innovative, answers, since they save the trouble and the money "misspent" on bilingual education. The money does worse than waste resources and keep immigrants ignorant of English, on this view. It panders to divisive ethnic pride and unravels the nation.[11]

One popular defense of bilingual education plays on the same theme of efficiency, maybe to convince fiscal conservatives in their own rational terms but also to register that immigrants come to this land of economic opportunity to make good on the "American dream." They want to learn English in order to maximize their prospects. But learning is a process, so saving money on multilingual programs looks irrational and inefficient to many immigrants and to their friends. Effective assimilation, they say, is a gradual transfer from one language/culture to another. It finally costs more to throw immigrants (few swim) into immersion programs than to train them to use new strokes.[12] Maladjusted "foreigners" drop out of school, drain welfare budgets, and make worse trouble. The cold turkey cure is inefficient and mean, critics say. It's also an embarrassment to democracy when "live free or die" (I'm writing this from New Hampshire) sounds like a fair choice.

Another bid for bilingualism downplays efficiency and promotes "richness." Many languages represent social capital, is the argument. Bilingual programs create value, not as scaffolding to get immigrants into English, but through maintenance and development of our diverse social stock. Two-way programs do in fact double the advantages for both natives and newcomers. Diversification (varying stock is a sounder strategy than concentration) can venture some long-term risks and resist the narrower rationality of efficient transition. But even this defense of cultural difference as a source of diverse values and perspectives stays stuck in market (or is it ecological/romantic?) metaphors. Lose a language, and you've impoverished the world, because each language constitutes a distinct "psyche of a people." The argument can fail to convince even the friends of bilingualism, let alone skeptics who know how to abstract a single translatable value from the variety. Let me mention one example of this Herderian axiom about different strokes for different folks in order to illustrate a range of examples that, paradoxically, follow the same broad strokes. Speakers of Lakota object to a "thingness" about English because it allegedly reifies spiritual meanings into objects. The "sweat house," for example, is a wooden translation for a mystical ceremony called *iníkagapi* ("with it they make life").[13] But the contrast between sacred Lakota and secular English is bogus. It ignores the heated mystical tradition in Standard English, where, for instance, communion means much more than wafer eating. The Lakota case shows only that one tradition doesn't easily understand another. More significantly for me, the case performs a cultural/political *desire* to value a particular language for its inherent qualities. Difference becomes content (thingness?) rather than the effect of opacity for outsiders and satisfaction for insiders.

Differential effects are what matter. (Wittgenstein joked quite seriously that the essence of language was grammar, relation, not the things language can point to.)[14] This is close to a recent conclusion that contrasting grammars of social relationships between East and West issue in different ways of thinking.[15] Even if I can say the same thing or idea in more than one language, switching from one to another performs points of entry or exclusion, and it sets off different sounds-like associations or etymological echoes.[16] These are asymmetrical effects to reckon with. The days of the one ideal reader or education have been numbered and spent in our segmented societies. A "target audience" can mean the target of exclusion or confusion. And feeling the unpleasant effect is one valid way of getting the point, or the kick, of a language game. "The more he dwelt on the humiliating episode, the less humiliating it appeared to him," muses the émigré translator in Zinovy Zinik's story. "The humiliation itself, paradoxically, was the only exciting aspect of his otherwise innocuous past existence in South London." " 'I should have bought them a round,' Victor would repeat to himself each time he recalled the episode, restless and lonely in his North London bed."[17]

Even more basic than these hide-and-seek games is the fact

that overloaded systems unsettle meaning. When more than one word points to a familiar thing, the excess shows that no one word can own or be that thing. Several contending words point, each imperfectly. Even a proper noun like Hamlet is game for competition.[18] Of course Hamlet worried enough about precarious arrangements (without code switching) to be an inviting target. "Whenever you were reduced to look up something in the English version (of the Russian *Gamlet*)," Nabokov's Pnin complains, "you never found this or that beautiful, noble, sonorous line that you remembered all your life . . . Sad!"[19] Words are not proper and don't stay put. They wander into adjacent language fields, get lost in translation, pick up tics from foreign interference, and so can't quite mean what they say. Teaching bilinguals about deconstruction is almost redundant. ("Big dill!," Pnin might have said.)[20]

Meanness about bilingualism, therefore, damages more than immigrant transfers to the promised land, though that is bad enough. It is harmful to use bilingual education for language replacement, and worse to cancel the programs that do it gently.[21] Worse still is the emotional stinginess of one particular language that cringes to hear others. But much worse even than these (arguably transitional) offenses is the civic and intellectual rigidity that meanness makes possible. Stingy defenses of monolingualism don't hold the country together. Instead, they rend immigrant children from parents who don't speak English and then wonder why the children lack respect for authority.[22] The stinginess also stunts early cognitive development,[23] while learning a new language quickens the mind for adults too. The exercise turns out to be especially good at an advanced age. It keeps the mind agile and forestalls senility.[24] The *uneconomical* effort of language learning improves general lucidity and also does something more specific: a new language opens routes of thought that can detour around decayed or clogged pathways of a first language. The United States is mature enough to take this advice seriously.

When it was young, the country practiced a bilingualism of sorts as it combined classical and modern political languages. Between those sources was wiggle room for an iconoclastic republic. Skeptical about established meaning, the founders refused the absolute claims of divine right. Then, popular reformers refused the conventional property restrictions that limited enfranchisement. How did the democratized republic manage to flex far enough to avoid failure? I'd like to suggest that the room for maneuver opened and stretched from the pull of different political languages. "Democratic republic" sounds familiar today, but the term is practically oxymoronic. It braces together the language of equality with that of freedom, preserving enough tension between the two to stay dynamic and philosophically bilingual, code switching between John Locke and Jean-Jacques Rousseau, contract and constitutional protection.[25] The liberal subject of politics (pluralist, variously associated) depends on this doubleness or multiplicity of perspectives. Historically, liberalism counted on the tensions between the languages of church and state, public and private, to sense the thrilling and risky emptiness of social arrangements that could be rearranged. This condition is good and necessary for democracy today, but it needs refreshment from another kind of bilingualism. This time it is cultural rather than political. When the design work of politics was new and daring, iconoclasm kept the designers vigilant about ready-made answers. By now the design has matured into a heritage with an enduring constitution, weighty amendments, and a history of trial and error that adds up to the bedrock of national values and practices. The emptiness at the core of liberal arrangements is today a heuristic device to think through possible reforms, not a license to trash institutions. (*Anarchy* is Brian Barry's word to dismiss multicultural thought experiments that locate an empty moral center.)[26]

What will keep us agile and vigilant today, while the threat of terrorism sets off presidential moves toward empire abroad and a garrison state at home? Democracy needs more perspective on its besieged condition than it can get from defensive Patriot Acts that would protect us by undoing constitutional protections. Perspective on rights comes sharply into focus around speakers of foreign languages (mostly Arabic now, as it was German during World War I and Japanese in World War II). Their violated rights signal the precariousness of rights for the rest of us.[27] We stay on edge by tolerating unfamiliar languages while staying vigilant about the danger that they represent and that monolingualism exacerbates. Learning those languages might open a detour around racial profiling and mass detentions toward distinguishing the blameless from the suspect.[28] Long before September 11, 2001, language differences were already presenting the most audible risks and opportunities for Western democracies. With mass migrations and stubborn or dignified (perspective matters) defenses of particularity, differences don't easily go away. They make both natives and newcomers uncomfortable and self-conscious, maybe self-reflective. Is that bad for democracy? I invite you to consider how good it can be.

A few years ago, I wrote a sober "Advertencia/Warning" to preface *Proceed with Caution, When Engaged by Minority Writing in the Americas* (1999). That book offers provisional names and examples of bilingual and other tropes that maneuver in the asymmetries that classical rhetoric, counting on cultural continuity, doesn't consider. The new tropes call attention to the culturally coded unevenness of information and power. Moves can hold out a chance for intimacy with the reader, and then hold back. "Slaps and embraces" Toni Morrison called the syncopated rhythm of minority performances. So far, there's been little response to my "rhetoric of particularism." Possibly, the general point about putting readers off is off-putting. *Bilingual Aesthetics* develops that point with a more welcoming approach. I learned the difference, and other lessons, from Sigmund Freud. He published his little joke book, *Wit and Its Relation to the Unconscious* (1905), barely five years after the major tome *The Interpretation of Dreams* (1900). That book disappointed readers and the readings disappointed Freud, as he explains in a pause between jokes that work like dreams, but more enjoyably. The heavy book left readers confused or skeptical, if not upset; the light one was sure to entertain and maybe win them over.

To honor the master, chapter 1 starts with two good jokes by and about immigrants. The humor depends on a home language that lets immigrants laugh with and at authorities. I hope that the title, "Choose and Lose," will sound funny too, after decades of one-way melt-down assimilation. The choice between home and host languages sounds downright un-American, as we will hear from Marilyn Monroe. Many of us have refused to choose and lose, even when we feel strange, dis-mis-placed, and unidentifiable. My own refusnik adolescence occasionally experimented with choices, starting from Yiddish speakers at home and Puerto Rican partners at play. I serially impersonated possibilities, as I said in a prologue to a book about the foundational fictions that constructed new nations from foreign misfits.[29] For each language or foreign inflection there was another persona. Much later, I understood that real authenticity means being more than one.

A more illustrious immigrant, like Hans Kohn (author of *American Nationalism*, 1956), wasn't playing games. He was congratulating himself and us for coming to this country, where Liberty holds her lamp (a lady and light that were fogged over when our boat came in) and where we were all equally free to be patriots as a matter of civic contract, not ethnic pedigree. But my new world was no freely entered agreement; it was a cluster of accents with a hollow cultural center that gave us misfits some wiggle room. (Need I say that Woody Allen's *Zelig* is my favorite film?) Where I grew up, only children spoke English without an accent, so the occasional adult who spoke that way (say, a teacher) lacked the linguistic density that made our Italian, Hispanic, Chinese, Jewish parents so admirably adult, and so embarrassingly out of place. With my double consciousness of would-be American and European has-been, desire and dread stayed deadlocked, thank goodness. Between them was the playground where surprises happen.

"Aesthetics Is a Joke," chapter 2, links art and humor through the effect of surprise. Bilinguals are full of surprises whether they like it or not. Borrowing cognates that turn out to be "false friends" or collapsing high and low registers that don't sound so very different from a distance, even correct usage delivers double entendres to double-talkers. Foreigners are often artful and funny. Freud found this a double advantage, since outsiders know enough to laugh at themselves whereas nativist one-way jokes victimize outsiders. Almost simultaneously, formalist Victor Shklovsky was pointing out the connection between art and surprise in essays that track the aesthetic effect through difficult and rough writing, often in funny texts. Surprise refreshes perception and rekindles love of the world for the formalist. For Freud, the spark of surprise relieves repression and prepares for another cycle of liminality and laughter.

"Irritate the State," chapter 3, suggests what foreignness can do for the country, politically. The gains for hosts can be more than narrowly economic. Difficulty itself is a goad to procedural neutrality, just as it promotes aesthetic effects by blocking habitual perception. Cultural habits and preconceptions can mire due process, so that confronting other cultural assumptions makes procedure a necessary lingua franca for self-government. The subjects of such confrontations belong to two cultures, at least. Double consciousness is, then, the normal and flexible if somehow neurotic condition of late modern life. Anything less seems cruel as well as politically dangerous.

"The Common Sense Sublime," chapter 4, recommends more, not less, refinement for facing the fear of foreignness. Kant is an ally for multiculturalism, despite some conservative claims on him. While some teachers object to cultural particularism because it allegedly dismisses aesthetics, the aesthetic attractions of foreign, even fearsome, cultural differences can claim our attention. The disturbing sublime offers more intense effects than does easily lovable beauty. The sublime elicits respect, not love; and it offers a thrill of survival close to catharsis. Few of us avoid fear today in a world where neighbors are often strangers. Can strangeness be our nonviolent commonality? Perhaps, but it will take the refinement of a new sentimental education. We will have to prepare reason to process the pain of incomprehension into the pleasure of contemplating a complicated world.

"Let's Play Games," chapter 5, ends the book by teasing Ludwig Wittgenstein. This last chapter could have been the first because Wittgenstein prescribed a general and radical therapy for all those philosophers and language teachers who worry about what is correct in language: What can we know? How are we and the world constructed by language? The therapy was to stop worrying. Language may not work the way we expect it to; it may not be neat and predictable, but it works in particular uses and contexts. Describe language, don't explain it, was his prescription. Why, then, doesn't he describe normal uses that mix "natural languages"? Wittgenstein himself begs the question with lessons that wean us from false problems and with his own bilingual performances that he doesn't deign to describe. Was he residually attached to universal validity in a univocal mode? Other iconoclasts, including Freud and Derrida, have also held back from breaching monolingualism. Mikhail Bakhtin noticed the cost of such caution: human sciences miss their targets of study precisely because they limit evidence to one language at a time and ignore the normal clusters of living language. Most people live in, or at least alongside, more than one language. This makes switching codes (cultures, perspectives) common. Switching complicates meanings, intentionally or not, both for players who are "in" on the intricate language games and for those who play odd man out. From any position, playing can be, and feel, funny.

Enjoy the varied company. Enjoy yourselves. Abraham Lincoln recommends it.

Bilingual Aesthetics

"*No bueno*," said the doctor grimly, as he walked in with Barbara's X-rays. He told Mima, "Ask her if she had TB."

Mima turned to Barbarita. "He says if you have a television?"

"Tell him yes, but in Havana. Not in Miami. But my daughter has a television here."

Mima told the doctor, "She says she had TV in Cuba, not in Miami. But her daughter has TV here."

"In that case we need to test her daughter for TB too."

Mima translated, "He says he needs to test your daughter's television to make sure it works, otherwise you cannot get your green card."

"Why the television?" asked a puzzled Barbarita.

"How many times did I tell you you needed to buy one? Don't you know, Barbarita? This is America." (Roberto G. Fernández, "Wrong Channel")[1]

"Ask the defendant, in Yiddish, if he stole a horse."

"*The judge wants to know if you stole a horse.*"

"*I stole a horse?*"

"The defendant said he stole a horse."

"Ask him if he needed a horse."

"*The judge wants to know if you needed a horse.*"

"*I needed a horse?*"

"The defendant said he needed a horse."

"Ask him why he needed it."

"*The judge wants to know why you needed a horse.*"

"*Me? A horse? I needed it oyf kapures* [to sacrifice, meaning for nothing at all]."

"He said he needed the horse for ritual purposes." (Jewish American joke)

1 Choose and Lose

The first joke is on the Cuban women who want to be American. One doesn't know enough English to take the required medical exam for immigration, while the other thinks she knows enough. You can just imagine these two in other ridiculous situations: getting busted for ordering "coca" (cola) at the corner store, or driving past the exit sign they discount as self-help advertising (*éxito*), or even getting lost in the precise alphabetical order of phone books that hide people under second (and secondary) surnames. Immigrants and foreigners are funny; they make people laugh, especially—and this may sound strange—especially similar folks who mix languages and become the butt of jokes. That's the funniest part of it. Henny Youngman told Jewish jokes to Jewish audiences; Roberto G. Fernández teases Cuban Americans with riffs that put them on and put them down as pitilessly as the playful *choteo* in Havana;[2] Bert Williams made a spectacle of being black in both black and white spaces;[3] Cheech and Chong poke fun at Latino angelinos in Los Angeles.[4] They are not abject, despite a guilt-ridden Anglo interpretation of self-directed ethnic humor, but active in the game of shuttling between insider and outsider.

Knowing more than one language is not necessarily risible, if you can afford the extras. Middle-class bilinguals almost always outperform monolinguals on tests of cognitive agility since thinking in simultaneous and competing codes trains people in multiple perspectives and uncharted possibilities. It is what linguists call creative "divergent thinking," as distinct from convergent thinking, which assumes that questions have one correct answer and which defines intelligence testing.[5] For the elite and well educated, multilingualism is a decided advantage. It allows them to travel easily, to get good jobs, read books in original versions, sparkle in conversations between puns and private codes, and to enjoy the sheer virtuosity of knowing more than enough. Some researchers wonder what comes first, intelligence or bilingualism. Are bilinguals smart because they know two languages, or do they know two languages because they are smart? The question hardly takes stock of the range of native talents in whole communities that are bi- or multi- or monolingual. In any case, research from several disciplines agrees that intelligence and bilingualism go together.[6]

But the value of the more-than-one is discounted for the "popular classes," a term I take from Spanish to name poor and often dark people. The same researchers who notice the bilingual benefit for privileged students know the bilingual blues of the poor. The variable is the difference between high and low expectations among authorities. We know that predicting success will enhance performance, while low expectations can crush students.[7] This damaging difference calls for a realignment of feeling, that is, a new sentimental education.

Think of the difference between the cosmopolitan prince, played and directed by Sir Laurence Olivier, and popular Marilyn Monroe, in *The Prince and the Showgirl* (Warner Bros., 1957). He can switch from English to German and French thanks to an elite education and to the requirements of international intrigue. Political plots thicken (in London, 1910) when he stops a seduction scene with the luscious girl to make an urgent phone call to an ambassador. "Yes, I'm alone," he begins, "there's no one else here." Offended and half drunk, the showgirl pours herself another glass and toasts President Taft. By morning, his telephone orders to arrest dissidents (democratic forces working with the Americans, "You know what children the Americans are") have leaked to Olivier's son, the legitimate heir to the throne. The boy steals into his father's study and asks Marilyn to place a call. After she indiscreetly says that the King of Carpathia wishes to speak to the ambassador, he grabs the receiver and speaks freely, as his father did when he claimed to be alone in Marilyn's company, but imperfectly: "*Vorstein . . . er ist unseren Plänen zuvorgekommen. Schlagen Sie dem Kaiser vor, daß ich mein (inaudible) . . . meines Vaters erzwungenes Exil sowie meine eigene Thron besteigung am fünfzehnten August bekanntmache . . . Ja . . . Es ist aber nötig, die bulgarische Armee marschbereit zu halten. Mehr kann ich jetzt nicht sagen. Ich danke Ihnen. Auf Wiedersehen.*" Afterward, with a smirk of satisfaction for the discreet maneuver, he thanks Marilyn and extends an invitation to his future coronation.

5

     —Oh, really? When is that?
     —Sixteen, eighteen, months.
     —Not sooner than that?
     —(delay) Sooner, Miss Mariner?
     —Yes, I speak German. I was born in Milwaukee.

The punchline shows that the underestimated girl had understood every detail of the dispatch, the fast-forward date, the backup of the Bulgarian Army, and the filial treason. Tsk, tsk, that's no way to treat a father, even if the regent had already betrayed his own son. Decadent (but irresistible) Europe is on the brink of Oedipal disaster. And New World viewers probably enjoy the cathartic pleasures of being spared, from their distance of time, space, and moral register. It is a timely reminder of anti-imperial ethics. Maybe the movie viewers thought it was better to be simple, "childlike" and democratic like North American monolinguals who don't play dirty. ("In England we speak only English," the father demanded, just before his son's secret conversation in German.) But the contrast is too stark, and the audience knows it.[8] Working-class Marilyn is no simpleton. What were the princes thinking? That class status is an indicator of intelligence, or that open and democratic spirits are easy targets for treason? Marilyn is a cure for un-American prejudices about "foreign" language incompetence.

It is time we noticed that working—and also underemployed—bilinguals sparkle too, and for similar reasons to elite code switchers. Both know the risks of language and the magic of making contact when communication could have misfired. With an exquisite consciousness of conventions, and a keen skepticism about what can or should be said, bilinguals develop the everyday arts of maneuvering and self-irony.

Some educators and politicians consider nonelite bilinguals to be damaged raw material that needs to be pressed into simple and transparent form before it can bear complexity.[9] Attitudes toward bilingualism correlate quite well with politics, Suzanne Romaine observes, as support rises and falls with immigration quotas and as regimes tighten or loosen control of civil society. How many wars have been waged in the name of a single coherent language and culture? Curiously, Romaine adds, linguist and activist Noam Chomsky fails to see what language has to do with politics.[10]

Color is a clue. Today, language difference is a metonymy for racial hierarchies. It segments a population into majority and minorities.[11] If it were not for color-coded linguistic differences, what could the language marker "Hispanic" or "Latino" mean in response to Anglo-centric questions of race? Latinos don't jump to congenital conclusions; they can lose one language too easily and to gain another takes effort. Starting with the bilingual advantage, immigrants face a linguistic paradox. Foreign languages are prized in elite education and dismissed for "foreigners," despite the cognitive advantages that linguists acknowledge as divergent thinking.[12] The counterproductive pattern runs parallel to the paradox of declining health in the promised land for the children and grandchildren of sturdy immigrants.

Melancholy Marilyn

The white-out policy for "foreign" speech, along with a blame-the-victim approach to language loss, misses Ms. (Marilyn) Mariner's charms. She speaks English Plus, not English only.[13] And she provokes a laugh of satisfaction among homeland viewers for outsmarting the Old World princes who imagined that we are monodimensional.[14] Being "American," in her case and in many others, means adding one (home) culture to a national lingua franca (she was born in Milwaukee, is the explanation for both). Ms. Mariner stands up to the unsettled prince, sturdy on her doubled cultural ground. "I'm American," she dismissively answers his threat; "you can't do anything to me." Let's take a lesson from this pride in her complicated country, and from the laughter provoked by misprising it, to shake free from the habit of forcing "foreigners" to forget native languages.[15] Cultural subtraction need not be the price of admission to this country. In fact, Alejandro Portes and Lingxin Hau recommend language maintenance, that is, "selective acculturation," because forced forgetfulness and the corollary disrespect of parents cannot yield strong societies.[16] "The price of uniformity" is too high.[17]

Strange—not to say funny—as it sounds, subtraction continues to be the conventional logic of assimilation, throughout the Americas and beyond. It urges us to get past complexity, to choose one common denominator of language and to lose the others. Children who develop a keen but common sense of contingency by straddling cultures when they translate for immigrant parents look promising as new Americans, though they should look like admirably accomplished assets.[18] Roberto Schwartz gets a laugh at the expense of Brazilian purists in "National by Subtraction." Practically nothing remains in the new world country after cultural cleansing.[19] He prefers the capacious cannibalism of Brazil's modernist "*Manifesto antropofagico*," where foreign elements are delicious, edible in fact, to a country nourished by the spice of difference.[20]

8

The advice to get on with one's new life by putting the old one to rest not only sounds like the prescription for mourning as a cure for melancholy, it is the core of a collective prescription. But mourning is chronic in countries that demand full assimilation and don't allow it. Melancholy haunts minority lives, doubled between an undead particular identity and the "new" person, embarrassed (literally burdened) by a former self. Refusing a full dose of the modern cure is a kind of affirmation of one's old self. Dragging one's feet in the game of odd man out defends a necessary measure of pride in personhood. One such foot-dragger was Dadaist Tristan Tzara, who dared to do almost unspeakable things with French while also writing melancholic rhymes in his native Romanian.[21] This doubling is an Irish option too, when England prescribes forgetting to cure subaltern sadness. Pride and cultural autonomy resist cures and prefer an almost perverse sense of agency. The recalcitrant art of keening for the dead is an affront to the Empire's good taste and good advice to bury the dead and be done.[22] Better not to give up the ghost.

Hygiene against haunting would kill off complicated patients, not cure them. Cures, in any case, can only be partial in an asymmetrical world, where some relief from envy comes from disdain for the healthy.[23] Either/or responses are out of line because patients both advance and hold health back. The double-take makes a little melancholia normal for those of us—all of us—who live inside or alongside more than one temporality and more than one temperament. The condition torments and titillates us through that perverse complicity between pleasure and pain that aesthetics has had to consider.

A conventional and dour description of melancholia reduces it to the guilty love turned into hate, when one beloved is supplanted by another. Competition is structural, we are told, as if it were bad for one clinging to provide escape routes from another. If a home culture stays hovering ghostlike in a new context, it can overshadow and undo new relationships. But denying the structural doubleness of immigrant lives doesn't promise much relief. There is, I want to suggest, a therapeutic charm in melancholia, like a dose of disease that vaccinates us against worse conditions. A measure of historically understandable sadness may even defend undervalued people from more serious depressions. The joke, of course, is that the malady is also a defense against those who would cure it.

Grief sometimes turns to grievance, we know. But this is hardly a remedy. When ghostly feelings materialize as damage, Anne Cheng says, the legal language highlights a fault line between ideal color blindness and the lingering racialism that goads North Americans to new rites of purification. Minorities, she says, are as haunted by racial melancholia as are the whites who refuse to see colored bodies and who can therefore erase them.[24] This is the tragic situation she decries.

But I have a hunch that racial or cultural melancholia has more than pathological consequences. There are elements of the undead past that play like dangerous but creative supplements to ideal self-constructions. (This is where aesthetics matters.) The supplements can conjure up an irritating presence from a haunting past, but like prosthetic compensations for missing members, they can enable agency in people who suffer losses. Ethnically or linguistically specific consciousness, Ms. Mariner knows, can be the extra elements in a country's culture that give it wiggle room. And unlike the scary psychic system attributed to melancholia—loss of loved one, incorporation of that undead love, and defense against its return—cultural ties don't need to be replaced in favor of new attachments. They are add-on pieces. Literary texts can show us why not to wrestle down foreign interference, when friction from the awkward extra pieces makes sparks of aesthetic pleasure. The add-ons irritate conventions and tease them open. Look at the extra capital letter and the superfluous accent mark in *AmeRícan*, Tato Laviera's modern and melancholic identity. The Spanglish *mot juste* proclaims his binational love of country. Are two loves too many? Not if you ask Tato, or other brilliant bilinguals. Better to be capacious than to give up the ghost.

Freud must have known that some jokes are melancholic, especially the profound ones that locate a human failing and refuse to remedy it. Do we need remedies for everything that hurts? Are humans perfect? This is the lesson of wisdom that he appends as the deeper level of the joke about the disgruntled young man who whispers to the marriage broker a list of faults about the prospective bride: "You can speak up," says the *schadchen*. "She's deaf too." "But here, as it often happens, the jest betrays the seriousness of it . . . The suitor really makes himself ridiculous when he collects together so sedulously the individual charms of the bride which are transient after all, and when he forgets at the same time that he must be prepared to take as his wife a human being with inevitable faults." Almost luxuriating in the incurability of the human condition, Freud makes self-deprecation a stable feature of his Jewish jokes.[25]

Melancholia was not a likely word for Freud's description of wit-work; it dams up the circuits of pleasure with unconscious repressions while wit releases them. One haunts; the other sets free. One acknowledges unspeakable loss; the other dares to speak it with the tremble of laughter. But by the 1927 essay "Humour," the difference had become a paradoxical partnership.[26] To the joke in the 1905 book about a convict on the way to his execution who asked what day it was ("Monday? That's a good way to start the week."), Freud adds the profound meaning he gave his best schadchen jokes: "'Look here! This is all that this seemingly dangerous world amounts to. Child's play—the very thing to jest about.'" Then he concludes, "The alternation between melancholia and mania, between a cruel suppressing of the ego by the super-ego and the liberation of the ego after this oppression, suggests some such shifting of cathexis; and this conception would, moreover, explain a number of phenomena in normal mental life" ("Humour" 219). A symptom of this alternation between choosing and losing is, I think, Freud's own reluctance to be entirely "cured" of his Jewishness. It made him funny (in both senses).

11

The word *melancholia* is out of vogue in the social sciences, where mourning now describes both normal and neurotic expressions of grief.[27] The single word is no doubt meant to suggest an unstable boundary between the two. That boundary has a particular name in Ricardo C. Ainslie's essay about the (melancholic) incomplete mourning among Mexican immigrants in Austin, Texas. He cleverly describes *La pulga*, the flea market, as a "transitional space" between the safe inside of Mexican culture and the threatening outside of an Anglo American world. La pulga extends the immigrants' ordeal of loss, he warns, "because they retain the hope of return, and cannot fully mourn" the place they left.[28] But the flea market is also a canny response to immigration, keeping used goods in circuits of exchange. Peggy Levitt asks Ainslie why he seems eager to move beyond that space between Mexican and Anglo cultures. Is it simply a matter of health and maturation, as if psychological trajectories were one size fits all? Does the space have no value in itself? Is it merely a crutch, a scaffolding, a transition?[29] In fact, Chicano cultural critics call it "a third space," and they call it home.[30] Living there, in the cultural overload (*en el desborde*, to use Norma Alarcón's inspiration), also preserves a taste for home cooking and for Spanish. Both are indicators for healthy Latino households, saved from the "Hispanic paradox" of declining health after immigration.[31] Without this mildly melancholic taste for food, music, ritual, and family of the undead past, unmoored people attach to shaky "color-blind" promises.

Over a century ago, Ernst Renan understood a profound paradox of patriotism. Successful countries, he said, consolidate their identities, not through collective memories, but through collective forgetting. Logically, peoples who are forgotten by that process respond differently. They refuse the therapies that probably serve the oppressor better than the oppressed. Why should they forget the trouble that turned people into the oppressed, when forgetting would forfeit an account of the present? Without memories of historical cause, other causes might be invented, such as alleged deficiencies, a lack of talent or industry. Ainslie, among many others, would cure perversity and purge the ghost. He might prefer a slight deformation (quite normal to my Puerto Ricanized ear) of that flea market from la pulga to *la purga*. But I like the original as a gadfly to assimilation.[32]

More is More

The cognitive advantages of bilingualism (in terms of flexibility, creativity, agility) promise superior education to native children as well as immigrants, but the promise stays out of policy debates.[33] Add psychological advantages to overdetermine the preference, since bilinguals develop a "metaconsciousness" to coordinate (Bakhtin might say orchestrate) alternative ego-positions and to withstand shocks with more mechanisms than monolinguals deploy.[34] If bilingualism represents a problem for mental health, it is not that two languages add up to an overload of voices called schizophrenia, as professionals had assumed in the first half of the twentieth century.[35] The difficulty is not for speakers, but for the doctors themselves who may well be outmaneuvered in sophisticated games. How, for example, do you tell a defense mechanism from "rhetorical devices used to create a dramatic or a comic effect?"[36] (In the next chapter, **13** Freud's bilingual reading of the *Glanz*/glance symptom is an exemplary response.)

Gloria Anzaldúa called this skill to maneuver a special *facultad* for shifting perception. It's a decided advantage even if it comes at the price of pain for "those who do not feel psychologically or physically safe in the world."[37] Think also of Junot Díaz's title character in the first story of *Drown* (1996). Ysrael's Hebrew name starts with a "Greek I," as the letter is called in Spanish. Doubled by the two ancient sources of Western culture (as in Derrida's Greek-Jew, Jew-Greek), the young man is also divided by a childhood disaster when a pig pulled off half his face. His surviving half is hidden by another layer of blue cloth mask. Maybe Díaz designed this double and divided Ysrael as an emblem for the bilingual bind, being too much and not enough. Early researchers had mostly pitied the condition as "semilingual," because, they alleged, bilinguals lacked competence in either language. But lately linguists have grown used to what Mary Louise Pratt called the contact zone between languages.[38] They are more likely to admire the verbal agility that comes—in Ysrael's masked image—from an extra layer of prosthetic persona over the "natural" one.

—I wonder how much of Ysrael's face is gone, Rafa said.
—He has his eyes.
—That's a lot, he assured me (8).

Though local children warned the narrator, "he's *ugly* and . . . that face of his would make you *sick!*" (8), the boy notices that Ysrael "was about a foot bigger than either of us (15)"; and that he was so agile you couldn't catch him: "coño, could he run" (7).

Bilinguals who laugh at immigrant jokes can take pride in a quick wit that gets to a level of self-reflexive humor that Freud located close to wisdom. Error is a part of meaning, not apart from it.[39] From this perspective, knowing more than one language is humbling, because two languages make each one precarious, and also because adding one to one leads to a mathematically sublime world of languages where two or three or more are never enough.

Anglos in the United States (or the French in France, Germans in Germany, Hispanophones in Spanish America) may not notice the invitation to this sublime depth of humor, but they can learn to read the exhilarating signs even in one language. If monolinguals miss particular "foreign" words, that's understandable. But hardly noticing that they missed something is ridiculous, to use Freud's distinction between this slapstick and the mature mechanisms of wit (*Wit*, 762–70). African Americans also know how silly white people can seem when they don't get the difference between an inside reference and the fact that it's for insiders.[40] Concern about the self-deprecation of migrants who both incite and enjoy ethnic humor sounds paradoxical and paternalist, as if the underprivileged newcomers didn't take pride in the wisdom of self-irony, as if they didn't know better than to laugh at themselves.[41]

Does it occur to critics that migrants have a knack for abstraction (literally distancing themselves from home and host rigidities) that deflects ridicule from ad hominem into a role to play? Is it also possible that they get pleasure from the attention and from the chance to turn jokes back on the jokesters? Such a knack for abstraction and irony is saner than the abjection that John Limon vindicates in ethnic humor. He does raise abjection from the at-your-feet posture to performances in-your-face: "The one-sentence version of the theory of [his] book would state the claim that what is stood up in stand-up comedy is abjection. Stand-up makes vertical (or ventral) what should be horizontal (or dorsal)."[42] But irony moves sideways; it knows the sane self-flattery of knowing more than the inflated opponent, though never enough. It closes ranks against the *goyim* even when they remain objects of desire. Ask Freud. Does it occur to nativists that migrants may be laughing at the real "Americans" for getting only half a joke? Probably. Otherwise, why would they be mad with anxiety? "Wha'd'ya think they're doing, Martha?" Richard Pryor ventriloquizes. "Are they laughing at us?"[43] Well, are they?

Take the doctor in Fernández's microstory "Wrong Channel." He is laughable from his first words, "No bueno." It's bad Spanish ("No está bien" is better). The mistake wouldn't be quite so funny if the doctor actually did try to know something about the language, for instance, the obvious way TB sounds like TV. But he knows next to nothing, which makes him ridiculous for showing off. No bueno, doctor, is the listener's diagnosis. Those of us who laugh at the joke know more than he does, and also more than the women who don't pick up the mistaken pronunciation either, unless—of course—they purposely miss it in order to play the doctor for a fool, taking a dangerous question for harmless chatter. Freud called such ruses purposeful naiveté. Mel Watkins runs with the technique in his study of "Black Humor."[44] And Wittgenstein's work shows "an intentional, or cultivated, naiveté in his method."[45] The rules for a game of tennis or chess are one thing, but the recommendations for playing are another. Sometimes playing "badly" may be a good strategy.[46] (In my neighborhood we used to challenge outsiders to a contest: Let's see who can hit the other most softly. You go first. Now me. BAM. I lose!)

We laugh harder when bilingual games make our particular group the target of the laugh attack. It's a lesson monolinguals can learn, not in order to switch roles from target to marksmen but to enjoy the double-dealing and distancing satisfaction that can make one's own ignorance the trigger for laughter. Knowing that you don't know is not exactly ignorance; it is to know something, never enough, and to be—as Socrates knew—deeply human. This sane and humane humor is the other side of pathologizing speculations about abject or self-denigrating minority humor. The double-dealing gives real humor its extra, self-inflicted kick, if you ask Freud.

Centripetal Centrifugal

Minority subjects, doubled by definition, often move in and out of labels, accents, or heritages. Practically everyone does this, given the normal range of distinct registers in any one language, but bilinguals feel the fissures unavoidably in everyday speech acts. The tragicomic and unsettled condition doesn't compute with dogmatism. No wonder Mikhail Bakhtin promoted mixed modes during the period of monologic Marxism. We need a refresher course during these newly imperial times. He favored the novel's dynamic play of codes against the single lyric voice of poetry. Bakhtin's study of stylistics in the novel works like a hinge that opens up, from the model of simultaneous competing languages in a good novel, to the multilingual complexities in the real world that should complicate all discursive practices. This is the general point of *Bilingual Aesthetics*, to be a point of departure to refresh a range of disciplines.

Bakhtin complained that a pretense of universality and univocity in the human sciences had narrowed the focus of scholarship to ideal, lifeless abstractions. Here is one of many passages that blame the murderous blockage on the monolingualism of philosophy, politics, linguistics, literary criticism:

> Aristotelian poetics, the poetics of Augustine, the poetics of the medieval church, of "the one language of truth," the Cartesian poetics of neoclassicism, the abstract grammatical universalism of Leibniz (the idea of a "universal grammar"), Humboldt's insistence on the concrete—all these, whatever their differences in nuance, give expression to the same centripetal forces in sociolinguistic and ideological life; they serve one and the same project of centralizing and unifying the European languages. The victory of one reigning language [dialect] over the others, the supplanting of languages, their enslavement, the process of illuminating them with the True Word, the incorporation of barbarians and lower social strata into a unitary language of culture and truth, the canonization of ideological systems, philology with its methods of studying and teaching dead languages, languages that were by that very fact "unities," Indo-European linguistics with its focus of attention directed away from language plurality to a single proto-language—all this determined the content and power of the category of "unitary language," . . . in the midst of heteroglossia.[47]

Life, Bakhtin observed, occurs in clusters of competing voices. That means through different registers of one language but also in alien alternatives. *Heteroglossia* (the focus of classical work on code switching)[48] refers to the variety of social and regional styles that make any language more than one,[49] and *polyglossia* pushes the description of discourse past the limits of patriotism. Together, a fractious home language and foreign codes combine to create compelling performances in literary prose. His lesson in the vitality of conflicting codes unhinges "scientific" ambitions to unification (Wittgenstein made a similar move) even in a single speaker. Bakhtin sometimes assumed that each discourse would have a particular vehicle and that the hybrid happens when different characters represent different registers or languages. But by the time he wrote *Rabelais and His World*, Bakhtin was touting the delightfully mixed man. Anyone less loses perspective on culture. Only on the multilinguistic borders, where Rabelais wrote, are reason, humor, and wisdom available.[50]

This is bad only when one is forced to take sides in a conflict, which is why patriots prefer monolingual and centripetal loyalties. What can a country expect from double-talking dual nationals in times of conflict? It can expect, I want to suggest, a level of ambivalence between or among intimate but precarious codes so unbearable that it might help to deter conflict. Double consciousness is surely a dis-ease of bad fits, but the cure of reducing two minds to one of them can be catastrophically cramping. For all of his complaints against double consciousness, Du Bois refused to take the cure of "bleaching" his black soul.[51]

Those who don't feel strained by the split may object that bilingualism doesn't necessarily lead to double consciousness, which is apprently true for some privileged subjects. Or they may object, more likely, that it is a luxury inappropriate for the poor who would benefit from simpler monolingual communication.[52] Such objections sound deaf to existing differences of class, color, and location. One reason the English and the Irish don't get along even in the same language, Terry Eagleton taunts, is that one assumes it to be for communication, and the other knows it's for performance. "Indeed the conflict has been not just between two languages, but between two quite different conceptions of language, since the English empiricist conception of language as representational has never had much appeal to the more linguistically performative Irish. The Irish have, on the whole, in the manner of subaltern peoples, tended to see language as strategic, conative, rhetorical rather than cognitive."[53]

Living in two or more competing languages troubles the expectation that communication should be easy, and it upsets the desired coherence of romantic nationalism and ethnic essentialism. This can be a good thing, I repeat, since confusion and even anxiety about conflicting identities are vigilant and insomniac; they interrupt the dangerous dreams of single-minded loyalty. But the condition is volatile and will demand solutions: either double loyalty can seek purgative cures that eliminate difference and induce more dreams of uniformity. Or it can develop a new, almost perverse taste for anxiety and irritation as stimuli for gradual and partial relief.

Not fitting easily or well, being both too much and not enough, can make ESL migrants aware of grammar (or relational) trouble with themselves, and with their neighbors, even after several generations. "Our identity is at once plural and partial," says Salman Rushdie. "Sometimes we feel that we straddle two cultures; at other times, that we fall beween two stools."[54] How is one to identify, when one is more than one? Two languages (often more than two) and loyalties can bind one to a home country and to hosts. This can seem intolerable to patriots on either side of the border, and on both sides of their own divided selves. "Say *perejil*" Trujillo's troops commanded the accented border people at the banks of a river already called Massacre in 1937.[55] Then the name was tragically reconfirmed by the slaughter of thirty thousand Haitians. Speak English without an accent, parents advise children, just to be safe. My parents too tell me stories of language games along the divided lines of Poland where pronunciation led to pronouncements of passing or failing vital exams.

But saying *shibbolet* with the accents of both Israel and Ephraim raises suspicions on both sides. To switch codes is to enter or leave one nation for another, by merely releasing a foreign sound, a word, a grammar tic, letting them slip into an always borrowed and precarious language. Ten American countries now recognize and even encourage dual citizenship, along with the generous remittances sent by U.S.-based nationals.[56] But the United States remains suspicious of disloyalty, in case of war or economic competitions. Is be-longing to two like bigamy, and living in two languages a pathology? Throughout the country, monologism is still the norm.[57] "Despite rapidly growing immigration, the U.S. Census reports that close to 90 per cent of the American population speaks exclusively in English and that the rest is formed mainly by recently-arrived immigrants."[58] This is bad for society, not good, Portes and Hau conclude. Language loss forfeits intellectual advantages and parental authority. An obsolete preference for full assimilation and its counterproductive success makes monolingual English seem normal, but the norm is dysfunctional. For François Grosjean this amounts to denial. Are statistics accurate? Do bilinguals deny speaking English-plus just to sound normal? One has only to listen to the many languages that complicate and enhance cities in North America—Boston, for example. Even twenty years ago Boston was the setting for Grosjean's *Life with Two Languages*. Monolingualism, paradoxically, is a symptom that too many people speak two languages. "There is probably a larger proportion of bilinguals in monolingual nations than in bilingual and multilingual countries."[59]

Migrants aren't at home, even at home. The word means somewhere else, a loss for the parents and a lack for the children who would be gringos there and may be Spiks here. In the Americas and throughout the modern world, national linguistic be-longing *is* identity. Johann Gottfried Herder was very clear about the monolingual core of national feeling.[60] Today again, the logic of language rights uses the same equation of one people equals one language. Consider Charles Taylor's "Politics of Recognition" as a contemporary milestone here.[61] It is only a step away from the late and generally forced program to distinguish Serbian from Croatian speech to keep the war going.[62] Nation builders have tried very hard to reduce linguistically complex societies to simple ones, usually by the force of elimination. Neither Du Bois nor the ideologues of *mestizaje* tampered with the imperial language.[63] Perfecting it was a sure step to active citizenship.

An Extra Twist

By now, monolinguals might notice the handicap of defending a single position on courts that allow lines to cross. Less is not more.[64] Any player may occupy more than one position. Bilinguals may be "targets" of a joke and still laugh because they double as superior interpreters of the double-crossing game. They feel smarter than monolinguals and laugh louder ("sudden glory" Hobbes called it).[65] But cagey monolinguals will know that the pleasure also boomerangs on bilinguals, when a joke targets their disadvantages. Does this mean that monolinguals can enjoy the inequality? If so, the cruelty abates to the degree that they admire jokesters who seem inimitable, even incomprehensible. Both sides win and lose.

Ethnic self-deprecation as well as the paranoia of privilege can be sweetened with revenge. "Swapping Dreams" is an African American sample of the double-dealing:

One morning, when Ike entered the master's room to clean it, he found the master just preparing to get out of bed. "Ike," he said, "I certainly did have a strange dream last night. It was like this: I dreamed I went to Nigger Heaven, and saw there a lot of garbage, some old torn-down houses, a few old broken-down, rotten fences, the muddiest sloppiest streets I ever saw, and a big bunch of ragged, dirty Negroes walking around."

"Umph, umph, Massa," said Ike. "Yuh sho' musta et de same t'ing Ah did las' night, 'cause Ah dreamed Ah went up ter de white man's paradise, an' de streets wuz all of gol' an' sulvah, and dey wus lots o' milk an' honey dere an' putty pearly gates, but dey wusn't uh soul in de whole place."[66]

A Peruvian parallel called "El sueño del pongo" is the Spanish translation that José María Arguedas added to his Quechua original. The privileged place of Quechua, on the first page, facing the Spanish concession to outsiders, already anticipates the twist of a story that reads like a folkloric joke: A slave dreams that he and his master go to heaven. The rich man is anointed with honey while the dreamer is covered in shit. "That's the way it should be," says the master. "Yes, sir," the slave agrees. "After that," he adds, "Saint Peter told us to lick each other for all eternity."[67]

One way to take rather harmless revenge on a host language, and to refresh it, is by twisting it out of shape. There is a guilty linguistic pleasure in getting it wrong, an almost benign but also thrilling transgression against assimilation. Among the masters of this license for mild linguistic abuse (called creativity) was Yiddish- and Hebrew-speaking Franz Kafka, whose bumpkin hero Rossman speaks an almost-English in Amerika.[68] Kafka, everyone knows by now, refreshed the German language because he dared to pull and push it out of its conventional shape. José María Arguedas was another master who managed to Peruanize Peru's Spanish with Quechua constructions that favor gerunds, for example, repeating.[69]

And who can forget the way Vladimir Nabokov grazed the level of slapstick by "Pninizing" English? So promiscuous a mix of registers would have been inverosimil for a native narrator or a native hero. But Pnin, our narrator reports, learns some "ordinary words like 'eat,' 'street,' fountain pen,' 'gangster,' 'marginal utility'" (14). Mostly, the storyteller's sentences start grandiloquently and then crash down to the banal, just like Pnin himself, who begins with an impressive head and torso only to end disappointingly, with spindly legs and "frail-looking, almost feminine feet" (7). (The taste for alliteration offers a traveler-friendly, portable poetic effect. In any case, Pnin—his very name makes "a preposterous little explosion" [31]—loves the p's and l's of his favorite line from *Gamlet, Vil'yama Shekspira*: "*plila I pela, pela I plila* . . . she floated and she sang, she sang and floated" [78].) The tumble of registers, from the dignified to the down-home, has no defenses against slang or local speech. Almost indiscriminately, it opens onto the heteroglossia that native stylists might have controlled. Pnin's job, for example, depends on his "disarming, old fashioned charm which Dr. Hagen, his staunch protector, insisted before morose trustees was a delicate imported article worth paying for in domestic cash." This "inexorable" move from lofty to low intends, I think, to taunt American readers about a national addiction to predicting high returns from high hopes. "Some people—and I am one of them—[says the narrator] hate happy ends. We feel cheated. Harm is the norm. Doom should not jam" (25). The lexical tumble and crash runs through as a structural leitmotif: "He had a deep admiration for the zipper" (13), we are told. And his father "once had the honor of treating Leo Tolstoy for a case of conjunctivitis" (21).

Ernest Hemingway does different damage to English, from

the inside straining out. His dialogue limps and lilts with the simulated sound of literal translation from Spanish in *For Whom the Bell Tolls*. Do we generally honor his experiments in *Verfremdung* when we canonize him as a great American writer?[70] Hemingway was tired of narrow nationalism, and he wasn't nervous about sounding too Spanish, the way William Carlos Williams was. Pound had made Williams nervous about not fitting into "the American grain." So Carlos developed more subtle moves than Nabokov's multidirectional mockery or Hemingway's studied clumsiness. You see, Carlos was Williams's intimate home name, the one his Puerto Rican mother called him during the long years she lived in this country and resisted belonging to it. The Anglo surname (Piri Thomas and Rubén Blades have them too) doesn't hint at the father's Hispanophone upbringing in the Dominican Republic nor the frequent business trips that made Latin America the area for his economic and erotic engagements. The insistent Anglo name that sandwiched what became a merely decorative Spanish middle was a demand for seamless assimilation, Ezra Pound counseled Williams. But the middle was the meat of the matter, his mother reminded him, in Spanish. Between Pound's beating Spanish rhythms out of Bill's poetry, and the riffs *de carretilla* by Doña Rosa (of the "red wheelbarrow/carretilla") about Caribbean values beyond Northern crassness, Williams stayed of two minds, agile and inventive.[71]

Pound loved to use foreign words too. His notorious taste for Italian had a fascist accent; and Asian languages spice his poetry with the occasional surprise effect of getting the words right. In the least case, his mixing and matching gave modernism its cue for a new shape of poetry.[72] Elite, discrete, or archeological languages titillated Pound, while the homey sound of Spanish put him off to the point of refusing the seductions that Carlos had indulged. Neither Góngora's baroque elitism nor the popular enchantments of Lope de Vega's stage moved Pound by the time he met Williams, though Lope had lured him in student days.[73] Pound had his preferential pretensions to high culture, and they pulled Williams away from his mother tongue. Bill's elegant mother resented the interference and disdained pompous Pound.

Disdain is a familiar defense against the limited reception that claims legitimacy. It is what the doctor orders in "Wrong Channel." Even minimally attuned listeners can tell, from the beginning, that the doctor is pompous. Two more self-inflated fools frame the defendant in the Jewish joke about an allegedly stolen horse: they are the humorless judge and his literal-minded translator. I need a translator? A longer version of the story ends with the judge sentencing the misunderstood man, who then curses the judge, in Yiddish. Finally, the judge curses him back, in Yiddish too, without changing the legal sentence.

These jokes work through English, but not entirely in it. They tease and stretch the language toward borders with other codes and cultures in ways that open up a single tradition to the dimensions of democracy. There are political enhancements too, as we will see in chapter 3, that come with bilingualism. It is an agent for interrupting familiar practices and forcing procedural solutions. When foreignness makes habit fail us, we appeal to procedure and to substantive norms.[74] Democratic institutions are different from any one linguistic culture, just as they are separate from any one religion. And one effective way to keep the distinction clear is to admit more than one language, or church, into the state. Thanks to interruptions of familiar sounds and beliefs, politics becomes the space for coordinating differences.[75] Of course a country needs shared values and projects, which makes a shared language necessary. Newcomers know this. They flock to ESL classes, or wait to get in, and they insist that their children learn English as the lingua franca. But it's the particular code, the one that doesn't quite fit everywhere, which keeps institutions flexible and alert to the distinction between familiar practice and good policy. If some citizens resent bilinguals, perhaps they can be persuaded to see things differently, especially since the new census finds a "richer, more educated, multilingual nation."[76]

Complaints about the dangers to national coherence can be downright funny. "Last week, the Oakland City Council voted unanimously to require certain city departments to fill vacancies with workers who are bilingual in either Spanish or Chinese," writes one irate journalist. "How can immigrants identify with America if they can't read Lincoln's words in the language in which they were spoken? Will we devolve from *E pluribus unum* (out of many, one) to a multicultural boarding house, whose fractious tenants babble at each other incomprehensibly in a welter of tongues?"[77] No need to be upset at this harangue. It's obviously a joke, even if the author missed it (a common asymmetry in bilingual humor). Notice that the translation from Latin assumes that English-only citizens don't understand the very slogan they hold dear.

Bilingual effects are everywhere, in the ways we think, feel, relate, and make art. Politics has begun to reckon with these effects, but aesthetics seems reluctant to enter the conversation. Maybe this is a reaction to allegedly too much politics, and too much critical theory over the past thirty years of literary studies.[78] Reacting to this reaction, scholars who defend the political value of literature are loath to favor the kind of aesthetics that amounts to a backlash against their own work.[79] Not all such engagements are pitched or personal, I am happy to note, because the other extreme, indifference to aesthetics, is a hard principle to defend for literary critics.[80] It is self-dismissive. What is literature, after all, but strange or beautiful writing that renews perception? Multiculturalism can seem irrelevant for art education, either because aesthetics stays unfriendly to politics or because politics seems insensitive to art. Yet it should be exciting to be invited, after centuries of monolingual taste, to the banquet of bilingual creativity.

It's not that diglossia vanished from literature altogether after the Middle Ages; anyone can name occasional experiments with the more-than-one language. Nor is immigration or mass displacement a new phenomenon. What is new are the great numbers, the visibility,[81] and the postmodern moment that unravels the dangerous identity between (administrative) state and (cultural) nation to recover the wiggle room between the terms. Now, again, multilingual experiments are a significant feature of literary art. The creativity is de facto.

Do we take seriously enough—as teachers and citizens—the responsibility to render the creativity visible and audible? As long as it stays out of sight, literary criticism misses its cues for analysis and for admiration of the unconventional as art. Politics continues to worry about foreigners instead of welcoming them as necessary agitators for procedural neutrality. And philosophy forfeits a predisposition to metacognition, that knack for knowing that knowledge is constructed, contested, and unstable. This predisposition to think about thinking, so common among people who think in competing codes, could keep us flexible, ironic, and in love with the world, not with just one defensive representation of it.

Modernity made us think that living in one language (and one political identity) is normal, not to say ideal. But given the real histories of military, economic, intellectual, and demographic movements, most people in postmodern times admit to living in more than one language and through multiple identities. They can look, to political theorists, like premodern medieval arrangements.[82] And people who don't live that way have to share cities and states—like it or not—with neighbors who may be playing language games that monolinguals don't exactly get. The choice of liking it or not is real, as is the choice of keeping or losing a home language. If we choose to, for example, we could register the initially unpleasant surprise of losing linguistic control in a conversation, or of not getting a joke, as only a first stage of an aesthetic response. The surprise, along with the unpleasantness, is unavoidable in Western democracies where unstable power relationships between hosts and newcomers make both sides anxious.[83] But at a next moment, there can be a pleasing aftereffect of having survived unpleasantness; it returns us to our senses through the operation of the everyday sublime.

Until now, people have mostly resented the moments of exclusion from conversations and the suspicions that they are the butt of some jokes. But alternatives to resentment do exist. At least they are imaginable and worth pursuing in countries that are learning to live with unstoppable migration and ambivalence about assimilation. Demographic shifts are sending mixed messages to all citizens and sojourners, natives and newcomers. Along with demands for national coherence are defenses of difference. The conflict won't scare democratic spirits who know that unity and individuality depend on each other, since rights refer to a collectivity and the collectivity is made up of particular people.

So, learning to love the language mix—in which all of us are insiders and outsiders to different combinations—shouldn't be too hard for citizens used to the contentiousness of democratic life. It is probably good political training. In any case, it will certainly be more fun to appreciate the jokes and the wily moments of disconnection than to flinch at foreigners.

esthetics is a joke. I mean that thinking about artistic effects is a lot like thinking about jokes, seriously. Russian formalist Victor Shklovsky was serious too when he found his favorite examples of aesthetic "estrangement" in the funny, smutty passages of *Tristram Shandy*.[1] The mechanisms that make language strange in Sterne's novel, according to Shklovsky, are digression, interruption, temporal displacement, and the apparent chaos that turns out to be intentional, "strictly regulated, like a picture by Picasso" (28). What he doesn't say is that this organized confusion makes you laugh. In other cases, it might make you shudder or otherwise feel "funny," because good jokes have that tragicomic, double-dealing quality that sends you coming and going between disturbing effects. ("Nothing distinguishes wit from all other psychic formations better than this double-sidedness and this double-dealing," Freud noticed.)[2]

Art, to get back from the digression to Shklovsky, is technique—not inspiration, and certainly not transcendent value. It is the intentional production of defamiliarization, a surprise effect accomplished by roughening conventional material in unconventional ways. Perception, not intention, is the measure of art, he concluded (8). It clears up a long-standing ambivalence in aesthetics.[3] *"Art is a way of experiencing the artfulness of an object; the object is not important"* (12, Shklovsky's emphasis). Art seeks difficulty of understanding and deliberate slowness of communication to detain readers just long enough to notice things as if for the first time.[4]

Standard romantic theorists of poetry believed that art was in the economy of expression, shorthand images that evoke transcendent values ("Images belong to no one: they are 'the Lord's' " [7], Shklovsky intones mockingly). Such loftiness and laziness provoked him to be naughty and unequivocal in "Art as Technique" (1917), which he illustrated with an essay on *Tristram Shandy* (1921). Literariness as effect, rather than literature as thing, should be the appropriate subject of aesthetics.[5] Disturbance is aesthetic, he insisted. Easy communication or habitual knowledge is death to the senses. "Not talking straight" is Bakhtin's paraphrase for literariness; this is a property of *skaz*, parody, verbal masquerade and of the complex artistic forms in great novels.[6]

Wordplay, distractions, detours, *foreign words* are among the devices of deliberate roughness that make up literary technique for Shklovsky. Roughing it, let's not forget, is a reliable English recipe for pleasure by way of discomfort. Ironically, and in the same spirit of Shklovsky's provocations, the delays or difficulties that English-only readers may encounter in a multilingual text probably make them better targets for aesthetic effects than readers who don't stop to struggle. That's why T. S. Eliot resisted translating the foreign words of "The Wasteland."[7] Roughness can irritate the senses pleasantly enough to notice both the artist at work and a refreshed world that may have grayed from inattention.

Sterne ruffles more than roughens his reader with performances of double meanings and roundabout intentions. The effect is relentless surprise, such as the small shock values of salacious innuendo in the passages that provoke and please Shklovsky most, even when his defenses are up because he expects to hear a joke. Citing Sterne as the master of innuendo, Shklovsky observes: "In the beginning, Sterne introduces an anecdote about an act of sexual intercourse interrupted by a woman's question: 'have you forgot to wind up the clock?'" (28–29). Then disquisitions about "noseology" occupy much of the essay, as they do much of the novel, through digressions about Uncle Toby's war wound in the groin and about our narrator, just born but already nose-damaged by Dr. Slop's castrating delivery (34). Shklovsky's nose for technique obviously leads him from art to humor.

Freud digresses along the same line, but in the other direction. He goes from humor to art. Jokes are serious business for Freud, because they provide the best shortcuts from repression to the unconscious.[8] Why, he wonders in the opening paragraph of his joke book, have "aesthetics and psychology not awarded to wit the important role that it plays in our mental life" (*Wit*, 633)? A new joke is practically a public event, he observes, and distinguished people like to share them during their lives and to record them in autobiographies.

Though dreams open onto the unconscious too, they don't need to be shared, or to be short, in order to be dreams. Instead, dreams are private and protracted, defending repressed material with extra compromises and cover-ups (752, 755). Wit, by contrast, is economical, Freud says, short-circuiting psychic energy that was being spent on disguising familiar but embarrassing material (713).[9] Shklovsky might have objected, again, to the popular cult of economy (he traces it to Herbert Spencer),[10] because jokes can depend on the belabored defamiliarization, on the roundabout, complicated, or half-hidden information that prepares the explosion of a punch line. A punch line, in any case, comes as a flash of inspiration (752), says Freud, and depends on an audience for its success (760–61).[11]

Jokes are social pleasure-producers, whereas dreams are asocial personal pain-controllers. On other counts though, dreams and jokes have quite a lot in common, from the unspeakable information they harbor to the mechanisms for managing it: "condensation with and without substitutive formation, displacement, representation through absurdity, representation through the opposite, indirect representation, etc." (745).

The difference of effect between dreams and jokes recalls Paul Veyne's distinction between novels (that cut and paste subjectively selected data, and then speculate on — or invent — relations of cause and effect), and histories (that do the same). The only tongue-in-cheek but significant dissimilarity, he concluded, is that novels have to be pleasing and histories do not.[12]

By 1900, Freud had already published his major study of psychic mechanisms: *The Interpretation of Dreams*. Why would he follow up only five years later with a somewhat redundant study of the same mechanisms in *Wit and Its Relation to the Unconscious*? The reason, I think, comes down to an aesthetic effect. Maybe his latest book, he wondered out loud, would finally make his theory of the unconscious popular and social (like a joke). The big first book was disappointingly dense and confusing even for professional readers (*Wit*, 745). The lighter second one, he evidently hoped, would be fun to follow, illustrating as it does the theory of the unconscious by giving in to the pleasure-making function of psychic mechanisms.

On the one hand, Shklovsky and his formalist followers grounded a definition of art in a psychological effect. Aesthetics starts by noticing a response of surprise to "estrangement" and then traces backward to locate a technical disturbance that produced the effect. Freud took an inverted track, as I said. He based his analysis of psychic effects on artistic technique. For him, the most important devices of the unpredictable variations were displacement and condensation (literally poetry making, *Verdichtung*), the same devices on Shklovsky's list.

Whether you privilege Shklovsky's aesthetic pleasure that comes from psychological surprise, or whether you prefer Freud's psychic strangeness that comes from artful mechanisms, one thing is clear. Aesthetics and jokes stalk the element of surprise. Surprise at what we assumed was familiar is the trigger both for aesthetics, where it produces an effect of estrangement, and for humor, where it ignites an explosion of laughter. (Kant makes the connection too, though he denied wit the intrinsic worth of lasting art.)[13] So when the material or the treatment of language games becomes standard and predictable, both the fun and the fear of surprise can go limp with repetition.[14] (Vat, by the way, did Freud say was betveen fear und sex? The answer is "Fünf.")[15]

Games that repeat the same moves often enough to be predictable perform like clockwork rather than as invitations to play. Consider Spanglish, for example, when it means an identifiable language rather than the field for artful games of code switching between Spanish and English.[16] I mention the difference of meanings assigned to Spanglish in order to foreground the cleverness of the process over some standard switched products. The words *marketa* or *rufo* are no longer charming or funny replacements for market and roof. Like dead metaphors they litter the playing field of language with the kinds of corpses that Cortázar laid to rest in dictionaries.[17] Good code switchers will produce surprise effects, even if it means resorting to monolingualism where a code switch has become standard.[18] More familiar to scholarship than the unruly sport of switching sides is the habit of team loyalty that codifies relationships into one more or less coherent language. The standard goal is to win autonomy for the target language, even if the evidence suggests less distinction than continuity among neighboring codes, as in differences between Serbian and Croatian, practically manufactured to justify different nation states.[19]

Emerging vernaculars sometimes claim standard practices in order to establish a legitimate status, adopting the same nationalist criterion of cultural coherence that closes ranks against the "foreign" cultures emerging in the nation's midst. To read Miguel Algarín's manifesto-like prologue to *Nuyorican Poetry* of 1975, the goal of creativity was to harness a "disruptive, tense, informal street talk" in order "to arrive at an organized respectability."[20] Defenders of Spanglish make that appeal to respectability,[21] but some Nuyoricans prefer to stay disruptive, aesthetically. "Worlds exist simultaneously, flashes of scenarios, linguistic stereo; they conflict, they debate," Víctor Hernández Cruz writes. "Spanish and English constantly breaking into each other like ocean waves."[22]

Bilanguage games don't fit into the expectations we inherit from monolingual rhetorical techniques, so I will borrow and also improvise some terms to name bilingual aesthetic effects, if you will allow these as invitations for your own improvisations.

Double-talk

Code switching is less dignified and more daring than games that can tell winners from losers. It plays naughty games between languages, poaching and borrowing, and crossing lines.[23] Imagine one ball field where players make baseball and basketball moves during the same game, says Jesuit Bartolomeu Meliá of his work in Paraguay. The maneuvers are always surprising. They demand virtuosity from players, vigilance from competitors, and admiration from the public.[24] Creative talent is the norm for bilanguage games, says barrio-based linguist Ana Celia Zentella. She compares the moves to expert basketball passes and to the unstable set of salsa steps that—true to their name—mix and morph one move into another. These shared art forms provide vehicles for group solidarity by way of individual and surprising variations.[25]

When linguists venture beyond monolingualism and ask about the social meaning of code switching, they bracket the universalizing questions of structural grammar for a focus on functional grammar. Here linguists ally with anthropologists who care more about why people alternate than whether this is legitimate.[26] Literary critics have been slow to take the combined lead, although discourse analysis provides common ground for scholars of particular language arts. Until recently, both linguists and anthropologists have worried that switching is a symptom of deficiency in one language or the other, since they assumed that switches are triggered by the demands of referential "efficiency."[27] (Shklovsky cringes again.) Engaging a "foreign" word would apparently mean that the native equivalent was missing, rather than a clever performance. And while linguists have for some time been using descriptions of orderly and grammatical practices to legitimate such alternations as normal, anthropologists have switched from worrying about language poachers to celebrating their resourcefulness.

By now, even some linguists have strayed from the once standard "syntagmatic" rule-based approach to develop a "paradigmatic" preference for the messiness of overlapping language games.[28] Consider Wittgenstein on the philosophical depth of rules,[29] but language "games" are not exactly rule-bound in his double-talk. A new attention to choices, contexts, and variable effects rather than universals drives this post-Chomskyan linguistics and offers literary critics some tools for describing particular genres and styles.[30] This capaciousness is the hallmark of the hybrid field called sociolinguistics. It takes up Bakhtin's challenge to listen to the real world of living language.

Simultaneous options, hybrid performances, unprogrammed choices, rhetorical effects, these are Bakhtinian "concepts of a sociolinguistics that place bi- and multilingual speakers and communities at its center, rather than in their traditional place at the margins."[31] The change of heart about how to hear alternation sometimes goes to the other extreme, Peter Auer cautions, when each instance looks meaningful in the same "semantic" way.[32] But his warning signals the new consensus among those students of language carried away by admiration for speakers who had seemed pitiful only a genera-

36 tion ago.

Unorthodox moves can irritate monolinguals when they don't quite get what's so clever or don't stop to notice that something clever happened, whether they get it or not. I say monolinguals, but people who live in two or more languages can also bristle when the game changes codes and shifts them to outside positions. A little irritation though—just enough to get a rise out of people who think difference is an obstacle to level and leave behind—is good for liberal democracy, Robert Dahl recommends, because we cannot know (and may not want to know) fellow citizens.[33] It's good for aesthetic education too, the formalists would remind us. If English (or Spanish or French)-only speakers get upset when their linguistic competence falls short of a multilingual situation, at least this upsetness acknowledges a heterogeneous environment that plays games with us all. With some help to see the big picture, frustrated players may also appreciate their imperfectly comprehensible environment as the necessary basis for democracy in globalized, modern times. Irritation can be simply annoying, but reflecting on it offers some political compensation, as I suggest in the next chapter, "Irritate the State."

Code switching prefers the surprise element of an estranged

(literally foreign) expression to the predictability of one legitimate language; it values artistry over stable identity, and it invites an acknowledgment of aesthetic agency over a politics of cultural recognition. The game of recognition, after all, has a built-in crippling effect, given the universalizing terms of Western politics and philosophy. The most one can hope to win at that game is equal footing with antagonists. Success means getting an acknowledgment that you are as good as your opponent, not that you wield a "dangerous (alien) supplement" to help you parry with power. A second language is—at best—no liability, if you ask Brian Barry.[34] And even this uninteresting outcome is unlikely, given the trap that Hegel described in the master-slave dialectic of vicious and circular reversibility between the positions of powerful player and subordinate contender.

Neither winning nor losing at the game of recognition will make any difference to the values at stake. These stakes remain identity and cultural patrimony, not creativity or maneuverability. Where is the invitation to admire artistry and the corollary admiration for the artist, if language looks seamless and given rather than manipulated and strange? And where is the qualitative difference between a culture at the center of power and one that survives, and has fun, by maneuvering in the margins, if both are rated on the same scorecard and simply change places from one match to another?

The anthropologist Kathryn Woolard identifies some of these maneuvers in jokes about language loyalty in Spain.[35] With examples from humorists in Barcelona, she points out that bivalency (the same meaning in two languages) makes a joke of anxieties about being either Spanish or Catalan. A bivalent word can act as a turnstile from one language to another. Her attention to technique is a model for literary critics who might locate the aesthetic particularity of code switching and stir appreciation for the practice and for the practitioners. The aesthetic advantages of pulling language in strange/foreign directions should be self-evident to students of literature, though it helps to spell out such advantages, because skepticism and ignorance can and do conspire against the legacy of formalism. Schlegel, who liked the rough spots in literary translation, has sometimes fallen out of view for hermeneutic conquistadores.[36] There is an opportunity here, and an obligation, to generate names and descriptions for a broad range of rhetorical figures and language games that stretch and push a host language out of its standard, sometimes tired, shape. Bilingual creativity is de facto, as I said. But our stock of interpretive tools needs to recover premodern investments in deliciously mixed language arts (e.g., Spanish *ensaladilla*; Italian *macaronic* poetry) in order to render the creativity visible as legitimate contributions to contemporary art. One net gain will be an expanded toolbox that can refine other readings too. Another gain will be to make migrancy mean something more than stigma, more like an incentive for aesthetic and political creativity.

What, for example, is the rhetorical name for a code switch that works like an

(1) *escape route?*

"los dos avientan una buena carcajada
y luego siguen platicando
mientras la amiga, unaffected
masca y truena su chicle
viéndose por un espejo
componiéndose el hairdo"[37]

What do you call a

(2) *purposeful mistranslation* ("'Thank you, Barbarita,' as she pushes the Cuban out the door. 'For nothing,' Mrs. Olsen.'),[38] or the

(3) *sounds-like slips* between different languages: ELA, *Estado libre asociado*, names Puerto Rico's oxymoronic and tolerant political status. It also stands for Senator Hayakawa's restrictive *English Language Amendment*. Are you constipada? "Mami sent us to the campo in summer"; or the

(4) *prosthesis*, otherwise known as *calque* that keeps a code from crippling? Imeléame if it's kosher to tell Juan; he's good people. How would Wittgenstein have continued his philosophical investigations if he had described bilingual games? Is Freud's preference for Jewish jokes a

(5) *"black behind your ears"* moment revealing an ethnic tinge that unsettles his universalist posture? Does Peirce's third part of logic,

(6) *abduction*, along with induction and deduction, seem like a necessary addition to the critical vocabulary for reading bilingual texts that poach words from a parallel language and feed them to another?[39] There is also the

(7) *anemic-phonemic* phenomenon of missing sounds (TV is TV) and hypercorrection for the lack, as in "a shit of paper." "Knock, knock." "Who's there?" "Juan." "Juan who?" "Juan, two, three, four." Not to mention the

(8) *malicious-delicious* jokes made by listeners, not by tellers, as when you notice that *E pluribus unum* needs translation; or when the Yiddish-speaking philosopher at Columbia University, Sidney Morgenbesser, responds "Yeh, Yeh" to the English grammar restriction against two positives making a negative. A woman comes to buy socks and after looking disappointed at all the other merchandise exclaims, "¡Eso sí que es!" The exhausted clerk complains, "Lady, if you could spell it, why didn't you say so." Also, stay tuned for Wittgenstein's "peh" in chapter 5.

(9) *Translated and improved*, versions of *Gamlet* in *Pnin*, or the Hebrew Bible in King James.

(10) *Vagrancy* may be the general category of these figures, but as a particular move, it marks foreignness, as when a neighbor gone astray asked my mother to explain her directions: "Parallel? Can you say that in English?"

Work Sheet. Identify Each Bilingual Figure [Invent a Category if Needed] and Comment on Effect: Use as much time as you need.

1. "Please excuse my son . . . because of high fever," is the standard note to the school nurse that Miami Cubans copied from one another. Proud of her superior English, Angela Campa added, "He is intoxicated." The nurse, probably trained along with the doctor of "Wrong Channel," thought the boy was drunk, even though drunkenness doesn't cause high fever.

2. "We were on our way to the colmado for an errand, a beer for my tio . . . My brother was twelve, and he was the one who wanted to see Ysrael, who looked towards Barbacoa and said, We should pay that kid a visit." [Junot Díaz, *Drown*, 3; marking place, marking debt of English to Taino]

3. "Mami shipped me and Rafa out to the campo every summer." [ibid; bivalency]

4. "I dedicate this book to you." "You do? We only just met!"

5. "Fruit is good, you mention fruit . . . Not too hot, not too cold, you know, just nice." Mel Brooks, 2000 Year Old Man[40]

6. *AmeRícan*

7. Sgt. Hodell, in *Raining Backwards*[41]

If aesthetics stays deaf to the provocations of strange sounds, it will be guilty of ignorance and bad faith. In any case, those alien sounds have a tradition more venerable than upstart Russian formalism. "Idiota" was what the Venerable Bede called the single-language speaker in ninth-century England. Throughout medieval Europe, macaronic poetry thrived, alongside the diglossia of entire populations who knew enough Church Latin to play it in counterpoint to the vernacular language.[42] But the equivalence between linguistic narrowness and intellectual simplicity didn't seem to matter during Europe's long and often brutal efforts to consolidate modern cultures and to impose them elsewhere. Bakhtin tried to revive polyglossia as part of a campaign against monologism which he dreaded with a mix of fear and scorn. Single languages were narrow and dogmatic by definition, Bakhtin repeated, because a language is an entire culture, one culture, and that doesn't add up to democracy.

Bilingual Prosthesis

Bilinguals can get caught between bad fits at thrilling and risky borders. These split subjects are not pairs of self-sufficient monolinguals stuck at the neck, Zentella says, but overloaded imperfectly doubled systems where particular vocabularies develop in one language and not the other, and where the supplements as well as the missing pieces destabilize both languages.[43] Arguments for the social and psychological advantages of fluent—as opposed to limited—bilingualism underestimate, I believe, the added value of even faulty familiarity with a second language.[44] In strident times, there is a value to the humility and tentativeness that come from practicing imperfection. Swiss cheese is the image for imperfect bilinguals, with more holes than sticky matter. Verena Conley has unforgettable things to say about being literally Swiss, weaned in one official German language and educated in an unwelcoming French rival.

Even official multilingualism in Switzerland, also in Canada, Belgium, Israel, Spain, and elite multilingualism can breed unhappy consciousness. Sylvia Molloy's Anglo-Argentine schooling comes to mind, as does Elena Poniatowska, who learned Spanish from the maids and envied their authentic Mexican-ness.[45] How could that consciousness be happy, given the modern economy (Shklovsky cringes once more) of one consciousness per people and obviously one per person?

Herder had identified the single and unified spirit of a people as its *Sprachgeist*.[46] Two spirits of language were too many. He said they produce spiritual indigestion that leads to a material decomposition signaled by flatulence.[47] Could Herder have imagined that the word for fart in Spanish (*pedo*) means kiss in Mayan?[48] Would he have wanted to know this kind of perverse (neurotic) joke that cures gas cramps with laughing gas, or would it have compounded the pathology? For bilinguals, something is always in the way or in need of supplements.

"Bilingual prosthesis" was the inspired mistake that Dale Shuger made when she meant to say "bilingual aesthetics" as the subject of our course one semester. When a concept is lacking, prosthetic borrowings like Molloy's English teatime *cucharite* that stirred up Spanish into her underdeveloped French, or like the word *kosher* and the expression "he's good people" can patch up a few holes in English, while *imeliar* or *beipasear* keep Spanish from crippling.[49]

Jacques Derrida also describes monolingualism as a net full of holes, patched up with provisional prosthetics. For him, all language is hobbled together and hobbles along in the same universally unsettling way. This consciousness dawned on Derrida, he says, through the childhood trauma of being denationalized and disconnected from his "home" language during World War II. The French had closed fascist ranks against Jews in Algeria even tighter than the Germans had required; "they must have been dreaming about it all along."[50] Without the historical trauma, would Derrida have known how treacherous language can be? Bilinguals know the treachery, one way *and* another. Often they are victims of historical catastrophe. Think of the correlation between military war and cultural campaigns to eliminate extraneous languages. History over-determines the lesson that bilinguals learn anyway: that language is too much and not enough. The trauma is structural-existential for bilinguals, not necessarily for monolinguals. The difference between structural and historical trauma is worth marking for ethical reasons, Dominick La Capra warns. The distinction should dissuade those who have not experienced limit events from the vampirism or "victim envy" that rushes past particular histories to sound a shrill and sustained tone of transcendent despair, as if limit events were only extreme cases of the psychological (Lacanian) fissure that makes us all—universally—human.[51]

Both victim and vampire (he might like that Borgesian formulation), Derrida universalizes a particular historical anxiety about language. Maybe his elite monolingualism turns the difference between history and structure into just another undecidable slippage.[52] Yet monolingualism is not the unmarked norm that accounts for intense anxieties and exhilaration, as Derrida claims. To the protests of Abdelkebir Khatibi about belonging to Arabic and therefore not at ease in French, Derrida says he protests too much. Khatibi's *L'amour bilangue* is written in French. If the book chafes against the language, so do other books, inexorably, says Derrida. But despite his chuckles at Khatibi's performative contradiction of writing in French and claiming to belong to Arabic, Arabic words do rub into the wounds of French to irritate more acutely than Derrida's (narcissistic) folds and routes can describe.[53]

Why object to Khatibi's performative contradiction, after Derrida himself had dismissed the same objection when it refers to his own work? "Stop; don't play that trick of performative contradiction; only German or Anglo-American theorists like that strategy, a childish armory."[54] In fact, Khatibi's novel is an extended performance of the contradiction between languages that Víctor Hernández Cruz described as worlds existing simultaneously: "flashes of scenarios, linguistic stereo; they conflict, they debate." The Algerian announces the theme in a kind of allegorical preface:

> And in French—his foreign language—the word for "word," *mot*, is close to the one for "death," *la mort*; only one letter is missing: the succinctness of the impression, a syllable, the ecstasy of a stifled sob. Why did he believe that language is more beautiful, more terrible, for a foreigner?
>
> He calmed down instantly when an Arabic word, *kalma*, appeared, *kalma* and its scholarly equivalent, *kalima*, and the whole string of its diminutives which had been the riddles of his childhood: *klima* . . . The diglossal *kal(i)ma* appeared again without *mot*'s having faded away or disappeared. Within him, both words were observing each other.[55]

Languages foreign to one another, anthropomorphized as an Arabic lover and his French beloved, are the protagonists of the tangle that follows. Their mutual attraction and repulsion go as deep as the difference between Muslim monotheism and Catholic idolatry:

> He very quickly saw an old emigrant woman beneath a statue of Mary; she was murmuring, *Allah akbar! Allah akbar!*
>
> He observed her without stating who he was. Mildly sleepy. Was he dreaming? The statues crumbled at his feet. He picked up a few fragments and offered them to the old woman. She hesitated, then grabbed one piece and kissed it. Now, he stumbled forward, in the midst of poor

people praying. He was bathed in light from the central stained-glass window. At his back, the columns had left their straight lines. He picked up the face of Christ and shattered it.[56]

Derrida rushes past scenes like this. After all, he reasons, the words are mostly French. But why reason this way in order to defend an equal insertion of all speakers into French or any other language? Maybe Derrida's residual universalism survives (like Freud's and Wittgenstein's) in a denial of linguistic/cultural differences. But since when have Jews, as a particular case of minority peoples, felt secure enough in one language to forfeit escape routes into others?

Derrida does lament the loss of "safe-home" languages like Yiddish or Judeo-Spanish Ladino, but he revels in the purity of his French, as if it depended on the loss of home.[57] The impossible dream of going back to one coherent language (ego, nation) provokes a romantic anxiety that Derrida considers universal. Listen to this reverie: "One can, of course, speak several languages. There are speakers who are competent in more than one language. Some even write several languages at a time (prostheses, grafts, translation, transposition). But do they not always do it with a view to an absolute idiom? And in the promise of a still unheard-of-language? Of a sole poem previously inaudible?"[58] No, Jacques, not always. When bilinguals pause to worry about missing pieces, it may be to poach a patch from a parallel code. Sometimes the sutures flaunt their seams, to make worry an aesthetic or ideological effect. Artifice is a trace of art, as when transvestites let a hairy chest peek through an evening gown.

The clumsy prosthesis *miscegenation*, for example, often appears in quotation marks or glossed as a translation of *mestizaje*, the Spanish American mission of racial amalgamation that the Anglo version vilifies. English *uncle* for a Chinese speaker ignores the significant attribution of maternal or paternal, and *fair play* seems so particular to English that other languages poach it as fair game. *We* should be two words in any language, either including or excluding the interlocutor, for speakers of Quechua or Guaraní. Bilingual worries about words that say too much or not enough is a symptom of care, not of ignorance. But unwary monolinguals may mistake this exquisite and commonplace attentiveness for a speaker's deficiency. (Excess can also amount to deficiency, when it gets in the way of contact and leaves a wake of lack and loss. Among Molloy's memories is turning, half asleep, to a monolingual lover and murmuring something important, without knowing in which language the message came or why it went unattended.)

I could go on singing the bilingual blues, and I probably will, which is to recognize the bittersweet pleasures of *either/and* bilingual games. These are mature pleasures wrested from reflecting on pain, as therapists and art theorists will know, however slow they are to associate everyday bilingualism with sophistication. A tragic bilingual sense of life tolerates loss, not because it cancels sensual values, but because our deformed prosthetic selves survive losses with a perverse pleasure close to catharsis. This bittersweet maturity amounts to a taste for the commonplace sublime, an everyday experience and training process for bilinguals and their neighbors who live the daily shocks of disconnecting and who enjoy the satisfactions of reflecting on it.

Quotidian Metalinguistics

A tolerance for variation and the corollary sense of arbitrariness in language is the metalinguistic sophistication that sociolinguists notice in speakers of two or more languages.[59] Since most things have more than one name there's no mistaking the signifier for the signified, no forgetting that precarious meanings and relationships can fail you. On the other hand, the overload of symbolic systems underlines a reality that might seem illusory in one code. The world is real, and dear, because things and people exist beyond any one word that tries to capture them. And on yet another—third—hand (excess is the issue here) the risks—sometimes the anticipation—of failure make communication thrilling. Ordinary contact is close to the aesthetic experience. Running the risk of misrepresentation and misrecognition shows a kind of breathtaking vulnerability, a social death wish at the limit of bi-language games. Will addressing a stranger in Spanish be an invitation to intimacy or an offense to someone who prefers to pass? Will it reveal mistaken assumptions about someone who speaks Arabic or Hindi, but not Spanish? The question may not sound important to people who don't make these decisions daily and don't worry about the risk. Perhaps they counsel us to get over the complication and simply speak English ("This is how we do things here," is Brian Barry's bottom line),[60] as if worrying about which language to use were not an exercise in the interpersonal delicacy and caution that amount to civic behavior. Am I making any sense in English, to people who may be assessing what I say without offering to *asesorar*?

Letting a bilingual pun slip in, I ask for less judgment and more help. Between the prospect of failure and the promise of a miracle, the risk produces a schadenfreude of bilingual communication, a Freudian *Freude* of one word betraying another's meaning, except that the master was reluctant to follow slippery words past language barriers. Compare the correct German style of the *Wit* book to the Yiddishisms that speckle and sparkle in the letters to Fleiss.[61] The linguistic cleanup campaign can cost Freud some of the punch in his punchlines. For example, a funnier folk version about the doctor who pays no attention to the duchess who screams *Mon dieu* from labor pains, has him wait patiently playing chess, until the screams reach the desperate pitch of *Oy vey*. Wittgenstein too tried to be tidy, while he still hoped to organize materially grounded language into an enlightened graph that plots this for that. But the effort of the *Tractatus* was pure egolotry, he concluded. Language was not a totality, it was an infinity of unpredictable games. Logically, it needed room to play. And if philosophy closed in too hard with its own enlightened or stoic agendas that seemed frustrated by the contingencies and instabilities of language games, well, philosophy was making trouble for itself, not pointing out any trouble in language. Like Lacan's impatience with a "science" of psychoanalysis, Wittgenstein's response to the technocrats of meaning, in the *Philosophical Investigations*, was to stop arguing about correct answers and to start admitting a range of possibilities.

The departures from ego-psychology and from transparent language are urgent steps to follow, now that renewed and massive migrations fracture and fissure masses of people. Those on the move, sometimes back and forth to homes *unheimlich* on both sides, and those who stay put in places that migrants multiply through various frames, live in uncanny homelands that have foreign sounds, smells, cults, customs. Adding up to more than one, modern migrants (including my students) sometimes describe themselves, as half of one identity, half of another, and half of an additional something else.

This is not a cause for celebration, much as I'd like to count the excess as a gain and thereby counter anxiety over lost moorings with found riches. Anxiety about homelessness is real, for students and guest workers who may come and go, and also for reluctant hosts. One response is to treat anxiety as if it were a soluble problem, by restricting immigration, perfecting racial profiling, pronouncing English clearly enough for even foreigners to understand ("If English was good enough for Jesus Christ, it's good enough for you!") The response is possible, but not interesting, or fair, or even practical in a mature economy that depends on fresh foreign labor. "Enjoy your symptom," is another perverse but more practical and less damaging response.[62]

Hineini (Here I Am)

Not everyone will welcome anxiety in order to get neurotic kicks. Admiring the difficulties of communication is not (yet) an appealing practice for getting beyond conservative culturally biased rating systems for immigrant performance. A more common (and also reviled)[63] approach has been to multiply the criteria of value by the number of cultural centers and to treat cultural value as relative, translatable, despite some loss of currency in the exchange.[64]

49

Try to draw the multicentric cultural map. First, you collect the competing maps, each one with a particular culture at its center. Unlike premodern maps, each drawn around a center that claimed to be the true navel of the universe, today's composite will have to consider the cacophony of conflicting claims. One culture cannot, anymore, lie flat and tilt the world into alignment from its own centrality to peripheral declensions. Even Western liberalism, whatever pretensions it may have had before September 11, 2001, now trembles from the ardor of different imaginings.

To protect some maps from others that would edge competitors off the table, multicultural relativists arrange the maps into a manageable design by piling each navel-gazing view on top of the others into a palimpsest.[65] One culture is assumed to be no better or worse than any other. Each cultural navel is curiously disembodied, but at least they are all exposed with relative parity. In this game, the initial riot of hostility or the drone of indifference from one center to the others should turn into mutual recognition and respect for particular points of sensitivity. Touch here and black is beautiful; touch there and symmetry is perfection[66] ("God is a Lobster," as Deleuze and Guattari teased);[67] "touch-down" at evangelical points and make a sport of conversion.[68]

This is very touchy business as you can imagine, practically deadening for a sense of humor and therefore for a technical approach to aesthetics. I also think it is dangerously aggressive business, in its ambition to represent as much of the world as possible in an expansive language of value and measurement. It keeps the evaluator in virtual control, as his cultural competence grows ever greater. Well-meaning neighbors with a universalist bent may hope to redeem misprised minorities from isolation and devaluation, by straining to conquer more and more multicultural appreciation for beauty.[69]

Minorities, though, don't always want to be redeemed from difference. If they did, conversion stories would not need heroes or martyrs. Perhaps difference includes the relationship to beauty. Could the value of beauty be culturally specific? Maybe, sometimes, beauty is interpreted as a temptation away from holiness, or perhaps it is a corollary feature of godliness, or even too regular and boring to be interesting. No one, I think, knows enough to complete the chain of possible nonequivalences. Analogously, to assume that winning is better than losing takes only one model of gamesmanship as universally valid. Maybe there's more than one incentive to play (as Schiller tried to identify them, or as Latin American narrators perform in *Manuals for losers*).[70] Wittgenstein, as I said, knew the art of playing "badly."[71] Differences are of different orders, rather than dialects of the same expandable language. In practice, the crusade to be inclusive can be damaging both to the embracers and the embraced, because the hold is another pose for universalism in the name of respecting difference.[72] And a sign of back-door universalism, for all the cultural multiplicity of an expansive design, is that beauty stays centered as aesthetic value. ("Everything is beautiful in its own way.")

Embracing stable values through symbolic experience, even when culturally specific symbols multiply, is a natural response to the unnerving changes in modern times. Shklovsky's teachers embraced symbols to intuit eternal truths; Elaine Scarry still does.[73] The attraction of stability and immediacy was clear to Walter Benjamin too, but he cautioned against it. In place of the quick emotional fix of light and heat available from romantic symbols (or immediately discernible beauty), he recommended the irritating and tangled narrative vehicle of baroque allegory. The difference of formal preference, for Benjamin, amounted to a difference of political disposition. Gnarled dialectical stories were on the side of democracy.[74] Neat transcendent messages were on the side of fascism.[75] Caution against easy embraces (*abrazar/abrasar*) is one incentive to think of another, messier way to put together the heap of culture-bound maps. A (related) reminder is Mikhail Bakhtin's lesson about the liberating disarray of modernity, compared to the ideals of classical times. That's why he liked the novel the way Benjamin liked dialectical allegories. Novels let the roughness of history make trouble for ideals. True to their name, novels are new, unpredictable, not a formal genre but garbage heaps of other genres, battlefields for the conflicting codes that make novels messy enough to be modern.[76] Both Benjamin and Bakhtin would advise us to give up the ambition of putting all the maps into a palimpsest.

The very pretense of inclusion is pretty funny. Did you imagine that being in on all the jokes is the only way to get a kick from them? There is more than one way to get a joke, after all.

In order to regain a common ground we might multiply positions on a shared playing ground. Freud himself mapped out a few for Jewish jokes: (1) the teller, himself doubled between pride in his cleverness and minority self-hatred; (2) the listener who shares the blessing/burden; and (3) the gentile who may be the offended butt of the joke but who enjoys the reminder of his privileged status vis-à-vis the despised minority.

The irritated "outsider" position also belongs to Freud's barmaid, as she overhears the demeaning jokes that men tell when she comes near. If it weren't for her third position that incites intimacy "between men," there would be no jokes. Her embarrassment makes the stories funny. But she gets a laugh too, because all three know that when men get a kick from sexy jokes, it is a ridiculous and sorry substitute for getting sex.[77]

52

Who is the outsider in Roberto Fernández's joke about TB? Is it the imperfect translator, or her lung-scarred ward? Maybe it's the presumptuous doctor, or we listeners who know the many ways we don't quite fit any one position. The point is that ethnicity, origin, gender, and other social markers inflect reception; they don't block it. And the challenge will be how to process a range of receptions into the common sense *that a joke has been made* and that people are clever. Feeling offended and irritated are at least signs of collective life. A developed sense of humor can, perhaps, sublime those painful feelings into pleasures that depend on difference.

Humor and humility go together, to remember Freud's 1927 paper. So, before you even start to design a map of multiculturalism, get some distance and irony about your limited resources and leave cultural relativism alone. Relativism assumes that your ignorance amounts to the same thing as knowing that value is separate but equal. (For Michael Ignietieff, "Relativism is the invariable alibi of tyranny.")[78] It is also notoriously inconsistent: how can relativism be relative?[79] Ignorance (one's own strangeness) should figure, along with humility and humor, as a factor of aesthetic and political maneuvers. Losing control, being the butt of a joke, worrying where the border is and whether you've crossed it, these are aesthetic responses to the artful devices for gatekeeping on a multicultural map.

Humbled by the task, but also relieved of unrealistic goals, you can piece together the few more or less familiar (limited) multicultural maps that a person can manage to read. We can patch together the inherited and acquired pieces in a variety of designs and stitches. Strive for more flexibility than firmness, given life's changing boundaries, obsolescent technologies, trips, passions, and losses. Nothing is seamless in the hybrid patchwork:[80] voluble Greek city-zens, for example, look naked and idolatrous near the Hebrew nomads who minced words because they recorded them in hard stone. Liberal acquisitiveness seems unnatural next to ecological vegetarianism. English sounds funny to Spanish ("Ask her if she had TB/v.") And Spanish sounds funny to English (Juan who?—Juan, two, three.) Minority subjects are tragicomic because we also belong to a majority that hates us,[81] and majority subjects feel neglected by the particular cultures they can't quite understand. Double consciousness (and more) is no longer the bane of minorities, as it was for African American W. E. B. Du Bois, but the normal, unsettling, and dynamic way many of us live. (Freud didn't dispute the racist allegation that Jews were neurotic; he simply added that everyone else was neurotic too.) Eating, breathing, talking, loving, thinking bilingually—all have the slightly unhinged and unpredictable combinatory quality that brings them close to the risks and accomplishments of artistic innovation. Not that everyday bricolage amounts to making art, but the skills required to get through the day, and the obviously artificial arrangements, can and do unsettle convention and train taste to engage with aesthetic effects.

Feeling unsettled or unnerved doesn't necessarily please new-comers, but natives are more likely to consider uneasiness a problem to be solved rather than a condition of contemporary life. "How does it feel to be a problem?" white people are always asking under their breath, W. E. B. Du Bois complained in *The Souls of Black Folk* (1903), even when they are feeling kind. Monolinguals ask the same of immigrants, sometimes less discreetly but in a strange language. By the time immigrants or conquered people learn enough to answer, what do they say? Some deny being a problem anymore, having managed to forget the home language and to assimilate into the new one. Others will admit that living in two or more languages can make them a problem, which isn't an easy feeling. But it leaves room for maneuver. Doubling is a lesser evil, they observe, than full assimilation—which can risk self-hatred without gaining acceptance—or than refusing assimilation—which will cost them opportunities. An aesthetic sense of life will help to appreciate that sometimes feeling bad can feel good. This can be true for migrants and for hosts.

An extraliterary invitation to name and to illustrate the aesthetic devices particular to bilingualism is the political charm of linguistic overloads and underdeterminations. That charm holds out an opportunity for a new alliance between teachers of literature and policy makers. Aesthetic judgment, after all, depends on interpersonal assent, and interpersonal, political desires respond to aesthetic judgment about the beautiful.

Without an alliance between teachers of taste and public leaders, our polyrhythmic societies will continue to sound cacophonic instead of engagingly contrapuntal. Barbarous interruptions can make natives nervous, especially when color is a clue to foreignness. This makes pedagogy and politics lag dangerously behind creative literature. To take creativity's lead, we might cultivate a taste for imperfection and for irritation as features of democratic life. Civic life needs the predisposition for flexibility that a new aesthetic education could develop, and literary study needs something more technical if it hopes to recover an academic legitimacy for the social dimension of aesthetics.

Utopia is a never-never-land, an impossible place. For Ernesto Laclau "never" is also a warning, as in "never again."[82] The very desire for utopian fullness is dangerous. It wishes away struggle, and with it politics and desire. Fullness would banish the rights to challenge existing arrangements, because demands and creativity are responses to lack. Laclau conjures Lacan to warn us against wanting to fill in all empty spaces, since spaces make room for human maneuver. On the other hand, manuevers do need an objective and desire desires something fulfilling, though satisfaction may never come. Unmotivated maneuvers cannot add up to partial emancipations, David Harvey cautions. Don't be overly cautious: "The rejection, in recent times, of utopianism rests on an acute awareness of its inner connection to authoritarianism and totalitarianism (More's *Utopia* can easily be read this way). But rejection of utopianism on such grounds has also had the unfortunate effect of curbing the free play of the imagination in the search for alternatives."[83] Harvey recommends a "dialectical utopianism" (like Benjamin's dialectical allegory?)[84] that would take responsibility for closing off some possibilities by realizing others and that continues to play between dimensions of space and time.[85]

My point is that such play comes sharply into focus through bilingual bifurcations. To appreciate them as enabling and not simply destabilizing, desire itself needs to be retrained. Training, and the adjustment of feelings or preferences, can probably promote predispositions for one kind of politics or another. Without appropriate sensibilities even good laws don't work. Nationalism itself is a sensibility, Benedict Anderson explained, not an ideology that can be measured by cost and benefit.[86] A predisposition for end-of-history utopianism trains desire on one relentless track, but partial and plural emancipations will require a taste for risky sidetracks. Bilingual arts—in everyday code switching as well as in literary classics—make a display of risk, of artifice, and of the simultaneity of options even when choices must be made. The trainers who might be recruited include teachers of language and literature.[87] Perhaps they can refresh their taste for the risky and irritating maneuvers called

technique in language arts. Then language training, ubiquitous in public and private schools from kindergarten through college, can help to prepare hearts and minds for democracy.

Teachers of literature already appreciate negativity of meaning as room for interpretation and surprise (often called ambiguity), but they seldom make it matter for politics or deign to notice the exhibitionist ambiguity of bilingual arts. In fact, bilingual education is almost always a scaffold meant to get students from one language to another and then to fall away. Today, politics in literary studies seems inimical to the aesthetics of ambiguity. Can we deploy a taste for it to maneuver past identity politics into imperfect democratic engagements?

The Lacs

To refuse that taste is to court monologism (Bakhtin's metonymy for totalitarianism) in one form or another. And the danger should urge political theory to consider monolingual policies and their consequences. I have been urging Ernesto Laclau to engage here. His sagacious endorsement of partial and unsatisfying emancipations supports the defense of linguistic anxiety, because he values an uneven movement through the bad fits between structures of power and popular demands.

Anxiety need not lead to a lack of constraint or to the end of hegemonic power; it can acknowledge constraint and alienated power as the stimuli for political life. Laclau's patience for a politics that will achieve satisfactions but remain unfulfilled has a resemblance to the loose ends and split structure of bilingual subjects. There is, of course, a Lacanian parallel here, maybe an inspiration. Lacan had concluded that there is no help for homelessness, or for fragmentation and struggle. These are the unsettling ways that human beings are "at home" in the world.

Unheimlichkeit itself is a consciousness that goads creative responses and makes us human. Therefore, feeling good about feeling bad is the lesson, a perhaps unforgivably simple formulation but one that could be repeated, as unforgivably, for Laclau and for Roland Barthes, as we will see. It is also the lesson of a self-critical pause in the practice of psychology, that had assumed the unmitigated benefits of "self-esteem" for over a hundred years and is now considering the ravages of feeling too good about oneself.[88] Tolerating a measure of irritation and incompetence is an enabling condition of therapy, of aesthetic education, and of politics. But not all of us tolerate discomfort to the same degree. All are created equal, but in the real world some feel more equal than others, and these others feel more split. That heightened tragicomic feeling of being too much and too little can be a beacon for a new active political sensibility.

Low-degree fevers might perhaps prevent overheated utopian desire for coherence between nation and state. "Germany for the Germans" is such a desire. "Poland for the Poles" is another. Fullness of identity is an ideal that would overcome struggle, that is to say, creativity. But locating the lack of coherence in human identity, an imperfect materialization of a specular ideal, demands both creativity and the tolerance for imperfection that amount to humor or wisdom. Appreciation for gaps will need a new sentimental education, as I've been saying, to develop a taste for unfinished pieces. But for the moment, politics in literary studies seems inimical to the aesthetics of ambiguity, so we forfeit even the conventional techniques of interpretation that would foreground bilingual creativity. Political investments in literature are more likely to defend a particular identity inside the hegemonic language than to admire maneuverability between codes.

Le Marquis de Barthes

Any new alliance between aesthetics and politics can count on some incitations from language and literary theory. I'll claim good standard theorists as precursors for an alliance (as I am claiming Borges for this metaleptic move) in order to project a future tradition for reforming democratic feelings. For example, the advice to feel good about feeling bad, or at a loss, should be familiar from my references to Roland Barthes, even if you haven't read him. Shamelessly, he preferred the shock of sexual release (*jouissance*, translated as bliss because orgasm is too anatomical) over the feeling of fullness in pleasure. Doesn't this difference conjure up Kant's distinction between the sublime and the beautiful? Beauty describes repose; the sublime attests to movement: "The mind feels itself set in motion in the representation of the sublime in nature; whereas in the aesthetic judgement upon what is beautiful therein it is in restful contemplation" (*Critique of Judgement*, §27). Beauty derives from nature, Kant says, but the (neurotic) sublime "arises indirectly" from repressed vital forces, "making its discharge all the more powerful" (§23). Barthes doesn't mention Kant among the brilliant neurotics. He merely bypasses beauty, the "comfortable" pleasures that affirm a culture and do not break with it (14), in order to tarry at risky borderlines.[89] "Neither culture nor its destruction is erotic; it is the seam between them, the falult, the flaw, which becomes so" (7). At the brink between one culture and another, textual engagements are so intense that they disrupt consciousness.

Barthes is practically exhorting us to acknowledge a bilingual aesthetics as the core of literary theory, because jouissance happens when one tongue invades another: "the subject gains access to bliss by the cohabitation of languages *working side by side*: the text of pleasure [on the other hand] is a sanctioned Babel" (4). The Marquis de Sade, master of getting and giving textual kicks, taught the technique: bliss follows from collisions among "antipathetic codes (the noble and the trivial, for example)" (6). Collisions rip a gash, a raw seam at which the text, between shivers of bliss, comes to a brink between making sense and losing it. (Pnin evidently belongs to the school of Sade.) Rubbing words the wrong way feels right to hedonists and to neurotics. These are Barthes's best readers, because the wrong rub is shocking (4), always a surprise. Freud and Shklovsky knew this too, when they described wit and the aesthetic effect as an unpredictable release from habituation. "The subjective conditions of wit are so frequently fulfilled in the case of neurotic persons," Freud diagnosed (*Wit*, 760). A slap that heightens desire (Freud called it "the damming mechanism merely to intensify effect" [*Wit*, 714]) and surprise refreshes interest in the world to make life worthy, again, of our attention and of our care. (Is this Heidegger's link to aesthetics?) Kant himself knew the perverse pleasures of the hurts-so-good sublime: "Hence charms are repugnant to it; and since the mind is not simply attracted by the object, but is also alternately repelled thereby, the delight in the sublime does not so much involve positive pleasure as admiration or respect, i.e., merits the name of a negative pleasure" (*CJ*, §23); Schiller also kept his pedagogical finger on the edge of words that "cut the unwary."[90] Roughing it makes lust last. This is a personal incentive, of course, but the lesson in literary erotics should not be lost. Barthes knew that reciprocity is asymmetrical, and that the effect of fine literature is to leave the reader at a loss, panting for more contact but worried that it may come. Barthes's admission of joy in these frustrating engagements makes intermittent externality a necessary condition of intimacy. (See Winnicott too.)[91] It is also a condition of democracy. In bilingual aesthetics, externality is always visible and audible and it goads movement rather than marks impasses. Multitongued engagements are opportunities for a range of performances and asymmetrical receptions.

How Thrilling

Sometimes the disarming effect of estrangement titillates you. Other times it confounds expectations, or makes people laugh (or feel offended, maybe worried that they didn't get it). A chuckle, a raised eyebrow, a sigh of pleasure or even a silent reflection are some of the signs of marvel at a clever delivery of surprise. It is surprise that unhinges conventional associations and invites peeps into relationships (almost illicit because they are unconventional) just beyond your sober expectations. Barthes got the eroticized point of the aesthetic thrill when he theorized *The Pleasure of the Text* as the neurotic enjoyment of Peeping Toms and other lovers who would rather be teased than pleased too much. And the peepholes pried open by surprise keep the world permeable for (Neoplatonic) opportunities to improve creation and make it more stimulating for love.

Is beauty, then, the necessary or only value of aesthetic experience? I've already said that the surprise element seems more basic, although to read much of the debate on the virtues of aesthetic education today you'd think that Beauty (capitalized; pun intended) were the only measure of worth. Much of the left dismisses aesthetics as elitist, while the right assigns it the civilizing mission to save us from barbarism.[92] Barbarism's original meaning of *foreign* won't be surprising for either side of the fracas. It helps to ground the terms and the stakes of the argument in a classical language that conflates particular values with universal worth.[93]

I want to underline the surprise element here, and to bracket the little I have to say about beauty, in order to promote talk about art as technique rather than to get caught in the acrimony of evaluation. I'll reserve judgments for the chapter on Kant, "The Common Sense Sublime." But for now, in order to overdetermine an appreciation for clever code switching by appealing to more than one language of aesthetics, let's notice that jokes are not about judging; they are about immediate response. Audiences are neither right nor wrong; instead, they either laugh or they do not. "Because it is plausible to assert that an audience is wrong about, say, an opera (critics will judge) or a novel (posterity will judge), opera and literature can stake claims to seriousness. To be serious means to despise the audience—to reserve the right of appeal to a higher jurisdiction. But we can say what Freud says about the unconscious: there is 'no process that resembles 'judging' in its vicinity."[94] Freud dismisses judgment before it dismisses normally imperfect people.

A more conventional approach to form, unlike my (Bakhtinian/Barthesian) focus on codes in collision, would linger over the ideal (found, given, repeated) instances of this genre or that one, and it would deliberate over the relative success of these examples. It is a tradition that starts with Aristotle's description/prescription of perfect plays and continues with the legacy of Plotinus to equate beauty with form.[95] Alternative strains of literary formalism make foils of lofty ideals, or ideology.[96] This line of defense in the name of personal freedom recalls New Criticism and also the Russians' taste for quirkiness over habit. I prefer the Russian version because it makes more of roughness and uneasiness than of the beautiful polished product. In the same spirit, John Brenkman offers a roster of nonformalists: Lukács, Bakhtin, Adorno, Jameson, for whom "the beautiful," as Adorno calls the effect, is not the finished form but "the discontinuous moments of illumination that happen as a result of—or in a counter-movement to—the striving for formal coherence. 'Glory be to God for dappled things' —writes Gerard Manley Hopkins."[97] The mixed company of Marxists and renegades also recalls Wittgenstein's use for philosophy; it was to locate bumps: "The results of philosophy are the uncovering of one or another piece of plain nonsense and of bumps that the understanding has got by running its head up against the limits of language. These bumps make us see the value of the discovery" (*Philosophical Investigations*, 119).

Whether intentionally or not, beauty, as the value of art, favors eternal forms and nature over human effort. While emphasizing effort and technique comes from a revolutionary strain in romanticism that affirms man as a maker, talk of beauty calls us back through nostalgic romanticism to classical order and to veneration of what is given over what is made. Perfect poems, for example, achieve the gemlike quality of inalterable, natural objects.[98] I will grant, of course, to colleagues with a classicist bias, that the incentives to contemplate beauty may be greater in natural phenomena, like the sea, the sunrise, a face, a tree (a flawless poem), than from the tinkering of an irregular description, or a musical composition, or certainly from a joke. As long as the natural world stays calm and clear of sublime excess (an acquired taste for romantics and also for normally neurotic multiculturalists), it is perfectly *possible* that nature is more universally beautiful than the culturally constrained things that man can make.[99]

"Possible, but not interesting," is what Borges's favorite detective might say. More interesting for anyone concerned with history and society are the strange shock effects that the sublime offers, and also the technical devices that art shows off, like scars or stretch marks. Effect and technique are evidence of per-sonae who perform in the world. The unnerving effect can be the commonplace in-your-face foreignness that disables nativists and makes them outsiders to some games. "You don't know me. You don't own me," is the message.

What is the response? Anxiety, fear, and revulsion, are familiar reactions to incomprehensible strangeness. But you can't wish strangeness away without wishing away the strangers. No talk of gradual assimilation or even of multicultural pedagogies designed to domesticate strangeness can eliminate the frustration. Difference has a way of surviving domestication, especially when new and varied waves of immigrants keep upsetting the economy of tokens.

Since irritation is unavoidable, the only practical question is what to do with it. A primitive response is straightforward: it either rejects what it does not understand or it assimilates foreignness into familiar patterns, as if continuity between oneself and the world were the only bearable relationship to it. But a cultivated (Kantian et al.) response would do a double-take; it would feel fear *and* the satisfaction of having reflected on it. Strangeness can inspire passion without getting stuck there, because reflection allows one to take pleasure in the intensity and in the moral capacity to abstract from it. Reflection is a reflex that beauty demands too, so that anyone serious about art appreciation is trained to step back from the immediate response of pleasure and displeasure to turn private "taste" into public judgment.

But displeasure at finding yourself out of control or just incompetent to understand can cause you to take two steps back. Then reflection comes like the relief of pinching yourself after losing control. At two safe steps away, the scary effect, of foreignness, for example, is sublime. Nervousness about bilinguals isn't necessarily "paranoid," because the feeling may be justified. Latinos do joke about Anglos, you know, even when they deny it;[100] so do blacks joke about whites.[101] Bits of indigestible conversation—spiced by asymmetries of intelligence that favor bilinguals—can cause trouble for the troublemakers themselves, but the moments of superior control are too delicious to give up for transparent talk. If those flashes of subaltern control seem dangerous for democracy rather than healthy reminders of other asymmetries, one challenge for educators and intellectuals will be to reframe the fear of losing control. An aesthetic option is to call that loss the first stage of the "multicultural sublime." It promises mature pleasures in exchange for a moment of pain. That interpretive move might mitigate the bite of bilingual performances, if the desired effect were aggression.

But often these are love bites that tease and taunt to get a rise of attention. At least we could anticipate the playfulness, if we developed more aesthetic refinement. The games of inclusion and exclusion (what linguists call "gatekeeping") produce artful effects that depend on a range of possible receptions. One way to *get* a joke is to notice that you missed something, or that someone else got it differently. In other words, the days of the single, ideal or target reader are gone. Readers move variously in and out of games. Acknowledging that variety of perceptions will be no small advance for education. But it would hardly be radical for readers of literary criticism, if they remember the Surrealists' taste for strange juxtapositions. Then Barthes added the confession that taking one's pleasure from a text is a neurotic taste for the (mildly masochistic) kicks gotten from attractive bouncers and gatekeepers.

Strange art and techniques of estrangement open onto a range of engaging questions and answers about human creativity. But value judgments about beauty are doomed to either debatable ratings, or to "separate but equal" cultural relativism that often misses both of the intended marks: competent judgment and egalitarian norms. Separate is not equal. And "equal" is not interesting for aesthetics. That is why my own limited human efforts that miss more than they can hit prefer the Russian (multilingual) formalists who ask, What makes art work?, rather than worry whether or not it is good art. This preference for technical analysis over value judgment has the additional attraction of being more intellectually rigorous than conservative defenses of beauty (even when the defense claims to be multicultural). Scholarship, after all, is not in the business of assigning value but of pursuing information and analysis. That is why the genteel arbiters of taste who taught an earlier generation didn't call themselves scholars. They were priests, not professionals, and they reviled the déclassé professionalization of teaching. (Mister, rather than Professor, was the honorific title.)

Of course my own class of rank-and-file education workers also makes judgments when choosing books to read and assignments to write. And some left-wing and right-wing revivers of aesthetics describe these decisions as value choices. They are value choices. But the defense of aesthetics will miss a step if it equates *all* aesthetic value with "beauty" ratings.[102] More than one criterion should guide choices. There is, for example, the value of innovation that interrupts habit (think of Pound's review of important but forgotten poets),[103] and also historical effectiveness (foundational fictions), as well as exemplarity of particular techniques (Rigoberta's secrets). A renewed taste for technique is probably a better exercise for developing multicultural respect than the remedy that multiplies never quite separate or equal value ratings.

An effect of the bilingual blues is to notice that the positions of reader and writer are more than two. To Barthes's provocations against complacent "ideal" readers, bilinguals can add that there are many levels and angles of ignorance and bliss. All are less than ideal, because a single ideal would elide personal differences as if they hardly mattered. Is there a place for ideal (utopian) readers in irritatingly heterogeneous societies?[104]

Under His Nose

Freud obviously saw himself in the privileged place of the ideal reader. His irritating cultural foreignness put him there. The funniest thing about his joke book is that it holds out for universal validity by holding up a nontransferable minoritarian model. Being Jewish was like being normal, but more so, according to Freud. His contradiction seems staged, like slapstick: the universalizing project to study the (ahistorical, culturally nonspecific) unconscious slips on the banana peel of one Jewish joke after another. Jokes about paupers, about marriage brokers, about primitive habits and incorrigible outsiders . . . He can hardly stop, and ends up theorizing their particular and superior qualities. (In fact, Freud already had made "a collection of profound Jewish stories" before he decided what to do with them, as he tells Fleiss in a letter of 1897.[105] What is more, he can tell them *because* he is Jewish:

> They are stories which were invented by Jews themselves and which are directed against Jewish peculiarities. The Jewish jokes made up by *non-Jews* are nearly all brutal buffooneries in which wit is spared by the fact that the Jew appears as a comic figure to a stranger. The Jewish jokes which originate with Jews admit this, but they know their real shortcomings as well as their merits, and the interest of the person himself in the thing to be criticized produces

the subjective determination of the wit-work which would otherwise be difficult to bring about. (*Wit*, 705).

Freud's universal economy of the one who can stand for the all has to ignore what Derrida taught us to call the "dangerous supplement" of another (competing, despised) code and another be-longing, until the supplement that breeds self-hatred and irony explodes in Freud's favorite jokes. Jokes are supposed to be universal products of neurotic inspiration; they blast open the clogged paths of repression. But Jewish jokes, he insisted, do it best. "We demand no patent of nobility for our examples, nor do we make inquiries about their origin. The only qualifications we require are that they should make us laugh and serve our theoretical interest. It is to be remarked that both these demands are satisfied best by Jewish jokes" (657). Practically all his examples are Jewish. Sander Gilman noticed this too, but he read the contradiction as a symptom of thwarted assimilation. I want to add the note of sly vindication for the indelible difference. The difference was under his nose, but the "scientific" ideal of universality perched like a queer pair of glasses on that nose—in Wittgenstein's simile—and narrowed his vision.[106]

Even if Freud was careful to keep his High German scientific prose free of the *mittel hoch* variety known as Yiddish, he was used to hearing and playing the games of high and low, and couldn't help but notice the familiarity of linguistic vagrancy in other people's speech. Foreign words manage to slide (*verschieben*) past linguistic control and release clinically significant information, when you know how to listen to double-talk. Duplicity in language and the interpretive twist that Freud gave it are among Lacan's favorite lessons from the master. He mentions one of Freud's few textual examples from the 1927 paper on fetishism. There, Freud reported his inspired solution to an enigmatic "shine on the nose" *(Glanz auf der Nase)* that a patient needed to see in order to achieve sexual satisfaction. The glistening Glanz turned out to be a "glance," in English, because the bilingual patient was suffering from an early childhood fixation with "a glance" at the nose (the desired phallus) of his mother.[107] Lacan doesn't comment on the bilingual structure of the pun or on the bilingual response of Freud's witty analysis. He simply notes the general mechanism of sounds-like associations as a good example of the universally unstable bar between signifier and signified that he privileges as the core intuition of Freud's science, even before Saussure formulated it as S/s.[108]

Everyone can experience language as arbitrary and slippery; but bilinguals can hardly avoid the (aestheticizing) risk/thrill of slippery speech. Veering from one signifier to another, in ways that affect the signified, is a technique of disguise, or escape, or privileged association that marks multilinguals even when we're not trying to be funny. I remember old ladies in my neighborhood who had *veryclose* veins, because varicose made no sense in the English they knew, so they corrected it. They were the same funny ladies who figured that Giselle McKenzie of television's *Hit Parade* must be famous, because *mir kennen sie* (slurred as *me ken sie*). She was much more famous than the already forgotten Sean Fergussen.

Like Freud, Lacan reads for universals, as if the shining example of the nose were not revealing in a culturally particular way, and as if Freud's cleverness didn't depend on anticipating a sidestep, soccer's *jogo de cintura*, that switches from legitimate language to homey and hidden code. The glistening example certainly underlines Freud's point about the relationship between wit and the unconscious. But the double bilingual performance of symptom and solution could do much more: It could open up Freud's work—like the Bakhtinian hinge of stylistics that pries open linguistics, philsosophy, and politics—from the centripetal call to univocal order toward unruly living languages that pull away from centers. Speaking and decoding Glanz/glance are among the many moves that can double us up with laughter or send us sliding from one language to another to poach resources or to dodge dangers. The economic release of repressive energy that Freud describes turns out to be an effect of interpretation as well as of delivery. It has a family resemblance to other sources of surprise interruption that play language games called wit. Among those sources are the perfectly visible, legitimate, and parallel languages that play games with one another, like stealing a base or wiggling away from a tight spot onto another turf. Remember Evangelina Vigil Piñon's "amiga, unaffected / masca y truena su chicle." Wit would turn out to be the work of art as well as of unconscious mechanisms, and Freud would find even firmer grounds for code switching between psychoanalysis and poetics, and for calling the witwork Verdichtung.

But bilingual arts might also have upset Freud. They don't always depend on the unconscious economy of repression and release. And Freud does depend on it. Without the unconscious, he has no science. In Freud's theory of wit, desire needs to dip into the unconscious in order to free a repressed thought through a clever association. Without the dip, the flash of inspiration that amounts to a loss of control, there is no wit. But a good bilingual joke doesn't necessarily take the dip; it can sidestep from one language into a perfectly visible and shared playing field of alternate words and associations. I need an unconscious? Bilingual jokes are clever, and yet widely available. They are sophisticated but democratic, especially when they invert expectations of handicaps between poor and privileged players. Even a limited vocabulary in two languages can mire monolinguals in a quicksand of code switching. What would Freud have done with this riotous surface where TB is a television and Juan is the first in a numerical series?

Lacan didn't ask about surfaces. He followed Freud's digression down into an unconscious "noseology." Shklovsky and Sterne would also have joined the excursion, but moving sideways, tagging after Uncle Toby's digressions on glances toward unsightly anatomies. Too bad Julia Kristeva isn't laughing, says John Limon, and generally strange that laughter doesn't lighten "Kristeva's nosography. There are moments when its exclusion seems almost perverse."[109] Lacan, on the other hand, enjoyed Freud's joke book and concluded that desire plays witty games with language. So there was no point in simply getting meanings right if one hoped to read desire. The waywardness of desire that pulls words between intended meaning and precarious means also splits the subject. There was no therapeutic point to adapting the ego to the world, as the Anna Freudians presumed to do. The modern world that had unmoored subjects from stable patriarchal arrangements was no place to tidy up the tensions, but to acknowledge and tolerate them. Unrequitable desire may be a problem, but not one to wish away, any more than we should seek "solutions" for the split nature of language that abstracts meaning from means. People desire and language abstracts. Separation from self, splitting, irony, these are conditions of life, not curable mistakes. Maybe everyone knows this, but bilinguals don't forget it. Maybe they can remind monolinguals to stay on edge, where art irritates and jokes go off in many directions.

3 Irritate the State

There are some things within our social order to which I am
proud to be maladjusted and to which I call upon you to be
maladjusted . . . As maladjusted as Abraham Lincoln who had the
vision to see that his nation could not exist half slave and half free.
Martin Luther King Jr., "The Power of Nonviolence" (1957)

The world is shaken now, after the September 11, 2001
attack that brought down New York's Twin Towers and
left a gash in military headquarters, reduced to what cal-
low punsters were calling the Penta-gone. Picking up the
pieces and patching up the holes is not easy for people who had
never imagined that terror would touch them so closely and
continue to hover, in menacing circles. So much of that menace
is military, given the escalation of international campaigns by
the United States and the inevitable but unchartable reprisals.
The dread is immediately political too, as domestic precautions
crimp civil liberties and foreign peoples mix condolences with
reminders of the provocations and unpopularity of the United
States. Envy is not their only incitation, despite invidious protests of innocence at home. It was the United States, after all,
that ensured the Taliban's victory against the Soviet Union and
prepared Afghanistan to be headquarters for a global jihad.[1]

Islamic extremism was for Carter's cold war what the Nicaraguan dictator Somoza was for Franklin Delano Roosevelt's campaigns, and what so many other despots have been for U.S. interests, "a son of a bitch, but our son of a bitch."[2] And after "liberating" Iraq from dictatorship, despite relentless worldwide and domestic protest against the invasion, U.S. interests confirm the public's suspicion that going to war was going after oil.[3] Much messier than the Pentagon had predicted, war is now mixed with other worries about the aftermath in Afghanistan, about instability in Iraq, and about eroding personal rights while private and public resources seem exhausted. Optimism was strained anyway by an economic slump just waiting to sink, and then it went almost numb from terror.

Cultural responses don't seem urgent, to say the least, and those of us in the business of offering such responses may look interesting only as savings in budgets that can be cut in the name of a greater cause. But culture is at the core of this crisis, and exhaustion doesn't excuse us from taking the core to heart. While Islamic extremists engage in a holy war against the evil West, calls go out for a Christian crusade against the evil East.[4] And though terrorists blame the United States for supporting a Jewish state, they also defend Muslim regimes that dismiss secular Arabs.[5] The passion and prejudice make an alternative scenario both increasingly vital and dangerously delicate. It will have to cultivate a taste for secular heterogeneous states that can embrace religion without getting carried away. The taste is vital because democracy needs stamina for the precariousness that comes with conflicting demands, and it is delicate, since a terrified world will hardly welcome dissension. But if we managed to banish risk altogether, and be rid of the "negative" moments of disagreement and doubt,[6] there would be little democracy left to defend.[7] Self-defense itself needs more space for dissent than single-mindedness allows. "It's harder to believe [in convergence] today," after the invasion of Iraq, Richard Nisbett said as a coda to his book *How Asians and Westerners Think Differently . . . and Why*. "That's the hopeful conclusion."[8] Risk and doubt remind us not to second-guess other people and preempt what they have to say.[9]

That is one reason to notice bilingual jokes. I raise this without levity. The jokes punctuate the democratic signs of cultural difference and acknowledge them with a laugh. Democratizing differences survive the minor explosion. In fact they are brightened by the attention to difference as an enabling condition of freedom and pleasure. Most liberals, however, aren't laughing yet. Conflicts of creed, culture, and language are familiar but threatening for many theorists of liberalism. And literary critics can be so falsely secure that they don't even percieve threats to their interpretive authority. Few smart from the slaps that minority writing can alternate with embraces.[10] Critics still prefer to take off-putting comments as pleasantries on the shared road to universalism. For example, they familiarize *Beloved* as a great novel in the modernist tradition, and Richard Rodriguez as an exemplary American scholar. But political theory makes no mistake about particularism's challenge to the interpretive authority of liberalism. Seen as the shadow side of universalism rather than its irritating codependent term, particularism has the chiaroscuro effect of drawing a bold line between advocates for group rights on one side and defenders of universal liberalism on the other.

Without getting derailed into the long and detailed arguments between liberals and their (communitarian) critics, I want to draw the broad lines of the debate in order to frame my own defense of irritating brushes between peoples and among them. This is certainly not to endorse conflict among people but to acknowledge it as normal and functional. It is one thing to irritate the state in ways that tease procedural solutions from conflicting demands (as Habermas sees it) or that stretch a system by admitting foreign elements that thereby become familiar (on Niklas Luhmann's view).[11] But it is quite another thing to imagine that irritants are pleasant. The question is how to address existing unpleasantness. Denying the frustration will let it fester and perhaps explode. To acknowledge irritation, on the other hand, may stimulate more than one response. Aggression is a familiar option. Another is the normally neurotic thrill of aesthetic response. If we hope to mitigate nuisance with the pleasure of aesthetic effect, we will need a new sentimental education. Retraining responses to strangeness will also, I suggest, promote democratic life. Strangeness, opposition, and negativity, like the zero that enables mathematical operations, demand and therefore beg political procedure.

The debate between liberals and communitarians, about parameters of procedure, includes speculations on how fundamentally different national traditions, steeped in their own particular principles, might overlap on a set of universal human rights.[12] Some theorists have almost forgotten how normal cultural double-talk sounds among U.S. citizens (like Milwaukee's Ms. Mariner). Either/or defenses of belonging on behalf of compatriots whose families hail from elsewhere sound too simple, romantic, and outdated.[13] Sometimes, the indigestible effect of these unnecessary choices is "splendidly dyspeptic."[14]

Indigestion

"The mixed plate" of cultures, as Hawaiians call their heterogeneity, sits badly with some reluctant but defenseless consumers of multicultualism, since like it or not, "we are all multiculturalists now."[15] Given current rates of immigration and trends that refuse one-way assimilation for the foreseeable future, the challenge will be how to live with the mix rather than how to judge it. Upset liberals hardly hunger for the mixed plates, though they can generally live with multiculturalism as long as it doesn't interfere with the principle of personal human rights. But in practice, dissenters from classic liberalism complain, this is hardly a concession at all. Cultural neutrality barely tolerates difference, because the principle of personal rights is a priority that turns out to be culturally preferential. Based in collective beliefs and practices, real difference—they say—requires recognition of group rights and exception from a presumptively universal law that, in fact, favors one culture over others.[16] Hard-line liberals respond to backsliders by saying that group rights simply contradict the fundamental principle of individual rights, however subtly cultural rights are defended: either an individual takes priority, or the group does.

Skeptics of individual rights point out, persuasively, that the world is too asymmetrical for anyone to anticipate fairness from universal norms that are blind and deaf to differences among groups. Liberalism's alleged bias against disadvantaged groups (constituted by race, ethnicity, gender, sexuality, religion, language) drives some theorists toward the alternative bias in favor of cultural rights. Members of undervalued groups suffer, says Charles Taylor among others, when their collective rights to resources and representation fail to win debates because individuals are imagined to be autonomous from group identifications. The complaint seems unobjectionable, but the remedy of group autonomy has seriously insalubrious side effects. One is intolerance for internal difference, since the cultural dynamic to be defended is not irritation but a particular and untranslatable spirit of a people, a romantic Herderian coziness of one compact culture threatened by contamination from another.[17]

Authenticity, the right to live "*my* way,"[18] keeps a straight and narrow course in Taylor's politics of recognition, as if sidetracks lead us astray. Disrespected people seem pitifully damaged and distant to Taylor, rather than interestingly doubled. "Their first task ought to be to purge themselves of this imposed and destructive identity" (the way Herder prescribed purging as a cure for cultural flatulence) lest they share the "crushing" fate of Caliban (26). Caliban crushed? Has Taylor seen *The Tempest*, not to mention the many Caribbean sequels that turn the tide on Prospero's Eurocentrism? Readers and theatergoers will know that Caliban is not crushed. Shakespeare gave him credit for vengeful creativity, and Caribbeans continue to claim Caliban as the mixed man who maneuvers inside and alongside master codes.[19] As for the remedy of purging self-hatred, surely the medicine is worse than the ailment. An attack on a piece of oneself can only aggravate self-hatred rather than bring relief.[20] Better to add pieces, and thereby destabilize any one identity, than to pursue a purity that cannot tolerate our damaged selves. Some defenders of authenticity target nation-states (as did Herder, their patron saint) not minorities, to demand respect for sovereignty against liberal crusaders.[21] But whether defenders tout the obligation to ethnic minorities or to sovereign states, in either case respect is a *feeling* not a legislatable rule. How does one demand, rather than cultivate, a sentiment?

Respect is either felt or not felt, like jokes that either provoke laughter or do not ("to laugh over the same witticisms is proof of absolute psychic agreement" [Freud, *Wit*, 737]). By contrast, judgments appeal to understanding or to reason. Until the early eighteenth century, European philosophers generally understood that sympathy and moral sentiment bind the individual to a community. Affective links can also bind one community to another. Though Adam Smith wrote *The Wealth of Nations* to show the collective benefits of self-interest, he knew that self-interest can also be self-destructive for more reasons than the violence Hobbes had observed.[22] One reason is that man is gregarious and needs company, Smith had established earlier, in the *Treatise on the Moral Sentiment*. Sociability is a necessary condition of human life, so sustained self-interest knows the limits of other people's feelings and also the virtues of fictions that fostered relationships. Empiricists like David Hume also admitted that actions follow from sentiment, not from reason.[23] But Smith had little use for the authenticity that motivated Rousseau, for example, or Herder. Like Kant, Smith recognized that civilized personae were masks, necessary artifices that could not and should not be removed.[24] About Kant, he was so upset with the airless provincialism of his student Herder that he responded with the cosmopolitan *Critique of Judgement*.[25]

In both ethnic-communitarian and country-based cases, a preference for cultural coziness over cosmopolitanism and conflict can gag even a voluble practice like Bakhtin's dialogism. Taylor conjures the reference because it seemed opportune. For Taylor, Bakhtin's "dialogism" describes the formative process of human personalities, an allegedly intimate give-and-take of family and community that conditions human life. It is "what we have in common with people we love; how some goods become accessible to us only through such common enjoyment."[26]

Bakhtin would have been scandalized. For him dialogism meant struggle or irresolvable debate among many languages; it was conflict not community. Dialogism, the radical feature of the modern novel he first described in Dostoevsky's work, became the hallmark of all novels worthy of the (insubordinate, nonconformist, tirelessly experimental) name of a form too unpredictable to be a genre. Dialogism refers to unreconciled points of view and to particular uses of language that distinguish one character from an agonistic other. Even the author occupies one position among several competitors. Bakhtin countered critics who noticed Dostoevsky's multivoiced world but "found no other course than to monologize" it into a new artistic will. "Dostoevsky, like Goethe's Prometheus, creates not voiceless slaves (as does Zeus), but rather *free* people who are capable of standing *beside* their creator, of disagreeing with him, and even of rebelling against him. *The plurality of independent and unmerged voices and consciousnesses and the genuine polyphony of full-valued voices are in fact characteristics of Dostoevsky's novels.*"[27] This description surely seems better *taylored* to liberalism's renewed respect for cultural discontinuities than to communitarian idylls of nurturing continuity between a group and its members.

78   Another unhappy side effect of Taylor's communitarian remedies is the preferential consideration for all "actually evolved cultures" as bearers of a people's lasting spirit and therefore worthy of group rights. This leaves out evolving or emerging cultures, precisely the "communities" that most urgently demand a politics of fairness.[28] But even this limited degree of cultural relativism that claims to respect long-standing cultures can seem insincere. Given Taylor's Kantian intuitions about general human potential as the anchor for a universal claim to respect, we should anticipate judgments about the relative value of cultural achievements as having developed the potential to different degrees.[29] In any case, as I said, respect is a sentiment to be trained, not a rule to be demanded.

In bolder and less cautious hands than Taylor's, yet another damaging effect of community over individual has been to affirm the venerable practices of gender and generational hierarchies. "Is multiculturalism bad for women?" Susan Moler Okin asks.[30] Not if women know how to take advantage of the bad fits between home and host environments, several respondents answer. Liberating maneuvers between particular (collective) cultures and universal (personal) rights can trigger traditional mechanisms of reform in home cultures. Updating traditions avoids the trash-and-burn approach of liberal triumphalism that has demoted minority women, and men, as aspirants to authenticity. Nevertheless, defenses of cultural rights do run into ethical quicksand when demand for uncritical autonomy endorses moral relativism[31] and condones the damage that groups can do to their members.[32]

Groups need not go so far as autonomy, say defenders of liberalism, because the principle of personal rights has enough flex capacity to accommodate multicultural societies. Yes, liberalism favors individual rights, but an individual is anchored in collective beliefs and practices. A person does not think or feel in a cultural vacuum, Jürgen Habermas agrees with communitarians, so that respect for individuals implies respect and recognition for one's culture, race, language, etc. In fact, he adds that rights and obligations are themselves products of historical and cultural contexts and subject to adjustment as contexts change.[33]

Michael Ignatieff takes the interdependence of particular cultures and universal rights to an even higher level. If some worry about liberalism overrunning difference, his "claim is the reverse: that moral individualism protects cultural diversity, for an individualist position must respect the diverse ways individuals choose to live their lives . . . Human rights is only a systematic agenda of 'negative liberty,' . . . a tool kit that individual agents must be free to use as they see fit within the broader frame of cultural and religious beliefs that they live by."[34] Take, for example, the reciprocal benefits and "mutual transformation" of Latinos and labor unions.[35] Ethnic solidarity can reinvigorate unions and promote Latinos into labor leaders. Their promotion also obliges Latino leaders to defend the rights of mixed constituencies in multiethnic unions.

With these acknowledgements, there is no philosophical reason to distinguish, as Taylor does, between Liberalism 1 (the personal variety) and Liberalism 2 (the expanded variety that includes group rights), because one requires the other in logical and organic ways. The individual requires the group to anchor personal identity, as a source of taste and values, and the group requires the free and creative participation of the individual, if it is to thrive in a liberal constitutional state.

Habermas juggles this broad interpretation with liberal hands, two of them. Someone else might have wanted to deconstruct the unstable opposition between liberalism (1) and communitarian liberalism (2), showing that one term depends on the other in the very struggle for legitimacy. But Habermas doesn't dismiss the terms as equally deluded partners. Instead, he leads with one and follows up with the other. Liberalism gives two-way support for rights: first the restricted "respect for the individual," and then the stretch to groups since "individuals identify through collectivities." Keeping both meanings inside liberalism allows tensions between a particular culture and general political norms that might seem out of place in communitarian arrangements.

The democratic constitutional state, Habermas says, can require only "political socialization" not cultural assimilation. This "uncoupling" of politics from culture will be a relief from the stranglehold of nation-state ideologies, where, for example, Germany is for Germans. Always unstable—oxymoronic in fact since nation refers to culture and state to administrative structure—nation-states aggressively insist on their coherence. By prying the terms apart, Habermas in fact revives a premodern distinction beween nation and state that had survived until the League of Nations failed to defend it.[36] On firm historical ground then, Habermas says that liberalism can accommodate culturally distinct immigrants, but not by compromising legal principles even if the principles become objects of scrutiny and

80

reform. "Nothing, including immigration, can be permitted to encroach upon [the state], since that identity is founded on the constitutional principles anchored in the political culture and not on the basic ethical orientations of the cultural form of life predominant in that country."[37] Uncoupling sets constitutional norms on ideally neutral ground. But to achieve a degree of freedom from any one culture, norms will need to be irritated by foreignness in order to distinguish between principle and practice.[38]

This constitutional priority of personal rights certainly irritates groups that claim decision-making powers over their members. But the frustration itself can lead to internal dynamism and to reforms that benefit groups. "Even those with no particular pretensions toward democracy will be vulnerable to internal pressure," as in churches "pressed on by internal processes of discussion, reflection, and critique" to ordain women.[39] For minority women in traditional patriarchal cultures, this internal pressure can counter the "choose and lose" alternative between group identity and liberal rights.[40] Orthodox Jewish women in the United States have forced themselves into the strictly male rabbinate.[41] And Muslim women in Egypt took advantage of secular reforms to loosen religious constraints.[42] In other words, along with the advantages of clarity and simplicity for legislators and judges, liberal norms provoke dynamic responses to certain personal demands. For one thing, insisting on the universal rule of liberal law underlines the personal option to exit from a group when one's voice is dismissed, and this option warns traditionalists that intransigence can cause attrition. Tradition knows how to adjust and to change postures, after all, since "tradition" itself is often a paradoxically modern response to liberal modernity.[43] (Lenny Bruce, for example, reinvented an already lapsed tradition in response to his parents' move to the assimilated suburbs. To go back to the ethnic inner city he "had to memorize the little Yiddish he dropped into his act.")[44] Though liberal law doesn't tend to interfere with internal governance of churches, a high economic cost of exit that incurs personal damage to dissenters can give the state one reason to intervene for compensation. Notorious instances of sexual abuse give another reason.[45] But in some matters that would be actionable elsewhere, say in matters of sex discrimination,[46] churches are autonomous voluntary associations. It's not the law but the lure of exit for disgruntled women that can put pressure on exclusivist men.

The reform effect of liberalism on illiberal cultural practices may be self-evident or intuitive for advocates of universal principles, but what of the countervailing pressure from apparently illiberal practices on liberal procedures? Have liberalism's advocates considered what "foreign" traditions and disidentification from a powerful hegemonic culture can do for the value of neutrality? Judith Butler senses the value of disidentification, a feeling of oneself as foreign and cautious, though George Yúdice faults the posture because it can get to feel normal.[47] Michael Warner also warns about the trouble with normal.[48] What is normal? Novelist and critic Silviano Santiago proposes to stay precarious, or irritated, not disidentifying from one position, but attached to more than one.[49]

This self-conscious attachment to "more-than-one" is the missing piece of an otherwise dynamic defense of universal rights in a multicultural world. Particular demands actually do work for democracy. The demands nudge liberalism toward neutrality, when strangers "take" rights and activate the principles of sometimes sluggish universal law. Habermas's defense of liberalism's knack for uncoupling particular cultures from a constitutional state does not go far enough. We should ask why the liberal state might *need* cultural minorities. The reason is obvious. Minorities make culture visible and tangible enough to "uncouple" it from constitutional protections. Otherwise, the "cultural form of life predominant" in a country passes for natural or neutral. Without the uncoupling operation between politics and particular cultures, procedure might be confused with cultural practice.

So it is *thanks to the multiplicity* of national cultures within one polity that (cultural) affiliation can be distinguished from (constitutional) law. The two codes of belonging are often parallel and sometimes mutually interfering. It is time we envision them as codependent, since the conflicting tastes and demands of particular cultures interfere in what can become a dangerous implosion of the biologically and culturally predominant nation with the political state it inhabits. Such codependence shows collective law as a lingua franca among particular and otherwise uncoordinated language (ethnic, religious) communities. Can we get used to the advantages of irritating gadflies, and of the liberating double-talk in democracies, between lingua franca and mother tongue? Irritation can hold procedure to higher standards of fairness than can the drone of familiar practice. It will help to hear this dialogue of competing cultures, particularly the ways cultural minorities talk in constitutional principles back to the state.

Standard descriptions of the United States as a nation of immigrants represent newcomers as unencumbered by earlier attachments, happy to leave the old country for the superior benefits and values of the new one. We know, however, that mass migrations are usually effects of push factors from wars and famine at home, along with the pull of American attractions. When immigrants take liberties and resources, they can disappoint their defenders, who feel like abused or betrayed lovers. But democratic subjects always take liberties and provoke a double dynamic: they push liberalism into more culturally neutral shape, while they pull particularism into line with universal human rights. Reading this way puts me clearly on the side of liberalism, but on its reflexive side. For all its limitations in practice, liberalism has at least a self-correcting potential that alternatives lack.[50]

Democratic deliberations can bring liberals and defenders of group rights to mature conciliatory positions, Habermas and Seyla Benhabib conclude. After all, opponents differ over the means of achieving fairness and human dignity, not over the goals. Attention to particulars can ground the debates without letting constitutional principles run aground. The deliberative process can coordinate differences and neutralize irritation. Benhabib comes close to suggesting the salutary effects of irritation as a stimulus to democratic process, but this may be my wishful overreading. Perhaps, for good reason, political theorists are reluctant to risk enthusiasm for the trouble minorities can cause a state. But a literary critic can take that license.

Gothic Thriller

Tellingly, Bonnie Honig's theory of democracy's dependence on foreigners comes very close to literary criticism. She takes liberalism's fundamental respect for personal autonomy and its corollary precaution against thinking for others to a logical consequence: "It is important to rethink democracy in non-kinship terms, as a politics among strangers."[51] We have been telling ourselves the wrong story about politics, she says. It's not a projected romance of reconciliation, though the magical happy endings fantasized in "foundational fictions" still keep most political theorists in thrall. It is a gothic thriller. Democracy is a double-edged adventure, full of uncertainties about the hero's character and about the law that might protect the heroine.[52]

Israeli songwriter Chava Alberstein put the desire and dread to music and words:

> I love foreign letters
> They are like drawings
> They are like secret signs
> From magic places
> From different worlds.
> I don't know what they mean
> I hope they mean well.[53]

Gothic lovers both desire and fear one another's strangeness. Honig's brilliant adjustment of the narrative frame makes room for foreigners as the necessary and dangerous supplements to the *demos* that would be democratic.[54] She reads stories, from the biblical Ruth through Rousseau's and Freud's lawgivers to Hollywood's *Shane*, in order to uncouple (cosmopolitan) democracy from the ambivalent, good and bad, power of the national culture.

I want to take full advantage of the double-dealing, "passionate ambivalence"[55] between patriotism and borderless rights to argue for the democratizing effects of provocation. Provocation describes an inside-outside maneuverability (or aesthetics) between particularism and universalism, slaps and embraces, which uncouple culture from politics so that they can interact in restless dynamic ways. When a political framework flexes enough to neutralize irritation and to coordinate divisive cultural claims, is it refreshed and made strong by the exercise or just dangerously stretched? If improvement is the result, the irritant deserves some credit. Without trouble, where is the incentive to refine conventions? Without the pain of assimilating foreigners, there's less gain in democratic procedure for natives.

Irritation, in other words, can "roughen" (as the Russian formalists would say) the perception of fairness and thereby renew its appeal. This "aesthetic" effect can defamiliarize liberal laws and send international shock waves to the closed concept of national sovereignty. Ironically, liberalism's defense of individual rights encourages noncitizen residents to make claims based on human rights beyond the state courts. One consequence is a refinement of liberal democratic procedure. At the international level, especially in the European Union, Honig says, foreigners thereby exert healthy pressure on democratic constitutional states.[56] Why, then, she asks, "has there been so little attention to the complex, constitutive, role of foreignness as the necessary supplement to national democratic imaginations, in most contemporary debates about [United States] citizenship, and even about immigration?"[57]

Strange Remedies

Consider the notorious French case of the three Muslim girls (three, as in the frontier ballad of old Spain about Axa, Fátima, y Marién) that Seyla Benhabib reviews. They wore headscarves to public school after they were forbidden to do so, demanding permission in one ruling after another, from the school's principal to the judges of the high court, and back again to local authorities. In each decision, a bright line between church and state cordoned the scarves off from the schools. Why, the girls objected, were other students allowed to cross that line by wearing crosses to school?[58] Suddenly, the line looked fuzzy and in need of brightening.

Julia Kristeva, among others, defended the fuzzy crisscrossed line as a transitional, national stage on the way to more abstract cosmopolitan principles. In France, citizens belong to la République, not to hyphenated enclaves. But Honig objects that the defense of France misses a cue to bring national democracy to a better level and to rethink human rights as they release the limits on fairness in narrowly national concepts of sovereignty.[59] The (aesthetic) effect of the scarves and of the defensive affirmation of French custom, in other words, was to uncouple practice from principle and thereby defamiliarize liberalism by staring at it as if it were new. Foreigners have a knack for reframing familiar practices as strange or unnatural. Alleging, as the authorities did, that the scarves drew more proselitizing or separatist attention than did the crosses was tantamount to admitting: (1) that the crosses seemed "natural" or national, and therefore unintrusive in the state; and (2) that liberals were simply not used to the signs of other religions. Get used to them, is one message. Denaturalize the crosses is another.

Consider on the other hand the failed complaint of eighth-grader Anna S. Kaufman at the Portsmouth Middle School in New Hampshire in December 1991. Christmas decorations and caroling, she pointed out to the principal, were practices of a religious orientation and therefore not appropriate in a public school. "We can add Hanukkah decorations" was his accommodating response. Multicultural accommodation was apparently easier to assimilate than the demand to separate what should have been the separate spheres of church and state. Had Anna been one of three troublemakers, perhaps, or had the principal been less cautious about offending her particular religious culture, the complaint might have escalated into more irritation and more productive debate. To non-Christian citizens and residents of the United States, the line between religion and politics looks dull sometimes, and due for a fresh bright irritating splash.

Even more troubling for democracy than personal and public accessories is strange talk, because language more than looks is the medium of public life, and the sounds of strangeness can block or divert communication. In the law, for example, diversion can sidetrack justice into literally diverting, tragicomic parodies. United States legal scholars will remember the case against the prosecutor of *Hernández v. New York*, heard by the Supreme Court in 1991. In a 6 to 3 decision, the Court upheld the prosecutor's right to exclude bilingual jurors from the trial for attempted murder, because—he had observed—they might heed original Spanish testimony instead of attending only to the (possible vagaries of) offical court translations. The allegation against him was "racial" discrimination againt two potential jurors. They were Latino, and Spanish-language ability bears a close relation to ethnicity. As a consequence, excluding the Latinos violates the equal protection clause. Like the Muslim girls forbidden to wear scarves because the practice was "more visible" than Christian signs of affiliation, the terms for exclusion from jury selection in New York seemed mired in issues of visibility. For some critics, the criterion of language finessed the unspoken, racial criterion of credibility, the difference that cannot say its name. Race, after all, does often trigger objections to cultural and linguistic difference, as in the letters of support for English-only legislation. "To my surprise," writes James Crawford in *Language Loyalties: A Source Book on the Official English Controversy*, "racial anxiety was the motor for the Official English campaign of the 1980s. Bilingual education had become a lightning rod for tensions about demographic and cultural change, increased immigration from the Third World, reforms in civil rights, and the political empowerment of minorities."[60]

The Supreme Court was not convinced by the allegation of racial discrimination in the selection of jurors for *Hernández v. New York*. It was one (inadmissible) thing to *see* difference, but another (practical matter) to *hear* it. Nevertheless, Justice Anthony Kennedy's majority opinion did admit there was a loose end of the law, since language is often an indicator of race, and linguistic lines can exacerbate racial tension. He added, ruefully, that bilinguals were an undervalued resource for society; they "inhabit two communities, and serve to bring them closer." "It is a harsh paradox," he continued, "that one may become proficient enough in English to participate in trial, only to encounter disqualification because he knows a second language as well."[61]

The paradox is downright pathetic and funny in an earlier case. During *U.S. v. Pérez*, in 1981, juror Dorothy Kim asked the judge:

> *Dorothy Kim (Juror N.8)*: Your Honor, is it proper to ask the interpreter a question? I'm uncertain about the word La Vado [*sic*]. You say that is a bar.
>
> *The Court*: The Court cannot permit jurors to ask questions directly. If you want to phrase your question to me —
>
> *Dorothy Kim*: I understood it to be a restroom. I could better believe they would meet in a restroom rather than a public bar if he is undercover.
>
> *The Court*: These are matters for you to consider. If you have any misunderstanding of what the witness testified to, tell the Court now what you didn't understand and we'll place the —
>
> *Dorothy Kim*: I understand the word La Vado [*sic*] — I thought it meant restroom. She translates it as bar.
>
> *Ms. Ianziti*: In the first place the jurors are not to listen to the Spanish but to the English. I am a certified court interpreter.
>
> *Dorothy Kim*: You're an idiot.

Upon further questioning, "the witness indicated that none of the conversations in issue occurred in the restroom." The juror later explained that she had said, "it's an

idiom" rather than "you're an idiot," but she was nevertheless dismissed from the jury.[62]

"It's an idiom" is a clever punch line to this risky joke—
as well as a cover-up for lost patience. Idiomatic expressions
do mark the borders between linguistic insiders and outsiders.
Bilinguals can anticipate the trouble that idioms make, even
when (like Dorothy Kim) they may not master the target language. Think also of the recent brawl at the University of Con-
necticut where a tenured professor faced dismissal for threatening a colleague: "If you want to fight a war with me, you
will wind up dead." Dr. Moshe Gai admits to saying something of the sort: "He who goes to war should be prepared to
die," but this, he adds, is "merely a figure of speech common
among Israelis, particularly war veterans."[63] Maybe repeating
the risky "idiot/idiom" joke, or remarking on the literal reception of a figurative threat, should stir us to reconsider whether
it is too costly to teach languages. Even before fiscal adjust-
ments, we should raise our expectation of more than one if we
hope to be fair and flexible.

Visible racial difference, then, is only one cause for nativist anxiety. Language matters too, and unwelcome difference
can sound as strange as it looks. Sometimes the sound can recast the look, as when the Irish didn't look quite white, or
when my white face seems surprisingly un-Spanish, and when
standard Spanish speech seems to lighten the color of black
speakers. Often, language is practically synonymous with national culture, and therefore maps onto racial difference too. It
is the struggle over language rights (in Canada) that prompts
Charles Taylor and Will Kymlicka to develop debates over minority group rights in general.

Minority languages can make the majority nervous for reasons beyond the obstacles to understanding. Because strange
accents signal cultural and racial differences, unfamiliar

sounds raise hackles and interfere with rights. Mari Matsuda illustrates how perfectly good liberal law can stumble and fail over these anxieties in cases argued with an accent.[64] Her critique is an a fortiori defense of cultural tolerance in the courtroom, because the examples she cites don't depend on substantive interference from a foreign language, or on the attendant complication of unevenness among jurors regarding translation. More difficult cases involving foreign languages strain the very possibility of fairness in existing laws.[65] But Matsuda's examples were argued in standard English, with accents. Each case yielded an unfair decision, for no good reason she says, but that the courts favored the sound of native English over foreign inflections.

Take, for example, the Filipino veteran of the United States Army in World War II who retired from a good position in Manila and moved to Hawaii where his daughter lived. A modest job at the motor vehicle bureau seemed like a convenient, air-conditioned, source of pocket money. So he took the written exam, got the best score among four hundred applicants, and performed with confidence at the interview. He didn't get the job. Maybe it was his age, but the interviewers said it was his accent. Incredulous, and too mindful of the law to allow the injustice, the man brought the matter to court. Official records show that his command of English was better than that of the defendants and even that of the lawyers. When the judge required expert witnesses to testify on language competence, the plaintiff's lawyer called a linguist who explained the normal variations of English. The defendant's side countered with a speech pathologist. From the low court to higher appeals, the result of this dignified and dogged demand for justice was a loss of faith in the system. The obstacle, in this and in other cases, was not in the law, Matsuda concludes, but in the culture. The legal advice she gleans from this and other similar stories is to develop sentimental attachments to difference. Hear accents with the pleasure of the effort. Uneconomical effort is part of the aesthetic exercise. It is good training for keeping democracy flexed. Expect discomfort as a welcome horizon for freer communication, was also Eve Sedgwick's tip to women at Amherst College when we both taught there: if you avoid public speaking because the stress can make you cry, talk through your tears, she would say, and the public will learn to strain and to listen.

Nuisance is a gadfly to politics and to aesthetics; it stings and goads them to activity. Obstacles detain citizens and art lovers long enough to notice and to care for the beloved object of attention. Not fitting easily or well is a bother, of course. Being both too much and not enough can make ESL migrants aware of grammar (or relational) trouble with themselves, and with their neighbors, even after several generations. One is often more than one. From the beginning of the modern nation-building period, the founding fathers have tried very hard to simplify linguistically complex societies, usually by the force of elimination. These were campaigns that sometimes came into conflict with the universal, Catholic Mother Church during the period of colonization. She cultivated many languages in order to facilitate conversions that would build the Church, and to obstruct competing state consolidations that required a lingua franca.[66] But in areas where there is no one church, religious differences can complicate the lines of alliance. The paradoxical advantage is that competition between church and state can create codependence among autonomous spheres.

Thanks to Many, One

Allow me to defend an analogy between many religions and many languages, in order to bring home—after calls for jihad and crusade—the stabilizing effect of overloaded state systems. (Overloads, obviously, are also the precondition for what Rawls called "overlapping consensus" among peoples).[67] It is true, as Charles Taylor and Will Kymlicka, among others, object, that culture (let's say language as the basic part for the whole) and religion behave differently with respect to politics. Religion can be private and separate from the state, but a particular language is a public medium for the state.

Politics cannot decouple from a language nor, therefore, can it be culturally neutral.[68] All the more reason for vigilance and testing against strange cultures. The difference between public language and private church is significant, but difference doesn't dismiss an analogy. Analogy shows points of divergence as well as contact, Wittgenstein observed. Otherwise, comparison would be too close or too far-fetched to produce the witty (unanticipated but irresistible) relationship that we call analogy. It is the figure that describes genre for Wittgenstein, not the particular rule that governs a game, but the similarity of rule-making systems that establishes gaming or identifies an activity. Different rule-bound activities, gaming and drawing, are themselves linked by analogy: "The kinship [of games] is that of two pictures, one of which consists of colour patches with vague contours, and the other of patches similarly shaped and distributed, but with clear contours. The kinship is just as undeniable as the difference" (*PI*, §76). It is the difference that goes without saying.

The link I wish to show between language and religion is the effect of multiplicity on both. The effect is aesthetic because it estranges (or decouples) any particular language or religion from the presumption that it is natural or necessary. Multiplicity makes you notice that your own language or religion is one option among others, not the only legitimate vehicle for human life. Estrangement can provoke anxiety, of course, but it can also jog reflection about the artifice of society and perhaps about the normal proliferation of artful constructions. I grant that unhinging one cultural term (language or religion) from "natural" moorings is not the same as separating two different terms like public and private.[69] But defamiliarizing one's own unexamined practices and beliefs cannot be irrelevant to politics.

Two reasons come to mind: First, estrangement develops irony (which is close to tolerance). Estrangement may even develop a taste for the unfamiliar aesthetico-political goads to the pleasures of reflection. Distaste for reflection in the United States keeps the country from ratifying accords for international rights, including the Convention on Rights of Children. But under the pressure of cultural pluralism, Thomas McCarthy notes, institutional arrangements sometimes change and law becomes reflexive.[70] (Taylor's hope for a Gadamerian "fusion of horizons" where "the other becomes less strange" would reduce anxiety and along with it the knack—and the kick—of reflection.)[71] And second, overloads of linguistic and religious constructions can be unmanageable and therefore demand coordination at a different, political level.

If you think about it, the separation of church and state works when there is more than one church, each irritating the others. Different religious beliefs don't amount to a unified system that might stand in for state power, so that in practice, churches stay separate from government when there are too many to speak for the general body public. James Madison was unequivocal on this distinction. Religion was both a problem for politics and its own solution, because the cacophony of beliefs ensured so much conflict that a secular government and civil society became necessary structures of coordination.[72] Thanks to religious incommensurabilities, secular society stayed secure because the overload and excess of religious meanings demanded an order of coordination that politics can provide.[73]

In a similar way, I am suggesting that multilingualism demands an agile lingua franca. Competing churches and multiple languages keep any one culture from overlapping with politics in ways that might stifle its breath. Politics is robust and hard at work when it coordinates many cultures through the law. If there were no need to coordinate, if culture were only one, how might we see or hear the difference between culture and universal political institutions?

In other words, when politics is singular and culture is plural, decoupling makes sense, despite the skeptics. Then languages, religions, etc. need administration instead of offering a "natural" vehicle for it. Is the majoritarian language a practical choice for the lingua franca? Then members of the majority should learn at least one more language, in order to reflect on political convenience and to feel creatively distracted by divergent grammatical (relational) constructions.

Contemporary theorists have taken a lead from Madison in order to credit the inharmonious churches for helping to establish secular democracy.[74] Can we credit multilingualism for keeping democracy hard at work? (Harmonizing is the name for top-down control through diversity management in the European Union.)[75] Instead of dismissing religious choice as indifferent for democracies, and urging away ethnic or racial "choices" in preference for an ideal, color-blind liberalism,[76] religious conflicts and language differences can actually enhance democracy by forcing a bright line between cultural practices and administrative procedures.

The "negative moment" of the analogy comes, obviously, from the fact that everyone speaks some language(s) but by now not everyone belongs to a church or believes in God (despite salutes to the flag, emblems on money, and inspired speeches). At independence, United States religious sectarianism was the irritant around which liberal politics developed, like a pearl around a grain of sand. Today, one incentive to roughen and refresh politics comes from the "foreign" languages that both irritate English and require it as the lingua franca. Despite all the theory that comes from Canada, it is not, in my opinion, the best model of irritation, except maybe for the big cities where multicultural immigration makes trouble for official bilingualism. The reason is structural, not specific to Canada: official bilingualism doesn't require one lingua franca; instead it frustrates underrepresented (French) speakers and bothers the (Anglophone) majority that perceives no need for a second language. Debates get stuck between communitarian authenticity from the minority viewpoint and personal freedom from the majority. Any bilingual country, including a possible (but

unlikely) United States were Spanish recognized, can polarize like this. Switzerland and Belgium are no better models. A typical joke about Belgium is a series of riddles: "What do you call a person who speaks three languages? Trilingual. And someone who speaks two languages? Bilingual. What about a person who speaks one language? Waloon."[77]

Instead of Canada, think of India, as Robert Dahl does when he considers why democracy works there, in so linguistically complicated a country. It works, he says, precisely because it's *so complicated* that people don't understand one another without the lingua franca and its administrative institutions.[78] Thomas L. Friedman concurs, to the point of holding up India as a model of secular civility between Muslims and their neighbors.[79] Active citizens generally speak both (elite Hindi) or "associate" official English and at least one local language. India has the paradoxical good fortune to claim English as a mere convenience, to follow Nehru's modernizing line of statesmanship, rather than a particular native language that would favor some citizens and inconvenience others.[80] English never got under India's skin.[81] It developed alongside local codes, and provides a vehicle for sidestepping conflicts among them (as a secular state runs alongside contending religions). Had India been a bit more flexible and tolerant at independence, had it included Urdu among the many official languages, Pakistan might not have broken away. Frustrated language rights have a way of congealing into less negotiable, sometimes intolerable, religious differences.[82] Think also of the "ramshackle" multiethnic Ottoman Empire, where "ethno-religious groups remained culturally autonomous" under a hole-ly government. It was "far from a perfect political system, but it worked," unlike the disastrously streamlined replacement that the British imposed.[83] Perhaps the United States can take some advantage of linguistic loose ends to put democratic coordinating procedure to hard work, now that non-English speakers are coming to this country in unprecedented numbers. It will not be the first American country to wrest an advantage out of troublesome diversity.

Peru has been learning the lesson after centuries of official monolingualism that effectively excluded the indigenous masses. As late as 1990, Mario Vargas Llosa ran for president on a platform that considered Indians to be only potential Peruvians, once they left their traditions for modern ways. But today the country is trying to recast its self-image as incomparably diverse, with its citizens as beneficiaries of both indigenous and immigrant cultures. After the presidency of Alberto Fujimori, known as "el chino" though his roots and possible political future are in Japan,[84] and the election of President Toledo, who campaigned in Quechua (through his foreign wife) as well as Spanish, Peru experiments with a bicultural program of education that assumes all citizens should know Spanish plus at least one (of forty) indigenous languages.[85] The assumption is a bit romantic, though, as if being Peruvian imposes nativist cultural demands. In practice, Spanish speakers don't bother to learn even Quechua, let alone minor languages. Peruvians are diverse and many resent Mrs. Elianne Karp Toledo's efforts to Andeanize Peru. Can we imagine a practical adjustment that promotes respect, enhances education for all, and gets unstuck from damaging implosions of nation and state? What if Quechua counted as a legitimate language that, like English or French, conferred bilingual benefits alongside Spanish as the lingua franca? Bilingual migrants might be ahead of monolingual Creoles and serve, without essentializing their Peruvianness, as models for the country.

The United States too can take the hint about the broad bases of allegiance supported by migrants' double moorings that make the either/or choice of cultural identity obsolete.

Many a newcomer still feels pressed to lose a home language to the host, although relief from linguistic irritation weakens the ground for democracy. Neither Du Bois nor the ideologues of mestizaje saw it that way. They didn't challenge the exclusive stature of the imperial language; on the contrary, they perfected it as a sure step to active citizenship.

Lost in the Mix: *Juntos y Revueltos*

Latin Americans know several names for W. E. B. Du Bois's fantasy of amalgamation. This fantasy saved him from despair (for a long while at least) of a country that required assimilation, yet didn't allow it. Mestizaje is probably the most familiar name. In English, the counterpart would be *miscegenation*, a clumsy translation.[86] Miscegenation has been pronounced with mistrust or revulsion, while Latin American racial mixing has often been an official slogan in Spanish and Portuguese. Mestizaje endorses the particularity of New World peoples through rhetoric of national brotherhood that is meant to ease racial tensions, but not necessarily address material inequity. Latin Americans would immediately recognize as a conventional banner of cul-

tural pride Du Bois's manifesto for merging. This manifesto
served, for example, as a standard of the Independence movement throughout the continent. Simón Bolívar proclaimed that
Spanish Americans have many fathers but only one mother,
that they are neither Spanish, nor Indian, nor black, but all
of these.

A century later while Du Bois was writing, to mention just
one more of many examples, mestizaje reaffirmed Mexico as
a modern country with a mission to the world. For almost a
hundred years, the republic had been torn between indigenist
liberals like President Benito Juárez, and Europeanizing mon-
archists who replaced him with Maximillian. Both sides would
contribute, said José Vasconcelos, minister of education for
the triumphant Mexican Revolution, to making the new man.
Whites and Indians would join blacks and Asians in the unprecedented culmination of one "cosmic race." This would
happen in Mexico, Vasconcelos wrote in 1925, because no other
country was as free from the racial prejudice that obstructs
human progress. Anglo-Saxons (like Emerson and Whitman)
might seem to prosper by divine will, but, Vasconcelos underlined, *"they committed the sin of destroying those races, while
we assimilated them, and this gives us new rights and hopes for
admission without precedent in History."*[87]

In 1940 Fernando Ortiz proposed a new word for merging, in *Cuban Counterpoint: Tobacco and Sugar.* "Transculturation" would emphasize the rough process of cultural change
that contemporary anthropology had painted too gently. Ortiz's
innovation was to take account of the pain and the costs (mostly
to blacks) of amalgamation, even though the end product was
an admirable and fascinating Cuban culture. Existing words
like *syncretism* and *hybridity* described the results but ignored
the tortuous process. And a word like "acculturation" missed
the novelty altogether by reducing New World clashes of cul-

ture into a one-way process of transition from one culture to another, and its manifold social repercussions. "But *transculturation* is a more fitting term . . . Men, economies, cultures, ambitions were all foreigners here, provisional, changing, 'birds of passage' over the country, at its cost, against its wishes, and without its approval . . . All those above and those below, living together in the same atmosphere of terror and oppression, the oppressed in terror of punishment, the oppressor in terror of reprisals, all beside justice, beside adjustment, beside themselves. And all in the painful process of transculturation."[88]

Ortiz was a cultural anthropologist (he began as an ethnomusicologist fascinated by African forms that flourished in Cuba), not an ideologue. Unlike institution-builder Vasconcelos, who promoted *The Cosmic Race* as *The Mission of the Ibero American Race*, Ortiz was describing an already existing cosmic culture. Cubans were not all equally flattered by the black and white boldness of the picture, to be sure. An autochthonous culture that owed as much to Africa as to Europe could not have appealed to the elite taste for Europe and Anglo-America that official Cuba had cultivated since the conquest.

To the extent that *Cuban Counterpoint* affirms a more complicated culture, the book is a stretch for conservative politics. It requires acknowledgment of the difference within a culture, an admission, for example, that the cult of Orishas plays in counterpoint to the cult of Catholic saints. To this same extent, any further change to existing Cuban culture would be superfluous and distracting. The only sensible response is to celebrate. Understandably, transculturation (along with mestizaje and the cosmic race) has lately come under criticism as an ideology of social affirmation that amounts to control.[89] If difference (neutralized and melted down) is already part of the self, how can transculturation promote political vitality?

I wonder if this kind of stabilized merging is what Du Bois yearned for. It is possible, even probable. He was troubled by the incommensurability of a black and an American consciousness. But he was also offended by the demand to acculturate, to "bleach his Negro soul." Bilateral exchanges seemed to promise more. If Africa and America could produce a new consciousness together, the way Ortiz said they had in Cuba (and the way Malinowski had theorized in general about parent cultures producing a new culture that takes from both and yet is different from either one),[90] then black and white America could be equally proud of their future offspring. Until very late 101 in his life, Du Bois kept yearning for this bilateral creativity. Everything seemed to hang on mutuality and partnership of the best of both races. The elitism (and the efforts to arouse indifferent whites) keeps some of his best students at a dissenting distance.[91]

I want to risk a less likely but still possible reading of Du Bois. It hesitates at the point before differences would merge and lingers on the tension between ill-fitting partners. In part, this slightly willful reading follows from Ortiz's historically inflected improvement on effortlessly friendly words like *syncretism* and *hybridity*. But such a reading also departs from Ortiz, along the fault line he described between blacks and whites locked into a forced marriage. Transculturation is creativity derived from antagonism. The term puts a focus on Du Bois's scorn for the requirement to bleach one's soul and to ignore racial antagonism, and downplays his goal of a coherent consciousness. That scorn is an expression of pride in one's difference, and the energy that keeps cultural particularity in productive tension with demands for assimilation. Thanks to the tension, taste, and preferences, some space opens up for a non-normative, public sphere of rights and obligations. Does the Du Bois who would modernize through merging convince post-modern readers? Do we still believe in an incrementally truer and more coherent consciousness, along with the eugenic arguments for melting down difference into a single cosmic race?[92] Or does liberalism need to turn the dread of cultural difference into a political taste for it?

Acquired Taste

The advice to take aesthetic pleasure and political advantage from discomfort is probably easier to understand than to assimilate. A related, maybe counterintuitive distance between a simple message and the anticipation of a difficult reception describes the challenge of Emmanuel Levinas's writing. I mention him briefly here, not to presume that a short reference could do any justice to his profound work, but only to register two stunning lessons that I take from Levinas as guidelines for a bilingual aesthetics that can irritate the state. One lesson is the ethical value of *training over explaining* (probably inherited from medieval theology,[93] and maybe—pace the ironic company—also from Wittgenstein, for whom explanation was not enough, and training supplemented language lessons).[94]

For Levinas, the Other teaches that *asymmetry* is the normal design of relationships. Levinas's ethics begin with and keep returning to the unequal shape of the association between one's lowly, hostage self and the exalted, sacred Other. The ethical subject begins by literally subjecting the self to the Other. Beginning with an ontology of the self, he warned, dooms philosophy to "egolotry." This is not a hard concept to understand. But it is so fundamentally alien to Western subject-centered habits of thought and feeling that each new formulation of derivative and lowly subjecthood reads like a revelation. Adding one formulation to another was Levinas's way to retrain anticipation and sensibility. His recursive style, I am convinced, fills long books to keep readers busy and fixed on the unfamiliar point until resistance wears down.

Extended sessions with Levinas can indeed alter a reader's instincts about ethical behavior, upsetting the self-centered secular thought with a sense of awe smuggled in from metaphysics. Awful responsibility to infinite difference summarizes both the drama and the impasse of his thought. Levinas has been criticized, of course, for an idealism that keeps ethics clear of politics, because it keeps the self cordoned off from the incommensurable Other who commands and doesn't negotiate. How to "use" Levinas is a dilemma for many disciples and it has been a reason to desist from the effort. But the lessons in training and in asymmetrical relationships are too precious to simply forfeit them. Instead, they can lead to (artistic and political) ways out of the impasse between self and Other, whether or not Levinas the philosopher of ethics would have approved. He did admit, nevertheless, that the demands of justice (involving more than one Other) interfere with abstract ethics and break the enchantment of absolute otherness.

Ironically, the way out of impasses is made by awe itself. The tremor it provokes can pry open detours around the paralysis that awe imposes. We humans don't sustain the impact for long; instead we look away and survive. And surviving even quotidian shocks and unpleasantness produces a mature pleasure that we'll consider in theories of the sublime. To reflect on the pain of losing control is to gain an intellectual perspective that can flatter the fearful subject. As a result, the gratifying detour away from awful difference becomes (to follow Barthes's neurotic inspiration) an incentive to endure the pain. A certain taste for the risk and a tolerance for personal demotion allow the sublime to work its unsettling effects. In other words, if we can submit to the shock of otherness (in the face that stares Levinas's reader down, in Muslim scarves, in foreign accents), the impact can explode tired habits of reasonableness and open a path for reflection. The taste for risk and the tolerance for irritation, are—as I said—easy principles to appreciate but hard feelings to acquire. That is why a new sentimental education should be on our collective agenda. To put it differently, the predisposition for democracy cannot depend on assumptions about human nature. These are culturally coded and inconsistent. (Hobbes vs. Smith vs. Rousseau vs. Marx.)

Training programs are arduous but shouldn't put off seasoned teachers. After all, teachers tend to care less about what students know and feel than about what they might learn and value. Among the precursors already enlisted as guides for an education in artful endurance and irony are Schiller, Shklovsky, Freud, Benjamin, and Barthes. They lead in the general direction of aesthetics, through rough or gnarled detours around speechlessness (whether its cause is unremarkable familiarity or unspeakable passions). All of them know the byroads to politics. Political masters of the detour and unconventional maneuver are surely available as well. I'll mention the examples of Antonio Gramsci and a couple of his best readers as an invitation to recall others.

Paso Doble

"Scientific" Marxism would have advised Gramsci to wait for an appropriate historical conjuncture in southern Italy.[95] The forces that should have lined up neatly, from economics as the determinant root to culture as an epiphenomenal byproduct, stayed underdeveloped there. But the advice to be patient didn't paralyze Gramsci; it showed that historical determinants needed some roughing up in order to energize the logic of struggle. With peripheral vision from southern Italy (suggesting other southern and subaltern perspectives), and with hindsight after the Russian Revolution surprised orthodox Marxists by succeeding where it was least expected, Gramsci saw that workers could force change when the forces of history didn't add up right.[96] He detoured from the unbeatable odds of "scientific" structural determinants and from Lenin's political authoritarianism, with a sidestep to cultural incitations.[97] Since Marx had appreciated the mutual effects of the economy and ideology, Gramsci underlined the relative autonomy of each sphere, to get more play between them and make culture count.[98] This was a "jogo de cintura," as Brazilians call the cagey move in boxing and soccer (*jaibería* is Puerto Rican for the crablike maneuvers), a gesture from the waist, not forward nor backward, but sideways from conventions. Gramsci veered away from both the fatalism of orthodox, academic Marxism and from the deadlock of proletarian dictatorship.[99] To Lenin's antieconomism and political alliance under the working class, Gramsci responded with the wiggle room of consensual hegemony under a fundamental class. Unlike dictatorship, hegemony requires compromise and a new culture that counts everyone in. This is work for an intellectual leadership.[100]

Gramsci's gesture made mischief with historical fatality. He saw that the unity of an emergent class would depend on ideology, that is, an activity that produces historical subjects, not on any objective bedrock of economic determinations.[101] So he bypassed those unpromising economic determinants to intervene at the level of "superstructure," practically inverting its relationship to the "base."[102] The push of economic constraints and the pull of a usable culture describes Gramsci's dynamic interdependent two-step (between conjunctures and possibilities). For a literary critic, it might evoke the "dialectical allegory" between desires and disasters that Benjamin described as history, and also the alternating rhythm of "slaps and embraces" between particularity and universality that Toni Morrison describes in peripheral or minority artists. (Should I mention that *estrangement*, familiar from formalist aesthetics, described the working-class perspective on history for Gramsci?)[103] This inside-outside movement toggles between "science" and creativity to improvise the new and improved step of Gramsci's emancipatory politics.

Whereas Hegel and Marx drew the line between elements that could participate in society and those unredeemable elements that could not, Gramsci disturbs the distinction to stretch the limits of social hegemony. With one "scientific" step he marks the conventional exclusion of the rabble (for philosophy) and of the bourgoisie (for Lenin's politics). With the other "cultural" step he translates competing interests into a hegemonic ideology that facilitates alliances between "the rabble," the peasants, and the capitalists.[104] Adding the irritating and disturbing differences of the outliers to the chain of equivalences means that Gramsci recasts the logic of political participation to mean antagonism. He took his cue from the unorthodox excluded demands, lest they rankle and fester instead of fueling a united effort.

Containing those exorbitant demands by bringing them in was a step toward a sturdy and flexible theory of hegemony, which I translate as asymmetrical codependence: The ruling class depends on other classes agreeing to be ruled, and the other classes extract benefits in exchange.[105] The inclusive maneuver roughened and refreshed the logic of equivalences to activate social asymmetries into a war of position. Uneven and codependent class interests of hegemony disturb the "laws" of Marxism and turn it into an artful practice, something like juggling sticks that are on fire.

The salve or glue for antagonistic classes that were stuck with one another is a shared ideology or a "popular religion."[106] This expressive form of the common "people-nation" will surely develop toward internationalism, Gramsci explained, "but the point of departure is 'national'—and it is from this point of departure that one must begin."[107] Now what are we to make of this hegemonic management that speaks for the common "people-nation," as if state and nation were not coming unglued? Today, outlying sectors of society show cultural, not only class, differences from the hegemonic class; hence including them stretches the boundaries of permissible participants beyond the ideal of a single "people." The hegemonic class will woo its allies by preferring the *interruptus* of communication over fantasies of cultural reproduction. And the syncopated rhythm of equivalences among social groups will stop to notice cultural discontinuities and start to refresh the state as an enlarged space where cultural nations engage.[108]

Nevertheless, Gramsci shows the single direction of his war of positions, or "passive revolution," to win power for the working class.[109] His sidestep to culture kept an ideal outcome intact.[110] Outcomes, however, are more than one, Ernesto Laclau says. Liberally, he reinterprets "emancipation" by pluralizing Gramsci's term and multiplying the possible results of unhinging science from Marxism: "By playing within the system of logical incompatibilities; . . . by looking at the effects which follow from the subversion of each of its two incompatible sides by the other, [struggle can] drift away from any single operation."[111]

This is room to wiggle and to juggle today. Gramsci had already abandoned fantasies of absolute freedom (Levinas dreaded the egolotry) when he embraced compromise between the ruling class and the ruled. But his own defense of democracy and antagonism leads Laclau another step back from a single utopian goal into plural *Emancipation(s)*. Between the singular and the plural political grammar is a difference that Deleuze and Guattari had also heard. It distinguishes between faith in the right line of politics and a penchant for maps with many spots for troubleshooting.[112] For some activists and intellectuals, the goal is no longer the dusk of capitalism before the dawn of stable egalitarian utopias, but many smaller, often local, targets of reform. For others, losing a coherent Marxian goal means losing one's way, even if the post–cold war world makes radicalism rhyme with religious extremism. Apparently, monotheism migrates easily from single-minded religious devotion to single-minded sacrificial ideology.[113] Utopian dreams of final solutions, perfect and airless, cannot tolerate the dangerous supplements of dissent and politics. Fear final utopia and pursue politics (a variation on the Sages' "fear evil and pursue the good"), is my simple distillation of Laclau's lesson from Gramsci. Utopia can be absolutist and inflexible, beyond conflict and therefore intolerant of politics. That is why democracy (which thrives on politics, i.e., antagonisms) cannot afford to be utopian in the monological sense.

Democracy depends on difference, as I have been saying, and needs the healthy side-effects of homegrown diversity and of foreign immigration. Immigration, regional ethnic and gender rights, upset the stubborn compact between nation and state, while stretching liberal practices toward a greater realization of liberalism's own promises. Universalism itself depends on difference, to follow Ernesto Laclau's provocative formulation shared by some critical legal scholars. The universal has survived classical philosophy's dismissal of particularity as deviation, the medieval collapse of universality into Christ, and it has outlived a European Enlightenment that conflated the universal (subject, class, culture) with particular (French) incarnations.

Today's universalism is a paradox for the past, because it is grounded in particularist demands. They unmoor universalism from any fixed cultural content and keep it open to an "always receding horizon."[114] The corollary paradox of democracy, Laclau admits without embarrassment, is that it requires unity but depends on diversity. Tension and ambiguity are structural in democracy, which neither Habermas's ideal of communication nor Lyotard's lament over an impasse can acknowledge.[115] The point of politics is to win ground and rights from centers of power, not to dispense with the power that invites struggle. This is perhaps the closest that political philosophy comes to appreciating antagonism as democracy's normal condition, very close to Judith Butler's psychoanalytic twist that makes personal subjecthood depend on opposition.[116]

Struggles for particular freedoms don't presume to destroy the state; they need it as an antagonist in a contest for concessions. Without a power to oppose, there are no struggles and no victories. The object is to win ground in hegemonic arrangements that depend on popular consent. And the mechanism is to irritate the state in ways that stimulate concessions of more freedoms and resources. Of course, this reformist dynamic is disappointing to many critics of capital who prefer systemic responses to an unfair system, but the unquestionable virtue of this pluralized approach is the recognition of multiple agendas and many voices, whereas the single thrust of most utopian movements would subordinate or cancel the travesties that contribute defamiliarizing effects to politics. The knack for stepping aside from power in order to play upsetting games with it demands some flexibility from hegemonic power.

I Don't Dance

Political theory has been slow to pursue bilingual advantages.[117] Bonnie Honig takes flight through literature, but mostly theory gets mired in the anxiety aroused by migrant workers who strain or interrupt national arrangements. When it is not being defensive, theory responds with compensatory designs to make room for difference, often spelling out rights and responsibilities for citizens who no longer speak the same native language.[118] At most, in the politics of language, the one-people-one-language ideal breaks down regionally, where local language groups demand autonomy for the same "nationalist" identity-promoting reasons that the country in question favors a single coherent code. Some theorists favor regional autonomy and others worry about the disintegrating effect on the country. In either case, an assumption is that people choose between languages rather than live with both. Why assume this either/or choice? Most people have never lived like that. And it's a good thing.

Although studies in international relations are beginning to suggest that demands by immigrants enhance liberal politics,[119] except for Honig's work, we don't often ask how immigration at home stimulates our own liberal respect for difference.[120] Two stimuli seem obvious nevertheless: one potential advantage is the bilingual's unsettling sense of human arrangements as constructed and precarious. The tentative and fissured belongings of many bilinguals demand caution and respectful distance from others whom we cannot presume to understand easily.[121] That is why formal modes of address that cast interlocutors as distant third persons are more democratizing than the utopian dream of grammatical symmetry allows.[122] Another possible advantage of the migrant's feeling of fitting badly is precisely that Unheimlichkeit is unhappy and restless. (Herder called it indigestion.)[123] The benefit of being at a loss and cautiously anticipating unpredictable differences is that one experiences existing arrangements with a margin of disidentification and, possibly, with frustration that generates action.

These stimuli to democracy urge criticism and pedagogy to

catch up to multicultural creativity. The lag is alarming, even if social scientists remain skeptical about what humanists do. What we *do* is teach taste, judgment, sensibility, that is, a predisposition for one kind of politics or another. "Habits of the heart" is what Tocqueville called the disposition for democracy, though he grounded them in Christian sentiment.[124] Tocqueville should be nudged to more neutral ground, says William Connolly, because religious sentiment and politics feed on one another.[125] By locating belief at a "visceral register" his reading of Tocqueville brings religion close to aesthetics and casts belief as a matter of taste. This proximity between belief and taste steers politics clear of some sticky interfaith competitions and puts the training of democratic dispositions on shared ground.

Hearts and minds remain undervalued organs for democracy, according to recent reports on civil society.[126] Therefore, teaching those enabling habits at this late stage of democratic developments can renew an opportunity (and an obligation) for alliances between politics and literature. Laclau's proposal needs pedagogues who can teach a taste for irritation, and literary studies need to make technical expertise count as a social contribution.

Alter-nations

The training will be to think and feel on one's feet, both of them, as does Gramsci. With one foot in a shared political culture and another in particular religious or linguistic cultures, we move in syncopated rhythms that fall out of step with holy wars. Doubleness or tripleness is the sane answer to single-minded zeal. For Christ's sake, we might take Jesus at his word when he admitted two poles of obligation: one belonging to Caesar and to the other to God, "zu Got und zu lad" is the Yiddish version. This doesn't assume that monotheism relieves the faithful from secular duties, or that it leaves a suicidal void if faith lapses.[127] The world is not the kingdom of heaven. But the lesson in doubleness is lost on ardent devotees and patriots who insist on either this or that. In the Catholic tradition of Latin America, Jesús Martín Barbero notes, religion and radical politics are often Janus faces for monotheism. A pity, he says, in a continent where the Church developed a splendid baroque taste for hybridity.[128]

Just off the continent, Puerto Ricans typically tell Spanish and English-only devotees, "Hablamos los dos." From the margin and in the vanguard of both mainland and *patria chica*, they and other bilinguals play a counterpoint to nineteenth-century liberalism that claimed to harmonize public and private desires through double consciousness.[129]

W. E. B. Du Bois had complained that harmony didn't work for African Americans divided against themselves, because the minority and the majority double consciousness clashed and frustrated anyone who wasn't white. To him, dissonance, irritation, bicultural blues seemed unfair and unappealing. But today, double consciousness and bilingual binds no longer seem soluble nor require solutions. The split soul might look, if we focused right, like an intense experience of the general split structure of language and of living as human beings. This unhappy consciousness could be a vanguard for our best cultural defense of humane practices, because doubleness won't allow the meanness of one thought, one striving, one alchemical gold-standard of value.

Can we develop our taste for dissonance instead of feeling forced to chose and lose between identity politics and abstract universalism?[130] By definition, bilingualism cultivates both; it is no communitarian bastion that might resist learning the common code, as immigrant parents will tell you. They notoriously favor the lingua franca for children who would otherwise miss the opportunities that encouraged migration in the first place.[131] Can we adjust to the overloads of language, music, sense of humor, etc. in ways that let cultural difference sound good for democracy?

It is a challenge that we might seize like an opportunity. We cannot, frankly, afford to ignore differences among us, either ethically—given the practical redundancy of the term "democratic pluralism"—or pragmatically—given the inevitability of global migrations, transportation, communication. The differences are internal too, now that identity sounds like an oxymoron for multiple be-longings.[132] Defense from fanaticism will need more than military, political, and economic retaliation. The kind of dedication that inspires suicidal missions makes terror wax more than wane with the efforts to destroy it.

Continued threats of terrorism are bound to raise more demands for revenge. If the ardor of militants on one side and avengers on the other is difficult to diffuse, some of us should step back and consider how to mitigate future dangers of terrorist networks. These networks apparently attract new recruits and count on broad sympathies of people who object to the United States for both good and bad reasons. One reason has been the U.S. habit of cultivating a variety of democracy that sometimes plants and then feeds on tyranny abroad. Whether or not less damaging policies would win sympathy and support is, of course, a matter of conjecture. However, a finer taste for democratic culture in the United States might shore up the alternative to intolerance at home. Democracy, after all, is a cultural taste to a degree that some may be reluctant to acknowledge. "Alternative modernities" can include the well-educated and efficient extremism that produces terrorists.[133] Democracy's alternative depends on a preference for the hits and misses of coordinating mechanisms. Like the lingua franca that a democracy speaks in multicultural environments, democratic culture takes on meaning from its *convivencia* with particular traditions. It will sing the bilingual blues, because losses of meaning are unavoidable effects of *alternancia* (code switching) where no one speaker masters all the codes. Maybe that is not a pleasing option for everyone. But learning to love it will prepare hearts for a mind to be democratic.[134]

It's natural to be nervous now, as late modern life lets the loose ends of identities and values dangle without a sign of tying them up in any pleasingly coherent weave. Amid the messiness of porous state borders and contested political boundaries, the unraveling doesn't stop to tidy up, no matter how long we wait. Waiting seemed like a cure for everything as long as the social sciences had faith in social evolution, while religion preached progress from creation to salvation. Like secular history, the sacred story has apparently lost its way too, or taken a detour while monotheists fight each other to establish the one truth and the one way. All the stories we have been telling ourselves wear out with the movements of people across borders, interrupting national projects and reclaiming religious identities. It's natural to be nervous, I said. But staying nervous shows little cultivation, as if only the world acted on us and we merely reacted. Cultivated responses include delayed reactions, after reflecting on raw feeling.

Maybe the only reasonable response to the lasting unpleasantness is to develop a taste for it. I don't mean an inclination toward irritation. A desire for something would cancel the aesthetic effect of disinterested or surprising pleasure. I mean a faculty of judgment that counts on openness toward surprise and readiness to process interruption for effects beyond frustration.[1] Then the pain of feeling unsettled or overwhelmed could become a source of pleasure. Think about it. If conditions will not change, we can at least change our reception and adjust beleaguered bodies to strike more graceful postures.[2] Why not acquire some poise as we play among the loose ends, exercise human skills for maneuver, and appreciate the irritation that keeps us creative? Why not? Perfectly serious people have tracked this very move from anxiety to enjoyment. Immanuel Kant was one master of the move and Friedrich Schiller followed up, not to mention other (neurotic) aesthetes like Bataille and Barthes. Their hurts-so-good game was sublime.

Kant is especially attractive to engage. A beacon for critics weary of politics and impatient with multiculturalism, he is a convenient or unavoidable partner. Disinterestedness in aesthetic judgment and the free play of imagination are among Kant's gifts to aesthetic theory, conservative critics know. But Kant's gifts are prodigal, and they lead from aesthetic contemplation to the difficult work of achieving intersubjective agreement. The freedom that aesthetic judgment locates is a space for social agreement. To read Kant through to the sublime, instead of stopping at beauty, he becomes an ally for multiculturalism, not for the opposition. A slightly unorthodox twist will bring him up to date and ensure his support.

Sublime Common Sense

If everyone feels nervous to some degree, because life is insecure and experience is overwhelming beyond comprehension, then nervousness becomes a sense we have in common. This is what common sense means for Kant, and locating it is the first step to building agreement. He imagined that the same stimu-

lus would produce a universally common aesthetic effect, repeated in each person and shared by all. Today the stimuli may
vary among a range of cultural predispositions, but they add up
to a common judgment of life's delicacy and danger. Each of
us may achieve the sublime effect through particular audience
positions and reach an intersubjective agreement: an event was
terrifying; a gesture amounted to art whether you find the ref-
erent pleasing or unpleasant; a joke worked whether I am the
subject, the ideal listener, or the butt of laughter. The disconnect effects can be universally acknowledged (suffered and enjoyed) as twinges of vulnerability that revive the preciousness
of life. Kant considered that reminder a glimmer of transcendence. Secular translations can keep a spark of that wonder.

Ironically, bringing the sublime down to earth will return it
to a pre-Kantian meaning of rhetorical effect. From Longinus
on through the early eighteenth century, the sublime described
difficulty of comprehension or an elevated style, not the awe
that shocks the mind and turns it inward. The sublime was an
effect of language before it became an exaltation of the self. Evidently the rhetorical tradition of difficulty and interpretation
survives in Kant, as the hermeneutical procedures that make
up philosophy. This tradition offers a bridge of safety from the
brink of fear. In the section of this chapter called "Work Out"
I will ask if the bridge of rhetoric can be reclaimed today as
a space for working out anxieties about hard-to-take foreign
languages.

Since fear and even revulsion are uncomfortable, the feelings incite people to find remedy. This usually happens one way
or another: either the irritants are removed, often violently, or
the raw unpleasant feeling is processed through reason. In that
case, people can enjoy both the stimulus for intense feeling and
the victory over fear: "How thrilling is this incomprehensibly
complex world! I'm humbled by the fact that the people on

my block speak more languages than I could ever learn! (The mathematical sublime.) I hardly know when I'm in on a joke, and when I'm the butt of it! (The dynamic sublime.) It's glorious to know how delicate the difference is and how clever I am to know all this!"

To contemplate terror can be sublime. Simple as it sounds, this is a foundation of aesthetic theory—from the eighteenth century on. Kant put it—more romantically—like this:

> Bold, overhanging, and, as it were, threatening rocks, thunderclouds piled up the vault of heaven, borne along with flashes and peals, volcanoes in all their violence of destruction, hurricanes leaving desolation in their track, the boundless ocean rising with rebellious force, the high waterfall of some mighty river, and the like, make our power of resistance of trifling moment in comparison with their might. But, provided our own position is secure, their aspect is all the more attractive for its fearfulness; and we readily call these objects sublime, because they raise the forces of the soul above the heights of vulgar commonplace, and discover within us a power of resistance of quite another kind, which gives us courage to be able to measure ourselves against the seeming omnipotence of nature. (*The Critique of Judgement*, §28)

The effect comes down to a pleasant (empowered) reflection on (powerless) pain. Unsettled subjects suffer from feeling small or disrespected in unmanageable circumstances. But surviving the scary moment to contemplate the pain can feel downright flattering to one's faculty of reason. The operation wrests grandeur from the overwhelming experience to lodge grandeur in the self: "Therefore the feeling of the sublime in nature is respect for our own vocation."[3]

The sublime doesn't describe objects but an attitude.[4] Beauty is in the object and encourages harmonious play between imagination and understanding. The sublime outraces the imagination, outstrips understanding, and calls reason to the rescue. Can you step away from fear or revulsion to regain a kind of control without entirely giving up the thrill of an overwhelming experience? Can you turn sensual pain into aesthetic pleasure by exercising the creativity of human reception that will create a satisfaction instead of simply finding it? Does the "Uh, oh!" of overwhelmed senses trigger a step back for the "Wow!" when reason reflects on the big picture and enjoys itself as the vehicle of sane survival? You can manage the process, says Kant, if your position is secure. Standing at the high bank of a teeming river, or on a granite peak across from the tumbling rocks, knowing that that immigration is good for the economy and that people who speak more than one language are intellectual and political assets, enables sublime effects in what looks like a scary world. Without the distance or the knowledge, you could stay dangerously stuck in nervous demands to banish excitement and the natural world along with it.

The faculty to abstract from a sensation of pleasure or pain and to judge the sensation is called "taste." You may doubt whether the sublime counts as an occasion for judgment at all, since judging asks if the aesthetic effect harmoniously engages imagination and understanding. The sublime doesn't hope for harmony of the faculties; it controls a violent imagination through reason.[5] But reason can stand in for understanding where nature overwhelms, and where artistic genius takes control of materials. Unlike natural beauty that is *found*, art is intentionally *made*: "A beauty of nature is a *beautiful thing*; beauty of art is a *beautiful representation of a thing*" (*CJ*, §48). Making means a genius is at work, plotting and producing in the play of reason and imagination. Like the sublime, Kant continues, art can be inspired by ugliness: "Where fine art evidences its superiority is in the beautiful descriptions it gives of things that in nature would be ugly or displeasing" (*CJ*, §48). The transformation of displeasure into pleasure is hard work, for artists and for the subjects of the sublime: "Hence this form is not, as it were, a matter of inspiration, or of a free swing of the mental powers, but rather of a *slow and even painful process* of improvement, directed to making the form adequate to his thought without prejudice to the freedom in the play of those powers" (*CJ*, §48, my emphasis). Schiller would trouble this alignment of art with hard work (e.g., *CJ*, §54) when he confronted Goethe, the "naïve" phenomenon of nature, but he endorsed Kant's suggestion that the sublime achieves more freedom than beauty allows. "Thus the sublime affords us an egress from the sensuous world in which the beautiful would gladly hold us forever captive. Not gradually (for there is no transition from dependence to freedom), but suddenly and with a shock it tears the independent spirit out of the net."[6]

I want to underline Kant's engagement with taste and art to talk of the sublime for two reasons, one literary critical and the other ethical. They can add up to a sidetrack away from paralyzing responses to an awful world, away from intolerant responses and from shrill identification with victims of intolerance. Crisis is another name for monotone shrillness, says Claudio Lomnitz. A fullness of the present, with no memory of the past or projections of the future, crisis is a failure of narration.[7] Therefore, Lomnitz defends the historical imagination. Dominick La Capra defends it too, in his responses to Giorgio Agamben and to others who fill the present with high-pitched theory of undifferentiated limit events that leave no margins for agency. The unmodulated tone ("all exclamation marks") calls itself sublime.[8] But this is no aesthetic sublime. Aesthetics could lead beyond shrillness, and give history a dynamic hand.

For literary criticism, generally following Kant, the sublime describes stages of a powerful aesthetic effect, from mute wonder to volubility. Criticism cannot stay speechless and stay in business. The feeling of awe (or simply surprise in the classics) is only a first moment. Awe from the impact of incomprehensible grandeur or horror is the trigger for feelings that follow. Surviving the impact to speak of it evinces a transmutation from the (first) stunning moment to a (second) acknowledgment of fear as an intense perversely pleasurable feeling, and then to a (third) moment of deep satisfaction in one's faculty to take the step from feeling to thinking. Therefore, to call (rather loosely) an event or (more correctly) a response sublime is to trace a process past paralysis. The process invites aesthetic judgment, just as beauty does, in order to determine the nature of the pleasure produced. Was it disinterested? Can it be communicated universally? Does it elude existing concepts? Does it engage the cognitive faculties as part of the pleasure?

For Kant, it is this availability of the sublime for aesthetic judgment, not the wiggle room to get past awe (before an object) to pride (in oneself), that constitutes its greatest promise for moral reasoning. Forgive me for roughing over Kant's careful distinctions between aesthetics and morality, but he can hardly help himself regarding the sublime (§29).[9] In other sections too, "many of Kant's arguments read like thinly disguised moral arguments."[10] Taste is the link from pleasure to politics, the missing link that art can offer to defenses of history and the one that aesthetic training can develop. Only taste can yield universal agreement without coercion. It is a personal faculty that can do public work. Without an appeal to taste, sublime pleasures would lose the link to commonality and to public life.

Taste alone is free from the constraints of interest and even of reason, to follow Kant. And the free exercise of taste is the only sure grounding for universal agreement, on anything. (See *CJ*, §30–54.) This is why aesthetics has been so promising for a philosophy of freedom, ever since Kant located disinterested agreement as a "common sense." Judgments on beauty or on the sublime do not depend on the usefulness or on the interests that objects may have for particular people. In fact, disinterestedness is the defining characteristic of a pleasurable object judged to be beautiful or sublime. Therefore, "beauty" (to linger for a moment on Kant's first move toward intersubjectivity) is an attribute that can be freely acknowledged by all. And the common feeling for beauty amounts to a common sense. (For Freud commonality was a joke; either you laugh or you don't. Freud didn't trust judgment.)

Kant's *sensus communis* kept the term's popular appeal.[11] Popularity mattered to him. Unlike most philosophers, Kant never gave up hope that the "narrow footpath for the few would become a high-road [for all]."[12] Instead of meaning fuzzy judgment based on concepts "only obscurely conceived" (§21), common sense would now mean the sense we have in common.

Later Kant hints at his ambition for the term *sensus communis*, through taste as a public and collective consciousness: a "critical faculty which in its reflective act takes account [a priori] of the mode of representation of every one else, in order *as it were*, to weigh its judgment with the collective reason of mankind" (§40). For Kant, thinking for oneself (being enlightened) leads to thinking oneself into the place of everyone else (through an enlarged mentality). How curious, Hannah Arendt comments, that common sense and the business of judging between right and wrong should be based on taste.[13]

Arendt goes so far as to say that Kant never wrote very seriously about politics because he was doing that work through aesthetics, slyly on uncontested apolitical ground.[14] "Not until Kant's *Critique of Judgement* did this [taste] become a major topic of a major thinker . . . Conscience did not judge; it told you, as the divine voice of either God or reason, what to do, what not to do, and what to repent of."[15] Kant had read Baumgarten and Burke, but their expositions missed the opportunity to bridge particular subjectivities through aesthetic feeling.[16] Building that bridge, Kant established the basis of modern political life at a safe distance from received doctrine, inside the human capacity to judge. And judgment, Arendt adds, had always been an aesthetic activity for philosophy. Kant's important move was to bring the common sense of aesthetic judgment to the center of his project for the good, collective, and moral society. Arendt locates that move at the core of Kant's political thinking, typical of eighteenth-century moral philosophy that paid close attention to aesthetics because taste was only a step away from judgment:

> Kant says: "That is beautiful which pleases in the mere act of judging it." That is: it is not important whether or not it pleases in perception; what pleases merely in perception is gratifying but not beautiful. It pleases in representation, for now the imagination has prepared it so that I can reflect on it. This is "the operation of reflection." Only what touches, affects, one in representation, when one can no longer be affected by immediate presence—when one is uninvolved, like the spectator who was uninvolved in the actual doings of the French revolution—can be judged to be right or wrong, important or irrelevant, beautiful or ugly, or something in between. One then speaks of judgment and no longer of taste because, though it still affects one like a matter of taste, one now has, by means of representation, established the proper distance, the remoteness or uninvolvedness or disinterestedness, that is requisite for approbation and disapprobation, for evaluating something at its proper worth.[17]

Recursively, through talk of art and politics and history and nature, Arendt tracks Kant's construction of common sense as a product of reflection. Common sense of values needs first to step back from a thing of beauty or a feeling of horror, from an event in history or a fantasy of the future, in order to reflect on sensation. Spectatorship defines the citizen. Reflection will show the way toward freedom and will waken the cognitive faculties (understanding in the case of beauty, reason in the case of the sublime) to actively engage the imagination. In both the beautiful and the sublime cases, a dispassionate judgment yields the common sense that defines the shared life of society. Think of societies where one language interrupts another to disconnect communication and to syncopate the state. There the quotidian sublime makes common sense.

124

Human judgment, in other words, the kind that grounds modern secular societies in a sense of collective morality, depends on a common aesthetic sense. That sense is "a peculiar talent which can be practiced only and cannot be taught," Kant said.[18] This doesn't mean, however, that the talent cannot be trained. In fact, the *Third Critique* itself can be read as a training program to distinguish the merely sensuous from the beautiful and to process the frightening into the sublime.

> But the fact that culture is requisite for the judgement upon the sublime in nature (more than for that upon the beautiful) does not involve its being an original product of culture and something introduced in a more or less conventional way into society. Rather is it in human nature that its foundations are laid, and, in fact, in that which, at once with common understanding, we may expect every one to possess and may require of him, namely, a native capacity for the feeling for (practical) ideas, i.e., for moral feeling (*CJ*, §29).

Arendt's hopes for democracy also depended on "a mind so trained and cultivated that it can be trusted to tend and take care of a world of appearances whose criterion is beauty."[19] For teachers (including Kant, Schiller, and Arendt) the common sense that aesthetic agreement signals cannot be an innate feature of human beings. If it were, teaching and training would be unnecessary, redundant; so would writing books. Even if a universal aesthetic sense is what allows commonality to glimmer, that faculty is only potential as a vehicle for developing the glow of common sense through the exercise of judgments.

Painful Pleasures

The efforts differ markedly for lessons in beauty and in the sublime. And the difference makes teachers more or less necessary. Beauty is practically self-taught, as "a veritable extension . . . of our conception of nature itself" (*CJ*, §23). But the sublime requires guidance when nature turns unfriendly and refuses to extend itself. Beauty's bond with nature grounds its pleasures outside of the self, in objects that beckon and arouse our love. The sublime breaks with nature after it shatters concepts. "Thus the broad ocean agitated by storms cannot be called sublime. Its aspect is horrible, and one must have stored one's mind in advance with a rich stock of ideas, if such an intuition is to raise it to the pitch of a feeling which is itself sublime — sublime because the mind has been incited to abandon sensibility and employ itself upon ideas involving higher finality" (§23). Schiller follows closely: "The feeling of the sublime is a mixed feeling. It is a composition of melancholy which at its utmost is manifested in a shudder, and of joyousness which can mount to rapture and, even if it is not actually pleasure, is far preferred by refined souls to all pleasure."[20]

Horror, Kant and Schiller knew, can produce these paradoxical pleasures. The Marquis de Barthes would call it "neurotic." For him the shock, rub, gash, brink incites an almost physical jouissance. For Kant and for Schiller it is a cerebral rush, but just as neurotic and revealingly couched in terms that come close to Barthes's bliss: "the feeling of the sublime is a pleasure that only arises indirectly, being brought about by the feeling of a momentary check to the vital forces followed at once by a discharge all the more powerful" (§23). The sublime turns the self on itself, in self-defense, and storms its own bounded understanding. "For the beautiful in nature we must seek a ground external to ourselves, but for the sublime one merely in ourselves and the attitude of mind that

introduces sublimity into the representation of nature" (§23). Reason offers relief from having to understand horror and excess. And the pleasure of that humane relief is also pride in being human.

Beauty is a "positive" pleasure that needs no processing to be enjoyed, only judgment to determine if the pleasure is disinterested and potentially universal. But a taste for the sublime is labor-intensive. The predilection appreciates the almost perverse charm of shock (irritation, fear, even revulsion) as an aesthetic trigger for reflecting on displeasure. Then taste can take on its meaning as reflective judgment, to signify both the high cost of recovering peace of mind and the flattering trophy of humanity that reason bestows.

Arendt appreciated this general move from the senses to reflection as the motor of a political philosophy that Kant enables, but she depends on the particular stimulus of beauty to free up a path from the personal to the political. The sublime version of aesthetic effect makes the stronger case for sociability and for common sense. The process is a matter of survival. The sublime forces a reflection instead of just inviting it, because frightening (*gewalttätig*) or unpleasant stimuli demand a creative, reflexive reception.[21] Though all aesthetic judgment takes a reflexive pause, the pause is longer and the work harder for the sublime. The extra time and extra work make good opportunities for teachers to train taste. Beauty leaves little room for the meddling we call education. It is immediately pleasing, while the initially frightening sublime is a command to reflect on fear. The one is available to all, the other to cultivated people who explore the causes and effects of feelings. Beauty is a praise-word for objects rather than for the subject who praises them. But the sublime describes the subject, elevated through the satisfaction of surviving unpleasantness and reflecting on the arduous process.[22]

The contrast makes a significant sentimental, as well as pedagogical, difference. Kant concluded: beauty excites love of the world; the sublime elicits respect because it threatens love. (In Schiller's formulation: "Without the sublime, beauty would make us forget our dignity.")[23] The neurotic/erotic passage quoted above from Kant's preface (§23) continues in this engagingly perverse way: "Hence charms are repugnant to it; and, since the mind is not simply attracted by the object, but is also alternately repelled thereby, the delight in the sublime does not so much involve positive pleasure as admiration or respect, i.e., merits the name of a negative pleasure" (§23).

The thrill of almost losing it (losing love, control, connection) inspires reason to invent maneuvers for holding on to the world. There are good philosophical grounds for privileging the sublime side of aesthetics, as Kirk Pillow argues in *Sublime Understanding*, because philosophy's grasp is "the always partial, indeterminate grasping of contextual wholes through which we make sense of the uncanny particular in both art and the lived world."[24] For literature and other arts, that uncanny particular is what taste values, since surprising the public's expectations, or veering beyond conventions, excites aesthetic contemplation whereas mere correctness can be pleasurable but passive.[25] Kant himself aligned art to the sublime, because—unlike beauty—the arts rely on the artist's calculated reason (Shklovsky's technique). In the naïve (beauty), Schiller added, "nature is victorious over art."[26] The naïve of surprise describes human beings who achieve truth through affect, not reason.[27]

Today, we cannot afford to be aesthetically lazy and prefer immediately perceptible beauty and affect over the sublime triple-take of received pain, process, and achieved pleasure. Loss of control is the strong aesthetic response to sublime terribly strange (and also funny) stimuli, unlike the gentler response to beauty that can stir and distract. The difference seems overdrawn to Elaine Scarry, who complains that beauty is thereby demoted, feminized, to mean something more decorative than divine. With a rush of sentimental judgments, she hopes to level the difference between "clearly discernible" beauty and the so-called sublime. But the demolition should give formalist readers pause and staying power in an asymmetrical multicultural world where discernibility is a game of hits and misses, a war of position.[28] Her position wants to clear differences away,[29] whereas Gayatri Spivak marks the border between beauty and the sublime as the limit where Europeans worry about what they can and cannot discern and control.[30]

Where migrant laborers do much of the unwanted work for advanced societies, we should worry about beauty that goes down too easily. Both citizens and sojourners will have to process even unpleasant surprises into a kind of sublime "common sense." For both natives and newcomers who don't speak the same language, our most palpable commonality may be the loss of harmony between imagination and understanding. A close runner-up is the fear of losing control, given the specters of violence, scarce resources, or just clogged institutions. But the enormity that makes any one of us feel small might look inviting, if we developed a taste for the sublime. On reflection, society would exceed any individual imagination; the complexities would excite awe and contemplation, and our only partial understanding would safeguard the modesty that democracy depends on.

Despite the feelings of personal smallness, the very reflection on asymmetries between self and society will be a pleasurable triumph over fear. And the pleasure can repeat from one feeling and thinking subject to another, even if the stimuli are different, until the pleasure becomes a common sense. Without a taste for the sublime, can we imagine general attachments to societies that don't seem either benign or immediately beautiful? Today, the most urgent educational and sentimental project may well be to train a preference for the initially frightening but ultimately flattering sublime. Trained taste will tell the difference between mere gratuitous or sensational impact and effects that invite reflection. Learning to enjoy those awful moments as awe inspiring will amount to a new (post- or neonational) sentimental education.

Mono Is a Malady

A lasting lesson of the modern sentimental education was to desire the consummation of a republican romance, or foundational fiction. That story of star-crossed patriots who overcome every obstacle to establish productive unions gave revolutionaries the permission to challenge divine right and to topple kings. Rebels would replace regents in the name of a *gran familia nacional* that spoke, ate, played, prayed, and procreated together in one culturally coherent language.[31] What do we disenchanted postmoderns do with a chronic national desire for one culture, now that family ties don't hold us together, in one place or to one language? Often, we cannot understand our neighbors, let alone the newcomers and goers in and out of the neighborhoods. Even when immigrants become "naturalized" citizens, they don't necessarily give up their original passports, so you can't be sure where—or how much—they belong here or there.[32] To make things worse, today's countries worry about their very sovereignty being compromised as migrants make claims on a strain of democracy that stretches across borders. Human rights become everybody's business. And inside our countries, it is increasingly difficult to tell who is who and how anyone fits into a familia at loose ends, since members can now officially claim to have this, that, and the other ethnic identity on census forms. What, as I say, do we do? This is not a rhetorical question.

Two general responses meet the messiness of late modernity, the same two I mentioned in the management of nervousness. One response is to clean up the confusions (restrict immigration, enforce English-only communication, fuel militant patriotism, restore ROTC to campuses, answer jihad with crusade and conversion). The other response is to value loose ends as lifelines for democracy (to legitimate dual citizenship, practice bilingual arts, learn a tragicomic sense of humor, draw a bright line between religious particularity and the secular lingua franca). The first option is familiar and intolerant. Bornagain Americans, often monolinguals, can bristle at people who speak strange languages. Spanish-speakers are asked to leave bars; Chinese conversations grate on English-only ears; the polyphony of a place like Manhattan sounds like the Mad Hatter to people like Ron Unz [*sic*].[33] His own family name announces an intolerant populism that pits Us against Them, if you play a kind of bilingual game close to philology and bring back the German, or the Yiddish his mother gave up to become American. It's not the foreigners themselves who bother Unz, he insists against xeno-baiters, but rather their stubborn cultural ties that tangle the country in "The Bilingual Bind."[34] "They are talking about me," is one self-centered response. (Are you a Merdican citizen?) Self-centering seems self-evidently legitimate in a powerful United States where it's enough to speak one language, because less powerful foreigners learn to speak English. Here monolingualism sounds normal. I am normal. You should be too.

The second option is unfamiliar and fresh: it is an opportunity to develop a tolerance and a *taste* for the sublime and risky business of democratic life. Hearts and minds are the organs of political life; without them, the best designs fail. But our tired rhythms of desire and our cramped approach to reason can't keep step with democratic demands. A new sentimental education should be on the agenda for this period of global movements of people and capital through multicultural states.[35] It is a tall order for teachers, but an urgent one, because some of our inherited tastes and predispositions have become obstacles for democracy. It may be naïve to think that a bilingual question can adjust our structure of feeling to prefer the cultural blues of being too much and not enough, and thereby to lend some flex to the familiar and unfriendly politics of national solidarity. But teachers of language and literature sometimes secretly believe in the social power of aesthetic education. It trains preferences, after all, toward one political predisposition or another.

Today we need a sensibility that opens wiggle room (o jogo de cintura, Caribbean *cimarronería*, Gramsci's peripheral move) away from the compact ideal of la gran familia toward the unfamiliar spaces that require and therefore tolerate democratic procedures. International courts, for example. That the work is feasible goes almost without saying, given the astounding success of the relatively recent training program in collective feelings that made us modern subjects of nation-states. That program started only about two hundred years ago and had its effect within one generation. The very familiarity and apparent "naturalness" of desires for national solidarity across class and sometimes color lines is proof that sentimental education works. Had that effort failed, we would still feel that monarchy was the natural order of politics. The education that novelists, legislators, leaders, and mostly classroom teachers provided for the earlier republican national period practically overhauled the hearts and minds of entire populations. *L'education sentimental* means more than the title of a particular nineteenth-century novel by Gustave Flaubert. It is the program of an entire foundational genre and of a generation of republican fathers and mothers.

In nineteenth-century Latin America and elsewhere, nation builders knew that personal desire would either promote or mire economic and political developments. So they launched a sentimental revolution. Eros and polis (in their modern meanings as sexual attraction and republican states) helped to construct each other, since erotics accomplished the glorious mission of producing citizens, and politics performed the tender service of protecting loved ones. New citizens identified with heroes and heroines who desired one another across class and regional barriers in order to establish republican families; and the republican rhetoric of personal fulfillment fanned the flames of reproductive love. No wonder presidents, generals, and legislators were also national novelists; they trained people's unproductive (colonial) passions toward (liberal) desires for consolidated republics through interracial, interregional, and economic affairs. The training program took a little time, of course, because winning hearts doesn't follow the same rhythm as winning minds with reasonable argument. And the novel—in newspaper installments that could stretch stories and train desire over a year's time—was the preferred medium for a gradual republican sentimental education. National desire, constructed with the help of fictions and rehearsed from intimate bedroom readings to institutional curricula, is a preferential feeling for coherent cultures and for its gran familia or "imagined community" of overlapping sentiments. Be-longing to a nation state, and to "natural" heterosexual alliances, legitimated republics and trumped the authority of monarchs. It has seemed simply natural and incontrovertible, but we know that the preference for coherent nations that map as seamless states is a relatively recent taste for simplicity that may turn out to be rather nasty and brief.

Nations still exist, of course, but not necessarily in redundant relationship to states. At the unraveling seam between the two there is a space, and an obligation, to imagine political preferences beyond the intolerant ideal of cultural coherence. The call to aesthetic action is apparently in the air, since several educators have already responded with proposals for naming and shaping a sensibility that can help to feel—and to flesh out—relationships and identities in complicated times. Peruvian Antonio Cornejo Polar, for example, reconsidered his country's most promising performances in an essay about its best-known bicultural novelist, and concluded that migrancy is not simply a personal hardship and a social blight; it is also a dynamic aesthetic and political condition.[36] Uncanny echoes of the argument migrate to my reading of Stephen Greenblatt's meditation on "racial memory," which suggests that Unheimlichkeit is the name for a kind of familiar homelessness, almost consolingly familiar in one's life and across different lives.[37]

To these contributions toward a "migrant" sensibility, I want to add some specific considerations about language choice and thereby to ground the sensibility in everyday arts. And while it is fun to follow the games that migrants develop between home and host languages, it would miss the point of common sense to ignore the monolinguals who may feel excluded by those games. Naturally, they can be nervous and hostile. But Kantian aesthetics considers this kind of immediate and unreflective rejection of strangeness to be unrefined and unworthy of our human condition. A response of a second, civilized, order as I've said is to notice the surprise of losing control and to enjoy the experience of getting the point that you didn't get something. That perverse pleasure of the *sublime* promises a new liberation, not from the tyranny of kings but from the tyranny of totality, a general will, a single ideal type of citizen, all of which can misprise the internal diversity of contemporary democracies.

Our postmodern republics will need to develop a palate for the unfamiliar, for surprise, even irritation. Some tolerance for a cross-cultural sublime (the thrill of incomprehension) as well as for humor should spice our talk of aesthetics. Then particular subjects will recognize our own "migrant" condition as normal double consciousness. Whether more than one culture is inside or alongside the subject, the doubling or multiplying of codes amounts to a humbling consciousness of one's limits. And humility is a sublime double agent that collaborates with reason, to make feeling funny feel very good.

Nervous Invitations

Nervousness about bilinguals isn't necessarily paranoid, I said with a reference to Ana Celia Zentella's teasing about Latinos who joke about Anglos even when they deny it.[38] Sometimes the joke is on bilinguals who pay the cost of language loss because they actually buy the idea that less is more. But even paranoia can be a first stage of a "multicultural sublime" where pleasure depends on the pain of losing control. Another response to strange languages is condescension: "Poor foreigners!

If they spoke good English, they would be smarter." Early cognitive studies jump to this conclusion, seriously.[39] A corollary claims that if English was good enough for Jesus Christ, it's good enough for you. And another boldly decries the loss of coherence in this beleaguered country, but doesn't notice that the slogan for unity, E pluribus unum, is incomprehensible in English-only.[40] Bold—and simple—as the equation of American equals English is, it passes for axiomatic in a whole series of calculations for economic and intellectual developments associated with globalization. Another name for global coordination is Americanization, something like the conflation of democracy with the particular name of a country that made Walt Whitman a hero for his populist interpreters. But some of us are reluctant to choose and lose between cultures in a calculus too narrow for democracy.

Contemporary democracy depends on difference, not only of economic interest but also of cultural codes, cults, preference, styles. These apparently prepolitical variations often locate fault lines in the exercise of otherwise admirable rules in the United States, as when legal procedures founder over intolerance for cultural inflection, in foreign accents for example.[41] Therefore, the specifically aesthetic challenge—to reframe a fear of foreignness into an appetite for it—is partner to another (political) challenge: how to distinguish capacious constitutional procedure from the mean practices that vitiate the law and refuse to play fair. The challenge can take a lead from Kant by fixing on the common sense of taste that needs to be trained in the exercise of free play and reflection, in order to develop a general moral economy for democratic society.

As things stand, our romantic habit of identifying monolingual nationhood with a political state predisposes us to the goal of coherence. Therefore, difference looks like it did in classical or crusader times, like deviation rather than an aesthetic effect of art or a democratizing incentive to coordinate cultural difference through politics. That is evidently why the Associated Press predicted, or invoked, the congressional bill to cut bilingual education short.[42] There were those who worried about Hispanic children not learning in English-only schools, but "two years after Californians voted to end bilingual education and force a million Spanish-speaking students to immerse themselves in English as if it were a cold bath, those students are improving in reading and other subjects at often striking rates."[43] This glibness about cold bath cures—as if Spanish were dirt or a disease—doesn't worry about other losses and the dangers that follow. There are at least three, and each is disastrous. One loss is to the children and their families, since Spanish is not only a vehicle for learning lessons in school, replaceable perhaps by English; it is also an international code that could foster communication, commerce, creativity, with fellow Spanish speakers in almost two dozen countries. Another loss is something beyond, or alongside, the rational functions and advantages of a second language. It is the range of affective, respectful, intimate, and generally performative registers of a second, home, or subaltern language. "Indeed the conflict has been not just between two languages, but between two quite different conceptions of language," to recall Terry Eagleton's distinction between the cognitive English and the performative Irish.[44] Language recognized as art has the social virtue of noticing a creative artist/citizen at work. ("But where anything is called absolutely a work of art, to distinguish it from a natural product, then some work of man is always understood," *CJ*, §43.) A third loss has the broadest consequences for all of us; it is the loss of difference itself, the disturbance that today's democracy depends on.

Democracy depends on difference, we should insist, despite some current communitarian skepticism about how much difference we need. Against the skeptics, Ernesto Laclau offered his interpretation of universalism as the space for particulars to conflict and to coordinate, and Bonnie Honig reframed the narrative of democracy from family romance to gothic thriller. Homegrown diversity and foreign immigration exercise democratic institutions. The *Times* is right to celebrate student advances in English; all of us residents in the United States share a space, and we all appeal to a code of justice that should interpellate vastly different peoples. But the unfounded assumption that this is possible only with the loss of Spanish (or Chinese, just to mention two major languages) begs comparative questions: is bilingualism a liability if the other language signals privilege, like French or German? Are bilingual children at risk of learning in neither language if they come from the middle class?[45] Or has Spanish been racialized and stigmatized to the point that white Spanish speakers arouse inquisitorial skepticism because "they don't look Latin"?

It is time to expect more than one language (as background or playground) in the normal course of conversation and to unhinge facile assumptions from policy issues. In fact, the same state of California that turned its back on bilingual education has now come around to defending "the right of each child to know more than one language."[46]

Training America's ears to hear the tones of one language in the defamiliarized sounds of another may be an almost technical challenge for the kinds of courtroom cases that Mari Matsuda considered, but it can bring broad conceptual rewards. At least this is the kind of technical training for democracy that we can do in the fields of language arts and that cannot be done elsewhere. It won't be enough to teach everyone a single second language, let's say Spanish. If cultural difference stimulates democracy, reducing multilinguality to the two most common denominators overrides the difficulty of communication that could promote cautious civic behavior.

Organic communities may count on ties of affection, but diverse societies like ours need to develop respect. Without the problem of opacity or indifference—the necessity that mothers invention—there would be no need for civic solutions. Without cultural discontinuity there would be less urgency for procedural arrangements and exercised institutions. Another objection to official bilingualism comes from complaints against using Spanish in politics and in the academy. President Bush's inaugural Spanish speech sent off a range of angry and anxious responses that add up to "Bush's radio address a mistake." "President Bush's Saturday radio address in Spanish will guarantee that he will receive complaints from those claiming to represent speakers of Farsi, Khmer, Tagalog, and the three hundred or so other tongues spoken in the United States. Admittedly, political speeches in languages other than English are not unknown to American politics. But we now live in a time when America has turned its back on the importance of assimilation. A gentle hint that immigrants might have some responsibility to learn a minimal amount of English is considered beyond the pale of *polite political discourse*" (my emphasis).[47] Polite politics, on the contrary, depends on a lingua franca so that politeness can be perceived. What good are good manners if the company doesn't notice them? But lingua franca assumes a general availability of the shared code, rather than proprietary rights of particular parties, so that politeness in mixed company also depends on a measure of chaste discomfort and the dangers of misinterpretation.

In Spanish, the concept of America has always been polyglot, complex, baroque, excessive, overloaded.[48] The very fact of the conquest brought European cultures into crises of self-definition and produced the supplements that show how unstable or insufficient the "original" culture had been. European baroque art and thought were anxious responses to the shock of discovering America, a vast and variously sophisticated world that had no notice or need of Europe. Half a millennium later, after variations of migratory movements and shifting borders (when the United States grew by shrinking Mexico and then overtaking Puerto Rico), single-language neatness feels too cramped, even as a desire. New movements of peoples and patrimonies refresh the baroque patterns that make neatness an unnecessary design constraint.[49] To recover a flair for the baroque that can welcome these complicated times, and to wean ourselves from murderously rigid designs for national unity, we will need the spice of exasperation and a taste for working through hard-to-digest difference.

Work Out

Some worries about multilingual societies may be quite reasonable, but anxiety can block fair means for addressing danger. There is relief from irrational fear and rejection if we stop to reflect and to work through them. Working-through is a familiar term from psychoanalysis and it suggests a parallel with hermeneutics; both tackle opacity and offer interpretation. Thomas Weiskel accounted for the relationship between analysis and hermeneutics through their shared origins in the sublime. He saw "that the poetic and philosophic language of the primary sublime texts could be made to resonate with two quite different twentieth century idioms, that of psychoanalysis and that of the semiological writings of Saussure, Jakobson, and Barthes."[50] Perhaps the idioms can communicate again so that literary interpretation may speak to emotional blockage. Luckily, after its demotion in the eighteenth century, the rhetorical sublime survived in literary hermeneutics. It has some practical work to do now, once difficulty is reestablished as a defining feature of the sublime. Difficulty is a quality of texts and can be worked through; blockage goes nowhere and describes the tormented self. The distinction "may sound trivial," Neil Herz writes, "a mere difference in degree, but such differences, between the absolute and the not-so-absolute, often take on philosophical and narrative importance."[51]

Kant's sublime starts with the absolute but doesn't stay there. He brings imagination and understanding to a brink of death, in contrast to the rhetorical sublime that didn't go to extremes. But Kant regains calm through an arduous process that shows how difficulty—associated with rhetoric not passion—is central to his sublime. If confusion triggers passion, Kant shows that intellectual work disarms fear and provides pleasure. In these anxious times, when rhetorical effects of foreignness can trigger absolute blockage, a demand for translation or opacity often escalates to brinkmanship.[52] Today's rhetorical sublime is a volatile hybrid of linguistic effect and unprocessed emotion. Maybe the lasting link between language and feeling will suggest an option to process emotion through interpretive language games.

We can get from "Ay, no" to "I know." Language games and other risky contact sports can survive losses and unpleasant shocks. The sequence of plays acknowledges "blockage" or refusal and then harnesses frustrated energy to work through interpretation and wrest pleasure. This variation on Kant suggests a way to interpret foreign interruptions and thereby to back away from brinks. For him, interrupted cognition could lead to transcendence, the fear for one's life to an affirmation of life and beyond oneself. For us, interrupted understanding can come from foreignness, the shock of incomprehension that ignites other anxieties in multicultural societies. If questions about how we can understand each other, govern, educate, or do business sound merely rhetorical and blocked, can we unblock rhetoric for the arduous work of interpretation? Do we have a good alternative?

Kant is in vogue again. In a morally stand-still world, the mechanisms of historical dialectics have apparently tarnished or rusted. So moral philosophy makes a comeback, sometimes through Kant's categorical imperatives that should move us by the sheer force of will or by responsibility for self-perfectibility.[53] Some neo-Kantians put his lessons on ability and responsibility to collective work, especially the lesson about "Perpetual Peace," which they read for its global ambitions.[54] Others, the world-weary literary critics who have had too much of politics and too much of theory over the last thirty years, care less about morality and prefer Kant's lessons about the purposelessness of beauty. Beauty is autonomous from goodness. If it were not, taste and pleasure might appear so self-evidently contingent on morality as to preempt the value of affective response and judgment. But autonomy is not exactly independence, since beauty is a symbol of the good, Kant sometimes says, and the "purposelessness" of aesthetic experience has moral aftereffects.[55] Aesthetic judgment itself depends on the claim of assent from others, which is why Hannah Arendt followed Kant's contribution to aesthetics in order to get to politics.[56] Autonomy's sign is a pause, a necessary hiatus from overweening practical demands, like a flash of freedom that develops a taste for more freedom. Evidently, the weary are reluctant to follow the moral consequences of autonomy. But, by forcing open a space for freedom and thereby for the responsibility of judgment, natural beauty and art, like the sublime, promote the disinterested reflection that links aesthetics to ethics.

Arendt didn't make much of that difference between beauty and the sublime. Her gloss on Kant celebrates the general common sense of freedom that all judgment depends on and develops. But one can imagine sequels that would contrast the effects of love and of respect for culturally complicated democracies, where citizens should be fair, not necessarily fond of one another. Beauty can dull the distinction in a rush of immediate attachments, but the sublime hiatus puts analysis back to work.

"Ask her if she had TB?"

"He says if you have a television."

Communication teeters, unsure if contact was made or even how to make it when codes intersect out of one's control. This common sense doesn't blunt the boldness of disconnect effects. Is it irritating or even frightening? Perhaps. The interesting question is what to do next. Either you can stay irritated, or you can sublime the feeling into a taste for the clever move that stopped you short. To notice the interruption and to feel the irritation exercises the faculties of knowing and feeling. Why not wonder instead of just worry about the wily language games that stop and start and keep us alert to skillful moves and to the precarious medium for playing human games? Newcomers know how unsteady communication can be, the thrill of teetering and the satisfaction of recognizing what has happened. Natives know it too, once they anticipate the possibilities of moving though frustration toward refined contemplation.

Nature provided stimuli for both aesthetic effects as far as Kant was concerned. But though he attributed the sublime to natural phenomena that exceed human capacities for comprehension or imitation, he did note an analogy with inexhaustible attractions of artistic genius. The analogy brings back the demoted rhetorical sublime. The sublime was of course a rhetorical effect for the classics. As late as *The New Science* (1744), Giambattista Vico was still defending the rhetorical surprise effect of the hyperbaton as sublime, although the metaphysical meaning was already gaining a vogue. He was reluctant, though, to name the trope *hyperbaton*, perhaps because *in-*

version, as the figure was called since Longinus (*On the Sublime*, §22), seemed excessive and unnatural to his French colleagues.[57] Inversions and other rhetorical excesses that make up a "bilingual aesthetics" inspired Henry Abelove to describe *Bilingual Aesthetics* as "queering language."

It was *Peri Hypsous (On the Sublime)*, attributed to third-century Longinus but probably two hundred years older, that began to stretch the word beyond its narrow technical meaning of bold rhetorical effect toward spiritual greatness.[58] In both cases the sublime was a man-made effect of art for Longinus, not of wild nature. Variety and surprise, tortured syntax (§10), orderly disorder produce the greatest effect (§20).[59] Shklovsky may have learned his lessons here. Art was as much the cause as the effect of greatness for Longinus, who noticed a reciprocal relationship between noble rhetoric and exalted souls (§17).[60] By sliding from great souls to great poetry, Herz shows that Longinus manages to raise Homer to the rank of gods and heroes.[61]

Longinus seemed naughty to Boileau, who published a translation in 1672. A warmer reception followed in England and Germany, where French neoclassical disapproval of excess brought an almost instinctive vindication of it by Francophobes. Then the sublime took off during the Sturm und Drang of the eighteenth century, practically shedding its technical origins and acquiring the almost mystical meaning of greatness beyond comprehension. A particular moment of the transition from the artful to the awful is worth remarking.

Edmund Burke published his *Enquiry into the Origin of our Ideas on the Sublime and Beautiful* in 1757. Characteristically, Burke was reluctant to sacrifice classical grounding to the romantic times; he kept the sublime effects of human agency as brakes on the runaway concept of uncontrollable passions and overwhelming odds.[62] The *Enquiry* appeals to contemporary taste for the sublime as a stimulus for moral development, including Britain's "moral empire." In that context, India—he argued—should be recognized as sublime. Her culture, history, religion, and arts show both the (classical) signs of ingenuity *and* the (romantic) effect of wonderful strangeness. India is doubly sublime and therefore worthy of respect, fair dealing, even sympathy.[63]

Burke's feelings for India hardly make him a sexy bedfellow for the postimperial trysts between powerful nativists and subaltern newcomers, I know. But it is delightfully perverse to link onto his fascination with foreignness and then to move—on an inspiration from Barthes (and Sade)—toward frustrating the imperial fantasies of superior control by enjoying how the Other (or the lover) refuses to submit. The perversion, reversal, *choteo*, follows Burke in acknowledging an artful effect I want to call the "subaltern sublime"; it also underlines the intentionally irritating ways that India produced its stunning effect of strangeness on the Anglo authorities. In postcolonial times, the sublime need not derive from a grand and independent history of the human spirit; it can simply be the performance of commonplace in-your-face foreignness that disables nativists in ways that make them outsiders to some games. "You don't know me. You don't own me," is trophy. A taste for the subaltern sublime might develop along the asymmetrical fault lines between producers and consumers of signs. To feel only resentment is to stay at a primitive level of response, in Kant's line of thinking.

Apparently, there are constructions so strange, so incomprehensible, that they arouse fear and revulsion. Anxiety is the undeniable effect of irritations, and we cannot simply wish them away. Irritation is unavoidable, but strangeness can ignite passion without getting burned.

If the point sounds redundant by now, we can proceed to

some corollary considerations. (Boredom is the surest sign of progress in language lessons.) A funny sequel follows from Kant's admission of the insufficiency of understanding to comprehend natural phenomena, such as a teeming waterfall or a gusty mountaintop. They arouse shudders, not thoughts. Whether Kant or Longinus like it or not, says John Limon, the shudder is close to a chuckle and even closer to a laugh attack. He is disappointed that Kant didn't get the inverted sublimity in his own joke about the Indian who wonders, astonished, how the foam got into the bottle of beer. "In a precritical demarcation, he writes that 'nothing sinks deeper beneath the sublime than the ridiculous.' This formulation distinctly, if unintentionally, lends the ridiculous a sublime, even oceanic, depth."[64]   **145**
High and low, beauty and sublime, pleasure and displeasure vacillate in Limon's shake-up of Kant's categories, as they do in Cixous's "Laugh of the Medusa," until one term of the binary looks like a disguise for its opposite and "pain feels like pleasure," so that "antagonism itself creates a strange harmony" (57). For Limon, stand-up comedy in the United States stages the shock of human vulnerability against the backdrop of rational modernity. This is the out-of-control sublime and ridiculous scene of American assimilation. High-mindedness pulled immigrants up toward culturally neutral suburbs, while ethnic and accented cities pulled them down to abject low-life. The stress made American audiences lose control and break records for laughter when Lenny Bruce did stand-ups that really got down.

Limon doesn't exactly stand the diagnosis of groveling and supine abjection on its head; he stands it up.[65] The joke is to invert loss into a gain of attention, lowliness into the stature of a spokesperson. It's a good joke on good taste, mostly for insiders and other almost-Americans, while upstanding citizens felt offended. A variation of the abject as erect comes to mind in the

shape of *la Gorda de Oro*, Mirta Silva's nickname as a singer
in Puerto Rico and then hostess of a variety show on New York
television. During her fan-mail spot one night, she read a particularly insulting letter. "You're right on every count, señora,"
she sneered into the camera. "But I'm here on TV and you're
there watching me." There's delicious revenge in her tone.

Revenge on the gatekeepers of good taste, the satisfaction of
knowing more than your agonist who has presumed cultural
superiority, and the sheer relief of surviving in an unwelcoming world, these are familiar pleasures for migrants and minorities above or beyond Limon's stand-up riff on abjection.
Turning the tables on cultural competence is not the same as

dragging an audience down to a comic's low level. "I know German. I'm from Milwaukee," says Marilyn Monroe to unsettle
the prince. Franz Kafka knew German too, and he played it
brilliantly, as Clement Greenberg insisted against F. R. Leavis.
Kafka revenged himself on taste that was "too high-falutin', too
Gentile" for the bite of his clever self-hatred.[66] He wrote in
off-German, not off enough to call his competence into question, though he'd write ridiculous English through his alter-
ego émigré to America.[67] Off-center even at home, like Tato
Laviera in *AmeRíca*, Kafka's languages double up and Greenberg seems sure that the cleverness is simply self-destructive.
Unlike peasant humor that flaunts intelligence, "or at least,
shrewdness," says Greenberg, Jewish humor "makes fun even
of intelligence; it shows intelligence being put to the pettiest
uses for the pettiest ends—simply because intelligence can only
agitate itself in vain and split hairs when it is so completely
unaccompanied by power."[68] But in liberal democracies, agi-
tation is an effect to reckon with. It marks an active presence
of human agency.

The showgirl's move makes her present to the prince, and
Kafka's German brought marginal antics to center stage. The

misprised players manage to pull the rug from under more presumptuous partners. Tottering and titillated from the unexpected imbalance, the surprise can feel sublime to the surviving victims of the joke; it can feel close to catharsis. Suddenly life seems more delicate and delicious in its renewable joys. But the charm doesn't always work, obviously. Leavis was not impressed with Kafka, and foreigners didn't respond to Lenny Bruce. In fact, Bruce left his British and Australian audiences cold.[69]

Differential responses, we know from Freud and others, are part of the "science" of humor. Jewish jokes just aren't funny, for example, when Gentiles tell them, and American ethnic abjection is evidently boring to outsiders. It makes no com-

mon sense. Jokes and other language games depend on that aesthetic commonality. Otherwise Arendt might have left Kant alone, instead of stretching his notion of common sense in order to warm the public toward a res publica.

If commonality is lost, if an aesthetic sense doesn't move the general public, politics loses ground. This is where aesthetic education might take a new turn, as I've said, away from a single ideal or universal audience toward a variety of limited receptions. They intersect in the acknowledgment of a performance.[70] Common sense could lead to a kind of enlarged mentality that appreciates asymmetries, instead of thinking oneself into the place of everyone else. There are several ways to get a joke, as Freud said, and we can locate a common ground by noticing more than one position on a shared playing ground.

What does this make Unz and others who fear "foreign" talk and ignore the invitations to play see-saw language games that shift positions of power and sometimes make English-only speakers feel funny? It doesn't make them bad, just humorless and primitive. And what might our response be to unrefined fellow citizens? It cannot be removal or rejection in a democracy. So let's try a sentimental training program that favors respect over love, the sublime over the beautiful, and that can turn the dread of difference into desire for it.

Resend Letters: *On the Aesthetic Education of Man*

Training can take a lead from Friedrich Schiller's program in *On the Aesthetic Education of Man, in a Series of Letters* (1759). Schiller wrote these *Letters* to nudge open dead ends in politics and society. Later he would add *Naïve and Sentimental Poetry* (1795–6) in order to quibble with Kant's *Third Critique*. After meeting Goethe, Schiller was sure that genius owed nothing to reason but was a gift of nature. Most modern artists were not geniuses, pace Kant, but (sentimental) tormented technicians who strained to recover a connection to nature. The struggle reveals a freedom to act and a moral obligation that self-sufficient naïve nature cannot cultivate.[71] The difference gives overwrought practitioners like Schiller a moral advantage over godlike Goethe.

But the *Letters* had a greater ambition than profiling poets. They defended art as the medium for a humane pedagogy that teaches how to wrest freedom from contradiction. If the capacity for art were only "naïve" genius, there would be little opportunity to teach and no moral effects. The loss would be incalculable in a fallen world. But sentimental art can be taught; it thrives in the very distance from nature where poets have freedom to maneuver. Art outdoes nature as a vehicle for the spiritual refinement of "citizens." First, art is stable and available for instruction, whereas nature offers only moments. And more importantly, art is evidence of freedom and free play. "Since nature can be aesthetic only as an object of free contemplation her imitator, creative art, is completely free, because it can separate from its subject matter all contingent limitations, and also leaves the mind of the observer free because it imitates only the semblance, and not the actuality. But because the whole magic of the sublime and the beautiful subsists only in semblance, art thus possesses all the advantages of nature without sharing her shackles."[72]

The *Letters* offer an aesthetic education to intervene in the world. A first move is to get unstuck from the idealism that Kant represented. The trap of idealism seemed reciprocal and hermetic to Schiller: intellectual habits are based on moral biases; and morality depends on intellectual ground. His way out of the circle was to open up the "living springs" of both the intellect and moral feeling through the "instrument of Fine Art" because art, like science, makes itself known by pulling away from constraints and conventions.[73] Kant was the pioneer here (Letter 11). Freedom's dependence on self-consciousness, and the promise of a new spontaneity based on reflection, became the themes of Schiller's pedagogy. It turned Kant's lessons about the differences between beauty and the sublime, love and respect, nature and artistic genius into a progression of before and after aesthetic education. "A first phase of unself-consciousness moves through a second phase of highly cerebral lucidity, and then to a third phase which combines the virtues of both in what looks like a return but is in reality a progress."[74] Later, as I said, Schiller added that art could be easy, if you were a genius like Goethe.[75] They joined forces after Schiller overcame his genius-envy. In both cases, however, attention to freedom revolutionizes conventional education. Art bypasses constraints, either naïvely or through struggle, while "the understanding of the schools, always fearful of error, . . . severe and stiff to avoid uncertainty at all costs, employs many words to be quite sure of not saying too much and deprives its thoughts of their strength and edge so that they may not cut the unwary."[76]

149

Schiller's English editors of the *Letters* applaud him for playing loose with the Kantian categories. Allegedly Kant didn't descend to empirical grit or allow for enough process to get from the nature to culture. "Schiller appreciated Kant's distinction between freedom and interest, beauty and utility; but he noted that the beauty Kant considered was pure form, 'arabesque' Schiller called it, not the contingent art of tragedy and literature in general."[77] "If art was to educate, it had, surely, to make connection with the chaos it claimed to conquer, not to remain aloof from it."[78] The very idea of education implies, as practitioners know, contingent rather than ideal terms.

Free *play*, though, was also the code term for Kant, as the dynamic relationship between imagination and understanding (for beauty) or reason (for the sublime). Schiller merely reframed the creative tension to call it a "form drive" (for categorical abstraction) against a "sense-drive" (toward material change).[79] The difference between the theories has to do with the degree of antagonism they will tolerate. Schiller portrays hostile forces barely holding each other in check, while Kant and Goethe see the collaboration of faculties as mutual aid.[80] Whatever their differences of intensity, Schiller is Kant's active disciple, according to Paul Guyer. Maybe the master even took a lesson from Schiller for *The Metaphysics of Morals* (1797), where Kant takes up the work of cultivating an aesthetic sense.[81]

The case for pedagogical continuity falls flat for Paul de Man, who admired Kant for tolerating opacity in nature and reviled Schiller for allegedly tinkering with the sublime as if it were the raw material for busybodies.[82] Gayatri Spivak repeats this objection to Schiller and accuses him of derailing philosophy into anthropology or history. Of course Schiller himself had admitted to being queer, something of a "hermaphrodite" cross between poet and philosopher. Teachers take risks with whatever works. Sometimes he found the hybrid condition enabling, because he could persuade by argumentation and by delight, but other times he despaired of the mutual interference that ruined both his thought and his art.[83]

If Schiller did take a sidetrack from Kant, Spivak might have treated the step as an escape route past the Eurocentric privilege of inherited civilization that Kant represents for her. Instead she prefers to keep Western philosophy centered in its own blindness to the rest of the world, so that she can outsmart Eurocentric reason on its own philosophical grounds. Whether de Man and Spivak are fair about Schiller's philosophical credentials, they are certainly impatient with him. Why berate Schiller? Is philosophical rigor the only measure of his worth for literary and cultural critics who know the value and vagaries of asystemic creativity? I mention the critics to preempt a hasty dismissal of Schiller on narrow grounds, because there are other, practical ways to read him. One way, though, fuels de Man's dismissal of Schiller as too willful to be trusted. His willfulness had dangerous consequences, de Man reminds readers, through the Nazi minister of propaganda Goebbels, who used Schiller to launch a program called "art for the masses." Stronger arguments against Nietzsche didn't bother deconstructionist de Man.[84] Another way to read Schiller acknowledges that some drive that sustains attention to "the masses" is necessary to make social change thinkable. Goethe agreed with Schiller on this point. Their joint campaign "on behalf of *haute vulgarisation*, . . . to improve public taste, has suffered from a species of reasoning not uncommon in historical judgement," Schiller's editors explain, "because they proved unsuccessful they must therefore have been invalid (why not perhaps premature?)."[85]

Did Schiller mistake Kant's idea of a predisposition to culture in order to use it as an endorsement for education and

thereby recover the moralizing tradition of Burke and Shafts-
bury? Maybe. But Arendt and Guyer would hold out for Kant's
principle of universal reason as a promise of equality, and
they too might link that promise to a process of education. Is
Schiller an aberrant reader for taking a sidetrack from episte-
mology into empirical and psychological observation? Perhaps.
But even if Schiller's popularized version of aesthetics were
an "aberration," why not consider it an educational opportunity instead of philosophical backsliding? Having dismissed the
wayward Schiller, Spivak can return Western philosophy to its
"founding moment" when Kant squinted at everything outside
of Europe. Then she can trump the nearsightedness with her
own brilliant and impertinent readings. So the game of culture
and reflection remains an elite affair that apparently moves
west to east with her, but not up and down through classes and
levels of education where Schiller would take us.

Another point of resistance to Schiller might come from
some efforts to bridge aesthetics and morality by underesti-
mating the tensions between beauty and being good in a gritty
world. This is Elaine Scarry's tactic for clearing up the confusions about the talent for judgment called taste. She veers
away from Kant at several points, including the sublime. This
is where Schiller had played loose by converting Kant's coeval
alternative to beauty into a later stage of mature taste for sentimental art. At the same spot, Spivak plays coy with Kant, who
misconstrued non-European civilizations as the raw natural
material that European reason needed to control. But Scarry
rushes right by the invitations to favor or to process nonbeauti-
ful aesthetic experience. Her love of beauty would enlarge the
word to include the sublime. The leveling of difference should
give pause to readers in asymmetrical and multicultural societies, where unpleasant materials stay unpleasant without the
extra work that makes them sublime. Through ardor and em-

pathy, cultural and aesthetic distinctions fall away for Scarry; along with them goes the work of "being good," if you had asked Kant or Schiller. Enthusiasm for aesthetics today, in the wake of too much theory for the taste of many critics, apparently takes a holiday from philosophy. *Revenge of the Aesthetic* is the title of collected essays by distinguished dissenters.[86]

Schiller had dared to turn the penchant for aesthetic judgment into a pedagogical program, and we will need to revive his efforts for some urgent business. It is to imagine a new sentimental education that will take aesthetic and political advantage of multicultural societies, instead of just fretting about a breakdown in communication and fearing group interests at cross-purposes. The dangers are real, but not necessarily daunting either aesthetically, if you have a taste for the sublime, or politically, because the threat of breakdown is both a measure of the freedom to dissent and an incentive to develop fair procedures.[87] Procedures are not enough, though, if citizens lack the predisposition to make them work. "There must, therefore be something in the disposition of men which stands in the way of the acceptance of truth, however brightly it may shine."[88] Rules can be fragile, revocable, and vulnerable to ingenious or perverse interpretations. This is the theme of a renewed interest in civil society, that wiggle room to associate alongside the state: "The courts cannot, by themselves, sustain a stable system of justice over time. If citizens are not in some way attached to that system, if they do not respect it, revere it, or believe in it, then no number of court orders will sustain its viability. One need think only of the highly juridified system of the Weimar Republic to see the limits of a system of justice that is not mirrored in the hearts and minds of citizens. Both feminists and civil rights activists are learning this lesson the hard way."[89]

This is where a sentimental bulwark comes in, constructed

from the cumulative exercises of the form-drive wrestling with the sense-drive. Schiller's lessons are a lead for teachers of language and literature. We train students after all, whether we propose to or not, to wrest art from the material of everyday life. Can we train them to develop a taste for the mature art wrested from unbeautiful materials?

Schiller proposed his aesthetic education, some say in response to Kant. Maybe that's true. You can say that I'm writing in response to Schiller, but my overriding motive is today's social volatility, aggravated by an outmoded preference for nation-language-state coherence. That lingering taste makes trouble for multinational states in global times. Schiller himself was writing in the wake of a different modern breakdown, the Terror at the tail of the French Revolution. And his once-critical English commentator, Herbert Read, reconsidered to write *Education through Art* (1943) while modernity went mad in World War II. The challenge that Schiller proposed for himself—and for us—was how to intervene in a disastrous world through the language tools he had to hand: the same tools that we teachers of language and literature wield. However successful or disappointing one judges his results, Schiller dared to put instruction in language arts on the real world agenda. And teachers who squirm at this move from aesthetics to civic education, imagining that it is philosophically derailed, are due for an alignment of focus.

Those who steer away toward "the left" may object that the move from art to politics deflects commitment from the real material issues of class power and economic inequality. Striking that dignified posture, language and literature teachers might ask themselves why they pursue privileged careers in literary studies. If they come up blank or embarrassed, perhaps they can salvage some usefulness from privilege and from the aesthetic purposelessness. After all, purposelessness makes common sense and provokes moral aftereffects by taking a break from politics and enjoying a taste of freedom. If that taste can be stretched toward the sublime effects of migrant multilingual states, left-leaning teachers can make real contributions. And though steering toward "the right" avoids some of the bad faith of colleagues who discount the literary work they do, conservatism bears its own cross of contradiction. It turns purposeless art into professional gain. People teach literature for money. We defend the practice for higher reasons, of course. But the very defense of teaching art appreciation as a higher calling than other businesses brings one back to Schiller. It was his sense of aesthetic education as an opportunity to affect society that made training a social obligation. This debt, or trap, interrupts Paul de Man's tirade against Schiller: "Whatever writing we do, whatever way we have of talking about art, whatever way we have of teaching, whatever justification we give ourselves for teaching . . . they are more than ever and profoundly Schillerian."[90]

Bildung is Schiller's legacy, the business of students and teachers. De Man dismissed Schiller as a distraction from philosophy, and Spivak passed him by to fix on philosophy's stubborn Eurocentrism. And yet the promise of late modernity and democracy is in that sidetrack from existing practices, in education, where Schiller invites us to creative (mis)uses of philosophy. Isn't this the kind of unorthodox and ironic move that made Franz Fanon appeal to the Rights of Man, knowing that the doctrine had not been intended for his black constituency? Wasn't it also the ploy that Latin American statesmen used when they demanded U.S. protection based on a Monroe Doctrine meant merely to control them? Schiller may have read Kant right, or misread him. In either case, the reading was to good public purpose.

Encouraged by lessons in mischievous reading, I have

wanted to tease Kant toward a sentimental education and to engage a couple of Schiller's critics. Schiller is worthy of more interested attention than he has recently gotten, if only to remember the range of disagreements among European intellectuals even during intense periods of colonial aggression. The disagreements show lines of flight that have inspired colonial subjects to adapt Europe's traditions and to turn them against Europeans. Schiller responded to Kantian categories with a preference for process. His sentimental education turns oppositions into the dynamic for development. At what stage are we now?

Clear the decks and get ready to play more games! The "Invitation" at the beginning of the book has a multiplying effect. Once stylistics breaks out of monolingualism, the gates of other discourses open up and admit living languages, always more than one. Among the options for playing at this point, I want to take up the philosophical game of games that we have been teasing and interrupting in order to allow mixed maneuvers among codes. Then we can follow up with a Borgesian wild goose chase where the fun depends on treading false tracks. That game and other classic matches of multilingual wit show that sidesteps into foreign fields are standard ploys to keep a game going, whether or not the expert players hope to win in the end. A bit melancholic, these language games enjoy the virtuosity of graceful maneuvers in tight spots. Often, players do double takes on what it means to win or to lose.

In chapter 1, we forced open a field where bilinguals—both elite princes and popular showgirls—play admirably at everything including statecraft. Then, chapter 2 dis-played irritating and funny effects in order to appreciate the general relevance of bilingual arts for aesthetics and humor. Chapter 3 engaged the political enhancements that follow from foreign interference, which brought us in chapter 4 to make a pitch for a new sentimental education that would train dispositions toward the unsettling sublime. It is finally time to play the game of language games. I mean the philosophy of language. Let's play at least with the way Ludwig Wittgenstein flattened and framed philosophy. My move, following the spirit of his investigations, will be to add a self-evident but underremarked observation. The observation is that most people normally live in more than one language. This doubling or multiplying factor of languages should complicate practically everything (art, politics, philosophy, be-longing, desire, humor), as Bakhtin said decades ago of the human "sciences" that refused to open up. The refusal has been quite stubborn.

158

Allow me, then, to repeat the obvious, even if I don't presume to play *at* the game of philosophy, but only *with* it. Lacking the technical training to argue a good point, I can nevertheless point it out: the conventions of philosophy have been blind and deaf to the ordinary and engaging games that play between languages.[1] The difference that I admit, between playing at and playing with philosophy, is like the difference between an atheist and a boor. "Why, Rabbi, do you revile me while you revere the atheist? What's the difference, if neither of us believes in God!" "Tell me," answers the rabbi (with a question), "have you studied the Bible and the commentaries?" Learning counts, I know. It entitles you to take positions. Maybe some learned philosophical atheists will put in a good word for us unwashed game players. Perhaps they will even supply the right references in order to help win hearts and minds for a creed of sanity and creativity that plays language games instead of judging them to be out of bounds or foul play.[2]

This book ends with a debt to Wittgenstein and some fun at his expense, but it might have started with his advice. After all,

Wittgenstein's rallying cry for the game of philosophy should have lent legitimacy to bilingual games and thereby under-scored his therapy for false philosophical problems: "Do away with all *explanation*, and description alone must take its place" (*PI*, §109). (This may amount to enlarging what Kant called the faculty of judgment [linked to sensibility] and reducing the range of reason.) Look and see, don't think, was the way to win at philosophy. Very well, if we look and see and hear we pick up bilanguage games. Wittgenstein certainly plays them. He slides from German to English to poach a phrase or link up an idea, not to mention his game of publishing the *Philosophical Investigations* with face-to-face German original and English translation.[3] But these everyday ex-centricities go unremarked 159 while monolanguage games get tireless attention from Wittgen-stein. Maybe sliding, poaching, and face-off editions are already too obvious as the moves that bring him to the iconoclastic *Investigations*. "Wittgenstein was one of us," Eugene Gendlin commented, referring to his own Viennese childhood and to my displaced personhood. "He couldn't have brought home what language *does*, had he not lived between English and German expressions, so that he could say *look what happens*, rather than assuming that language names entity meanings."[4]

Perhaps, on the other hand, Wittgenstein's silence about bi-language games suggests a surprising lack of nerve, a reluc-tance to finally escape the prescriptions he claimed to dis-miss: "Don't say: There *must* be something common, or they would not be called 'games'—but *look and see* whether there is anything common to all," Wittgenstein instructed. "To repeat: don't think, but look!" (*PI* §66; §1c, 2b, 3a, 10a; §109; §340). Let unexpected evidence speak, exhorted the man who resisted philosophy's obstinate desire to find patterns and to fix mean-ings.[5] My favorite performance of the obstinacy of naming and fixing is the hilarious *Saturday Night Live* spot called "It's Pat."

The title character (m/f) has an (un)canny talent for frustrating efforts to fix his/her gender. The doubt drives everyone else crazy. Like Pat, Wittgenstein's practice of "queering" language by switching, sliding, and seeing double is probably his most effective therapy for the problem of philosophical rigidity.

Wittgenstein's linguistic restlessness reveals a world somehow anterior to or alongside language. There are experiences and ideas that don't yet have suitable words. Each time Wittgenstein strains against existing language, by inventing replaceable metaphors and crossing national borders, he locates the wiggle room beyond any one compact culture or code. If language speaks the individual, as we have come to assume especially since Foucault pronounced authors dead, then individuals with more than one language can exploit the contradictions spoken through them. Bilinguals gain some say in their lives because contradictory codes demand judgment and encourage creativity. Or, if Gendlin is right about life existing before or beyond language, the clash of codes is a sign of wiggle room, not its cause. Either way, bilinguals are likely to locate that space behind the prison house of language.

Wittgenstein insisted, repeatedly, that we look and listen. He must have been worried that colleagues and students would continue to force patterns on heterogeneous data, crushing the circumstances that meaning depends on.[6] To distinguish between language and situation misses his main point, that language is as language does. Specific language games differ from one another and morph into variations, as Wittgenstein shows in many examples. But all participate in the general game of engagements between words and the world: "I shall also call the whole, consisting of language and the actions into which it is woven, the 'language game'" (*PI*, §7). Surely that intricate weave describes more than one "natural" language. Either/or distinctions of this language or that one, like the uses that distinguish male from female, gay from straight, and home from host should show up as specific games among other options. If languages have barriers between them, they also share turnstiles where meanings get tangled up or pulled free.

Whatever happens at these relay points would seem to participate in the stuff of Wittgenstein's dispassionate descriptions. It follows that if people use more than one language at a time, the practice cannot be either wrong or negligible, but a feature to reckon with. Language is not obliged to be easily understood or absolutely accurate, only to be normal and useful. Wittgenstein thought it was just as wrongheaded to overcomplicate (as if the world were an unmanageable muddle of corrupt ideals, instead of an endlessly interesting range of circumstantial meanings [*PI*, §§81, 131][7]) —as it was to oversimplify (by forcing ill-fitting details into prescribed patterns). Wittgenstein avoids both the errors of dismissing vulnerable meaning and of conceding hands-off respect. Vulnerability is no excuse for condemning language as untrustworthy, or for scoffing at its accomplishments. He was as impatient with radical skepticism for not dealing responsibly in the world (*PI*, §67) as with idealism of essential meanings. If we hold ourselves to unreasonable standards, Wittgenstein sighed, "We feel as if we had to repair a torn spider's web with our fingers" (*PI*, §106).

The haunting and helpless image cautions Wittgenstein to stay his course. Maybe this kind of damage made him think of Kant's mockery at musty philosophical schools that discount the common man and "raise a loud cry of public danger when somebody destroys their cobwebs."[8] We must "not go astray," says Wittgenstein, "and imagine that we have to describe extreme subtleties." To notice the delicate contingency of meaning doesn't mean that you stand back in mute awe. It is an invitation to engage.[9] The contingent use-value of meaning "is not to say that we are in doubt because it is possible for us to *imagine* a doubt" (*PI*, §84). Now I am insisting, almost incredulous that this practical and engaged spirit might have missed a chorus of cues to link the polyglossia of living language to the wiggle room of a world beyond (one) language.

Let's play games, Wittgenstein was saying, including the game of appreciating the intricacies of "everyday thinking" (*PI*, §106). This is an ethical injunction, as you can tell; it is about doing damage to useless habits in order to avoid the greater damage that follows from neglect of everyday thinking. On one view, Wittgenstein was no "quietist" who might interpret established practices as inviolable, but a philosopher of human agency who enjoins us to leave prejudice behind and investigate how meanings are made.[10] (With a very different—transcendent—valence, Emmanuel Levinas would enjoin readers actively to submit themselves to the mystery of otherness, instead of incorporating the Other into propositions about ourselves. Jean François Lyotard was bold enough to link the modern metaphysician Levinas with Wittgenstein as allies in defense of a "sacred" residue of difference, lest one life is forced into the frame of another.)[11] On another view, Wittgenstein was so thoroughly ahistorical and apolitical as to be practically desperate about the future. "One must travel light," was his advice, and avoid entanglements.[12]

Since contingency anchors meaning for Wittgenstein, instead of undermining it, should we not include among the unstable anchors a strange grammar when I want you should get me a slab and also get the point that the grammar is strange? Or, might I ground communication at a doctor's office in contingent sounds-like associations that make the stuffy nose of *constipación* prescribe a laxative instead of a decongestant, and the food poisoning of *intoxicación* mean an end to barroom sociability? I'm simply spelling out the contingency of two (or more) anchors, and this is a common reason for more than one meaning.[13] That's why foreign speakers produce a particular surplus or dangerous supplement in one or both of their borrowed languages. (Once you learn a second language, the first can feel foreign too.)

Wittgenstein simply gives a French speaker credit for getting an English meaning right (*PI*, §208), but he misses the possible "*over*" (a Dominican word for American *plusvalía*) from the second language. Some sociolinguists get the point: "For example, the word for 'school' in Welsh (*ysgol*) also means 'ladder' . . . while the English word has no such associations." So in addition to understanding the word "school," "Welsh bilinguals may have mental imagery . . . which allows them to create metaphorical links, e.g., the school is a ladder to knowledge."[14] In addition to understanding profit, Dominicans know that exploitation means American capitalism.

Or, take the example of the squiggle in *PI*, §166. For Wittgenstein it's an arbitrary mark that could elicit any corresponding sound. He chooses to call it *u*. But to anyone who knows Hebrew script, the squiggle is a "*peh*," the seventeenth letter of the aleph-bet, originally a hieroglyph for "mouth" in its written form and still its common name when voiced. *Mouth*, a metonymy for speech or spoken language, *peh* becomes the emblem for the whole project of Wittgenstein's investigations! In language games like this one, the point (*Witz*) is often in the bilingual reception, not in the delivery. (We called the effect "malicious delicious" in chapter 2.) Vagueness or impurity doesn't rule us mixed-language players out of the game; it gives us more maneuverability (*PI*, §100).[15] Certainly in my Spanglish and Hebrew examples, impurities help to make meanings, because meanings depend on asymmetrical contingencies, more than one. Yet Wittgenstein simply calls foreign misappropriations "wrong" (such as "a whole series of sounds as one word" [*beipasear* for example?], rather than describe them as existing variants [*PI*, §20]).[16]

Intentions, mistakes, misappropriations can be part of communication, just as losing or stumbling onto shortcuts and long shots is part of a game. Keeping these eventualities in view, as "queer" uses Wittgenstein might say, is part of language. Queer uses look queer because conventional uses do exist (*PI*, §142). But without availability for queer variants, how does one account for metaphor or any other rhetorical roughening of normal uses? In any case, some sparks of "friction" normally fly, as particular uses rub against standard definitions. Where conditions are ideal (everyone understands the same thing), there's no need to talk and we're on "slippery ice . . . unable to walk. We want to walk: so we need *friction*. Back to the rough ground!" (*PI*, §107) With this therapy for philosophical problems, bilingual friction should look normal. As soon as one opens eyes and ears, on the street, at the workplace, in the schools, and in courtrooms, bilinguals come into view and into earshot. Noticing the interruption of one language by another could cure some of the cramps in conventional expectations about the good and the beautiful with the remedy of acknowledging that alter-nation is normal everyday practice.

Wittgenstein's advice should have brought those bilingual games immediately into focus, even before we stopped to consider their particular aesthetic or political and pedagogical charms. The practices of code switching, (mis)translating, and gatekeeping, are evident almost everywhere, as long as you don't decide, a priori, to filter out foreign words, funny grammatical tics, and strange accents from one standard language. The point (Witz) or joke of some language games is—after all— to unsettle fixed meanings; they "require us to try to see it in a different light, to use our imagination in a variety of ways, to seek new experiences which help us to refine . . . *sensitivities we acquired as we mastered the language*."[17] Adults can recover that sensitivity to risk and thrill at the border of a strange or even neighboring language. If Wittgenstein's point is that philosophy should describe what ordinary language does and also how philosophy's own games sometimes hit and other times miss the point, if he sincerely cautions against the mire of rules that cannot always hold true for every case and that therefore mislead those who lust after clarity, then bilingual games should show up on philosophy's game board.

His most loyal disciples may be Deleuze and Guattari, given their penchant for errancy all over the map of meanings. The lines and chutes and tangents that they draw on a surface from one game to another take leads from Wittgenstein's lesson about language working through the "spread effect" of context, background, associations.[18] "The difficult thing here is not," Wittgenstein reminded us, "to dig down to the ground; no, it is to recognize the ground that lies before us as the ground."[19] Instead of tracing meanings back to a home base that might win some stability for words and for relationships, the naughty French philosophers discredit the binarism of origin and result, cause and effect, center and periphery. Thinking along inflexible binary either/or lines is dogmatic, and deadening. "God is a Lobster," they tease, with a full-page picture of the symmetrical comestible crustacean that looks like a visual joke out of *Tristram Shandy*. The lobster is a neat design, too simple and clumsy to describe the supple rhyzomatic map of meanings (Sterne drew squiggles). Symmetry cramps the signs that form and morph as lines get drawn, shoot off in different directions, or get overdrawn, crossed, erased. Curiously, for the lesson-giver about the contingent games of "chutes and ladders," surprisingly for the down-to-earth garden-variety philosopher who repeated the injunction to look and to listen, Wittgenstein doesn't discuss the contingencies of one language as it interrupts or poaches from another language. If he notices bilanguage games at all (how could he not notice, this Austrian in England), he doesn't stop to describe them.

I wonder why. Watch out for academics who stop to won-der, Wittgenstein might have warned you, because they start to speculate and to invent (mythic or metaphoric) fillers for the ignorance they cannot abide. So now (you are forewarned) to speculate on the silencing of bilingual games, one could imag-ine that, like Freud, who avoided Yiddishisms in his scientific writing, and like aesthetic theorists, who prefer symmetrical beauty over irritation, or like Jacques Derrida, who defends his prosthetic be-longing in one language as a universal Unheim-lichkeit, Wittgenstein may have censored the riot of mixed-up codes that would have marked him as a "foreigner" or a newly minted member of a modern adopted society. For him, I specu-late, code switching could have seemed a sign of instability, maybe a lack of mastery and therefore a threat to elegance of expression and to claims of expertise. Or, one can imagine that in the 1930s and 1940s, Cambridge was a place where English-only sounded normal, even to Wittgenstein, who had grown up in German, traveled, been a prisoner of war in Italy, and may have code switched in his own head all the time. Whatever the speculation about reasons, or motives, or denials which we can bracket on a cue from Wittgenstein, the dispassionate observa-tion that repeats with the regularity of a working hypothesis is that he describes meaning as if it depended on one language at a time. "The language in question" doesn't share its cityscape with other languages, but bloats with borrowings and novelties in function of its autonomous and imperializing self: an "an-cient city . . . surrounded by a multitude of new boroughs" (*PI*, §18).

Now if description is offered as therapy to cure a (neurotic) spiral of unrequited demands for clarity, demands that lead to disappointment, disappointment that deepens disenchantment with the world, disenchantment that urges desperate demands for clarity, Wittgenstein is obviously avoiding the cure. Maybe

he is in denial about his own code switching, in which case it might help for someone to tell him it's okay to alternate; it's normal; lots of people do it. Had Wittgenstein let himself off the monolingual hook, had he described the everyday frustrations and hilarities that make bilanguage games hard to miss when you look and listen, when you cringe and giggle, the delusion of "normal" rule-governed monolingualism might have become obvious to more people. But delusion is a wily player. It gets the better of very smart agonists (losers, in this case). Think of Freud, who translated the Yiddish out of his Jewish jokes in order to make a universal science of humor, though it was based on particular material that wasn't even funny if non-Jews repeated it. Think also of Derrida, whose monolingual blues
claim to be universal, as if all of us live, dream, write, speak in one language that is not our own. Ownership aside, it makes a difference to function in more than one.

Wittgenstein appreciated the wiles of delusion. To him, for example, Freud seemed deluded for confusing his own cleverness with wisdom, and the myths or metaphors he invented with scientific discovery.[20] Wittgenstein's most serious objection to Freudian psychoanalysis was the way it passes off speculation for scientific observation. Psychoanalysis may be an interesting practice, even an art, but it's not a science if you ask Wittgenstein. And without a science, how can anyone tell what exactly ails the patient or what a cure might be? Maybe analysts are not curing a patient's delusion by tracing dreams and jokes back to Oedipal desires. What is worse, analysts may be raising the delusions to a higher level where they become participants more than observers.[21] Who is to judge the success of the treatment, the doctor? the patient? Wittgenstein was evidently right about the deviousness of delusion. In fact, he demonstrates it, because—if I can be so bold—he was deluded too when he described the "normal" field of language games as if it were limited to one language. To be fair to his admirably ruthless rigor, Wittgenstein predicted as much, because "the aspects of things that are most important for us are hidden because of their simplicity and familiarity . . . The real foundations of his enquiry do not strike a man at all" (*PI*, §129).

Wittgenstein Writes a Letter

Listen and marvel at how elusive Wittgenstein's advice can be, even for himself. He evidently has trouble hearing the recommendation to get over our language "problems" by simply describing what works in everyday practices, such as writing a letter:

> What happens when we make an effort—say in writing a letter—to find the right expression for our thoughts?—This phrase compares the process to one of translating or describing: the thoughts are already there (perhaps were there in advance) and we merely look for their expression. This picture is more or less appropriate in different cases.—But can't all sorts of things happen here?—I surrender to a mood and the expression *comes*. Or a picture occurs to me and I try to describe it. Or an English expression occurs to me and I try to hit on the corresponding German one. Or I make a gesture, and ask myself: What words correspond to this gesture? And so on.
>
> Now if it were asked: "Do you have the thought before finding the expression?" what would one have to reply? And what, to the question: "What did the thought consist in, as it existed before its expression?" (*PI*, §335)

El camino se hace al caminar (the way is paved by walking) is the folksy Spanish equivalent for Wittgenstein's lesson in peripatetic practices. Don't we sometimes, he asks, "make up the rules as we go along? And [sometimes] . . . alter them as we go along" (*PI*, §83). Writing happens, pen in hand, starting perhaps with an "arbitrary doodle" (*PI*, §175). If you imagine the material of language to be delicate fibers (an alternative figure to stomping feet, both are Wittgenstein's images) they twist to become threads of communication through the activity of tying and weaving them into intricate texts. Texts, like spiderwebs, hang together suspended on precarious anchors, let us say on twigs that shudder in the breeze. Those anchors and the general context of the multidimensional loom enable the weaving, just as the terrain allows particular paths to be paved.[22] In other words, weaving or walking doesn't happen without the loom or the land, just as thoughts don't exist, exactly, outside the context of language.

Nevertheless—and this is Wittgenstein's daring move past the reigning determinism of language—he knows that one *feels* the intention to express something (to weave, to walk) before hitting on the right words. Intention, desire, the motor that drives speech is different from the spoken or written word. To miss the difference dismisses the particular—exhilarating or frustrating—force of inarticulateness. There is a world outside or alongside language, as bilinguals are likely to know when things remain things beyond one word or another. But the feeling itself, Wittgenstein goes on to say, is an effect of knowing a language to speak (or a terrain to walk): "in order to *want* to say something one must also have mastered a language" (*PI*, §338). Intention "is embedded in its situation, in human customs and institutions. If the technique of the game of chess did not exist, I could not intend to play a game of chess. In so far as I do intend the construction of a sentence in advance, that is made possible by the fact that I speak *the language in question*" (*PI*, §337, my emphasis). Language (should we call it *parole* when it's at work?) gives form to a desire that would be unthinkable without having learned language (*langue*, when it idles?).[23] What happens, though, when you know more than one?

Does *caminar* stop short at the border of "the language in question," as if the terrain for walking and talking dropped off into nothingness on some flat and finite pre-Copernican map? Does activity only shuttle back and forth from the cramped circumscribed possibilities of one langue to the particular conjunctures of its words? Not if you look and listen. Walking doesn't work that way, especially not in these global times of mass migrations, as linguists increasingly acknowledge.[24] Walkers and talkers don't stop at the limits of one language when they know more than one. And walkers—almost by definition—generally talk more than one. Even when they keep the codes straight and discrete, inarticulate desire wanders and error interferes in the sounds of bilingual blues, because the language in question may be new and unmanageable, or it may be old and faded, or cramped and unwelcoming. In chess, it is generally true, the moves are circumscribed to legitimate steps; one can play correctly or cheat, win or lose. The analogy between somewhat ungovernable language games and a regularized game like chess was one reason that Wittgenstein multiplied his metaphors and also reminded us of the negative moment of analogy. "Like chess, and not like chess," says Henry Staten, the lessons of the *Investigations* are also "like dancing and calculating and hearkening to inspiration—and like making an arbitrary doodle and then copying it."[25]

Dancing is a particularly agile likeness for language moves, including the turns from one language to another, the exhilarating anticipation of a surprise switch of position and the satisfaction of following it, as if the invention were a response to the partner rather than an effort to outstrip her. Dance can pick up moves from one rhythm into another, which is what gives salsa its multiflavored *sabor*, without missing a step or mistaking the mix for a coherent style. Salsa steps stay on the move, inventing ways to twist the fibers of rhythm and dance. This is why ballroom Latin routines look lifeless, like museum artifacts embalmed from popular arts. The charm of the Spanish *refrán* about walkways made by walking is that the activity of path making is really path breaking. Doing almost anything fearlessly is doing something new. It takes stamina to stay on a chosen track when signposts for established shuttle-routes point to easier sidetracks.

Wittgenstein set out to describe the ways that language works, and to locate some misleading philosophical sidetracks that established irrelevant rules for language. Anyone who has problems with philosophical language, he taunted, was making problems not solving them. The language of philosophy creates difficulties with its packaging, its memories and opinions, to keep philosophers busy and in business. One difficulty has been what to make of Wittgenstein's apparent change of heart. The analysts have overstated it, Eugene Gendlin observes, in order to claim Wittgenstein as one of them. Analytic philosophers distinguish too neatly between the *Philosophical Investigations* and the earlier *Tractatus Logico-Philosophicus* (1921), because the mature philosopher who allegedly stopped playing the game of "name that object" or build that proposition did not reject the young logician, Gendlin says. Only four years separate Wittgenstein's books, and he planned to publish them in one volume to show both what logic *can* do and what it *cannot* do.[26] It cannot, for example, account for the contingency of everyday language. There is little point to analyzing normal meanings down to their most precise particulars, as if tiny building blocks could be a foundation for secure and predictable combinations. That kind of discrete essential meaning in a word or in a thing was misguided because, Wittgenstein quipped, "*Essence* is expressed by grammar" (*PI*, §371). Just for good measure, he repeated the provocation. After all, professional philosophers might think he was joking. "Grammar tells what kind of object anything is" (*PI*, §373).

Along the way in his *Investigations*, Wittgenstein points out a few distractions from the path of description as therapy for hypochondriac philosophy. Grounded in everyday uses, like Ulysses tied to his sturdy mast, Wittgenstein can hear the sirens of error beckon and yet manage to sail by. To start with, Augustine's language lesson about pointing to things and naming them is seductive as a way to make the world and words correspond. This ostensive feature of language seduced, for example, the Vienna circle of logical positivists who imagined that Wittgenstein's *Tractatus* would make him a member.[27] But Wittgenstein never joined. On second thought, he showed that ostensive meanings can be misleading, as if naming objects this or that performed a baptism (*PI*, §38).[28] "That is the kind of proposition that one repeats to oneself countless times. One thinks that one is tracing the outline of the thing's nature over and over again, and one is merely tracing round the frame through which we look at it" (*PI*, §114). (Isn't the game of speaking louder and clearer for foreigners just as funny, as if volume and insistence overcome the disconnect?) Still, he might have made more of his intuition that Augustine's lesson worked for learning a second language (*PI*, §32).[29]

Then there was Russell's attractive atomism that offered analytical clarity, as had Wittgenstein himself. But Russell was wrong about words having essential particulars independent of context.[30] And the distinction between necessary and contingent by Moore and Quine was nice, but it didn't work for the "pragmatics and psychologism" which Wittgenstein pursued and which the logical empiricists had always dismissed.[31] Behaviorists are also wrong to pursue only visible signs of emotion; they tend to run in circles from sign to evident meaning that produces the sign and back again to meaning (*PI*, §304). Freud is practically irresistible, but he too was wrong to confuse psychoanalysis with a "science" that could fix metaphors into stable meanings.

Wittgenstein eludes them all. Unreliable as Homer's sailors, less grounded companions in philosophy would lead astray toward abstractions. But unlike the sailors who obediently stuffed wax into their ears on Ulysses's command, the philosophers seem willfully clogged and deaf to the real world of language. Only Wittgenstein honestly looks and listens, he says, unplugged and unencumbered. Sometimes the investigations steer toward the kind of anthropological observations that attracted Kant and that Schiller took up. The Viennese neo-Kantians, including Karl Krause, so influential in Spain, also veered into anthropology via cultural relativism.[32] What happens then—it seems fair to ask—when Wittgenstein writes a letter?

All sorts of things can happen, you may remember. Many more than most postmoderns might acknowledge. Along with the effort to find the right expression for a thought prior to language (an effort like "translating"), there was also surrender to a mood and a picture that flashes. Among the many things that can happen according to Wittgenstein, "an English expression occurs to me and I try to hit on the corresponding German one." Without stopping, he adds another possibility: a gesture that signals some words that might correspond to it. The bilingual moment flashed and faded immediately. It happened like all the other invitations to write, and it led to the same results. From thoughts, pictures, foreign words and gestures, the product is words on a page. The stimuli line up like a chain of equivalents to twist into a closed circle and choke a significant difference (Lyotard's *différend*). In fact, foreign words are not comparable, on most counts, to the inarticulate preverbal intentionality of thought, pictures, or gestures. They are language.

Here is a fork in the path. Here is an opportunity to notice a normal practice that is out of bounds in the single-language game and that proves his argument against linguistic determinism. This is where the negative, particular, and contingent dimension of analogy could have rescued a comparison from forcing the heterogeneous evidence into an established pattern. Wittgenstein might have stayed steadfast on his therapeutic path of description and paved the way of recognition for bilingual games and for the intricate world they describe. He could have noticed how normal it probably was to hear an English word in his head and how different pre- or nonverbal stimuli were from foreign words. But he doesn't stay his course, or notice the normal practice, or even the telling mismatch of comparing pictures and gestures with English words. Instead he goes from one thing to the other, as if from cause to inevitable effect. Wittgenstein rushed ahead, darted from an English stimulus to a desired German response, practically collapsing the two into one event. How strangely impatient he seems with the interference; how unexpectedly prescriptive this goal of monolingual performance appears, in the *Philosophical Investigations*, where flexibility is the remedy for philosophical "problems." Rather than theorize about what can and cannot be done with language, Wittgenstein got busy doing things with it, like writing a letter.

Yet he seems stuck in at least one abstract parameter of language philosophy, I mean its reduction of everyday functions to the operations in one linguistic code. The fact that Wittgenstein himself thought and communicated in more than one language (I suspect that many philosophers do) stays under-remarked and undeveloped. With the gate still closed around monolingual therapies, an English expression comes to Wittgenstein, and he acts indifferent to the ways it rescues him. He hardly looks, doesn't quite see, and certainly doesn't skip a beat before dismissing it "to hit on" German. How would the *Investigations* have developed if Wittgenstein had acknowledged that English came to him, unbidden and available, to free him from frustration? What would the playing field look like if the gates around monolingual therapies were flung open to philosophy, or pried open by a cagey artist like Jorge Luis Borges, just to name one who will lead in the last section of this chapter? It would surely look uneven, a complicated terrain of privileged vantage points and unavoidable handicaps, where players can mix rules and complicate a range of language games with the hide-and-seek moves of code switching or gate making. A second language may be as limited or treacherous as the first, but in different, occasionally liberating ways. Among the things that happen with a code switch, to read Wittgenstein, is that a thought finds appropriate words, in English. Why didn't he notice that, before he forced the words away?

Staying Power

Immigrants who hold on to home languages after coming to the United States are not necessarily ungrateful; they are complicated.[33] Offended neighbors may bristle at feeling excluded when they don't understand home languages spoken on the street (in bars, hospitals, businesses).[34] But displaced people will defend their freedom of speech and continue to live in normally double (or multiple) codes, sometimes for generations. If pressed to embrace the host culture after moving across the border—or being crossed by it politically or economically in transnational circuits—creative migrants are likely to double their responses. They defer and demur, in counterpoint. Their language games can thrive under pressure, as the charm of traditional cultures survives in posthumous displays of originality. They notice the charms of purposeful mistranslation, a postponed punch line, and relief from the law of one language by reprieve from another. The point is not to escape from the house, but to open it occasionally. (*Estirar la pata* makes "ethnic flight" or out-marriage too drastic a move, and unnecessary, ¿verdad?)

Some games flourish in the tight spots where one language rubs against another. When these somewhat intractable games hold something back from the universal embrace they are not quite modern,[35] but postmodern in the sense of postcolonial and doubled between political subalternity and cultural surplus. Surplus is not mere noise but difficulty. Bilinguals understand the arbitrariness of language even more intensely than do theorists who, after Paul de Man, call language allegorical because words are of a different order from their elusive referents.[36] Beyond elusive, everyday language can be downright opaque when it confronts another speaker, intentionally opaque sometimes, as a reminder of surviving cultural differences.[37] "We have a right to our opacity," begins Edouard Glissant's manifesto for Caribbean cultural self-determination.[38]

I have described some of the vanguard practices that relieve the conspicuous normalization of culture. They are the bi- (or multi-) lingual games that take advantage of dissonant residues of assimilation (or that bear the erroneous but often pleasing consequences)[39] after particular languages are forced into universal codes.[40] Interruptions, delays, code switching, and syncopated communication are rhetorical features of bicultural language games; they are also, as I argued, symptoms of democratic engagement that should not presume mutual understanding among citizens.[41] However much we may grieve over the real losses of cultural difference in the wake of modernity, it would be even sadder and counterproductive to let lamentation drown out the sounds of cultural counterpoint and creative survival. If you ask Borges, as we will, some of the most fertile spots in the field of language are the pitfalls and snags on the uneven playing ground between host and home languages.

To investigate the games played with that lingering linguistic attachment, we might take advice from Wittgenstein and shift the focus to see the games under a different (this time darker) light. Changing focus is a practice recommended for distinguishing prejudice from normal practice.[42] On one reading, the almost posthumous home culture haunts immigrant lives. It holds them back. Melancholia is the name for this danger, as I mentioned in chapter 1. I called it a manageable dose of madness that vaccinates displaced people against morose self-hatred, a measure of understandable sadness that defends people from more serious depression. Resistance to full assimilation is irritating, the way art is.

No irritation (Wittgenstein called it "friction"), no creativity, not even the creativity of normal, everyday language games. This is the stunning conclusion of Bonnie Honig's reading of Ruth. The biblical story celebrates the assimilation of a Moabite into Israel where she becomes a matriarch of the future house of David. But Honig shifts the conventional focus on Israel and asks after Ruth: why does she fall silent long before her end?[43] The point is that her seamless absorption leaves no time or place for a creative talking cure. Ruth doesn't play the transitional *fort-da* games of mourning that turn unmanageable attachments into the stuff of controlled appearances and disappearances, a game that should have counted on friendly witnesses to watch and testify to the transition. "Like Antigone's mourning of Polynices, Ruth's mourning of Orpah is forbidden for the sake of a regime's stability and identity. Thus, Ruth's mourning—like Antigone's—is endless, melancholic. Her losses get in the way of the closure this community seeks to attain through her and in spite of her."[44]

This literally tragic reading of Ruth in Greek dress suggests that tragedy could have been averted in the Bible, that mourning might have done its proper work to forestall melancholy if the community had allowed it. It seems to me a particularly modern conclusion, as if there were, necessarily, an appropriate remedy for pain so that life could proceed painlessly. In the case of nomadic peoples, however, one can imagine that assimilation is never seamless and that mourning is hardly ever an endgame. Settling in a new land would not override a previous be-longing. In fact, settling anywhere ignited the wrath of Israel's prophets. They railed against the idolatrous attachments of the people to one place or another, because the Spirit of the desert required more flexibility. To shift the focus once more, might we ask if, sometimes, a degree of melancholia is a normal condition of migration? Maybe geographic, linguistic, cultural displacements don't mean replacement but redoubling.

A Vindication of Double Consciousness

W. E. B. Du Bois worried about doubling. African Americans, he said, bore the burden of a double identity, a contradiction because identity should mean one consciousness not two. This is a symptom of melancholia as one be-longing gets in the way of another. In a country that refuses to face the past and to mourn the losses of millions of lives and of whole cultures, the pain festers and creates problems. "How does it feel to be a problem?" is what whites are always asking blacks, Du Bois complains at the beginning of *The Souls of Black Folk* (1903), even when whites are compassionate or feeling vicariously outraged at things "that make your blood boil." Du Bois reduces his own boiling point to a simmer, as he puts it, and ventriloquizes in order to air the question: Feeling yourself to be a problem, he answers, "is a peculiar sensation, this double-consciousness, this sense of always looking at one's self through the eyes of others, of measuring one's soul by the tape of a world that looks on in amused contempt and pity. One ever feels this twoness,—an American, a Negro; two souls, two thoughts, two unreconciled strivings."

Double consciousness was a double bind for Du Bois. Today the contradiction can locate some room for maneuver, but Du Bois resented the image he inherited from white Hegelians. Ralph Waldo Emerson coined the term as a neat solution for tensions between public and private life, for Anglo Saxons.[45] "One key, one solution to the mysteries of human condition, one solution to the old knots of fate, freedom, and foreknowledge, exists, the propounding, namely, of the double consciousness." I'll quote more from this essay of 1860, "Fate," because Emerson remains an icon of American self-making. The piece was no short-lived departure from democratic thinking, Du Bois would have known. Emerson wrote and rewrote "Fate" over the ten years immediately after the war that annexed half of Mexico to the United States, just before the Civil War.

Between Emerson and Du Bois, we inherit either/or positions regarding double consciousness. Either it festers in Afro-American frustrations, or it straightens out through Saxon single-mindedness. "Cold and sea will train an imperial Saxon race, which nature cannot bear to lose, and, after cooping it up for a thousand years in yonder England, gives a hundred Englands, a hundred Mexicos. All the bloods it shall absorb and domineer: and more than Mexicos,—the secrets of water and steam, the spasms of electricity, the ductility of metals, the chariot of the air, the ruddered balloon are awaiting you."[46]

"We like the nervous and victorious habit of our own branch of the family," Emerson admitted. So the condition of double consciousness didn't need a cure. Why tinker when Divine Law takes care of straightening out the divided self and overriding oppositions? Instead of cures, Emerson commissioned "altars to the Blessed Unity . . . Why should we fear to be crushed by savage elements, we who are made up of the same elements?"[47]

This is not a rhetorical question for everyone. Those who are crushed ask why differently from those who benefit by the crushing. Anglos cultivate themselves and everyone else turns into fertilizer, literally: "The German and Irish millions, like the Negro, have a great deal of *guano* in their destiny. They are ferried over the Atlantic, and carted over America, to ditch and to drudge, to make corn cheap, and then to lie down prematurely to make a spot of green grass on the prairie."[48]

Frustrated by the Anglos-only game, Du Bois described black double consciousness as pulling in opposite directions and getting nowhere but down. "The history of the American Negro is the history of this strife,—this longing to attain self-conscious manhood, to merge his double self into a better and truer self" (*Souls*, 215). Fifty years after Emerson's rhapsody on fate, freedom felt like another form of bondage for blacks. Instead of progress borne by conflicting forces, Du Bois describes an insoluble conflict for the black intellectual, as one force wastes the other. "This waste of double aims, this seeking to satisfy two unreconciled ideals, has wrought sad havoc with the courage and faith and deeds of ten thousand people, has sent them often wooing false gods and invoking false means of salvation, and at times has even seemed about to make them ashamed of themselves" (*Souls*, 216).

Ever since then, double consciousness has seemed the bane of American minorities. It has named the unproductive tension between contradictory identities, one particular the other universal. This is an unhappy melancholic consciousness by definition, as if normal meant happy or simple. The structural duplicity is braced together by hyphens (African-American, Jewish-American, Hispanic-American, Irish-American . . .)

Braced is a word that might point to a cure, like an orthopedic supplement to produce a better alignment, a necessary nuisance that will be removed once citizens achieve an attractive maturity. The young country was absorbing irregular citizens, and lingering ties elsewhere interrupted a sense of belonging here. The unhappy, but understandable and transitory, result was a fissured double consciousness that might be straightened out through time. The orthopedic image would have signaled unnecessary meddling to Emerson, since Anglos were aligned to history, as long as everyone else dissolved into guano. Immigrants who didn't blend or bend easily would become problems.

"How does it feel to be a problem?" makes a questionable assumption, Du Bois knew. The problem—as Wittgenstein said of standard philosophical questions—makes trouble instead of probing it. To unburden himself with that slow burn that boils away pretense, Du Bois shifts the focus from black to white, from contemporary misfits ("an outcast and stranger in mine own house" [*Souls*, 214]) to a mournful history. Melancholia offers a therapeutic dose of sadness and rage. It cures muteness and madness with narratives that link causes with their effects. Du Bois eulogizes the slaves' limitless faith in freedom and their heroic resistance, and then reviews the long and bitter anticlimax to that faith when Reconstruction broke one promise after another, the lynchings and the inability of ex-slaves to maneuver in too tight spaces. This unspeakable experience, as far as whites are concerned, fissures black consciousness into African and American. Double consciousness for Du Bois is doubly unfair. It shortchanges blacks in America, and makes them fall short of their own American ideals.

When authenticity means a single and solid identity, doubleness breeds the kind of self-hatred that members of any minority group may experience [since they also belong to the majority group] that hates them. Sander Gilman's *Jewish Self-Hatred* repeats the structure that Du Bois called "two warring ideals in one dark body," in another body. Gilman's prologue explains that his particular focus on Jews is circumstantial, autobiographical.[49] Paradoxically enough, the predicament of self-hating particularism is rather universal in modern times.

What does double consciousness mean today, in the company of words like "cosmopolitanism," "transnationalism," and "immigration"? The context makes the melancholic condition an almost unavoidable consequence of uprooted moving or of being interrupted. Unavoidable and probably incurable, we might notice with relief. Emerson's cure reduced doubleness to single-minded progress that squints at collateral damage to expendable races. And Du Bois imagined that amalgamation might combine the best of black and white into one American consciousness. But doubleness is no obstacle to democracy. It may be our best cultural safeguard for democratic practice, because doubleness doesn't allow the meanness of one thought, one striving, one measure of value. The gambit for a new sensibility prefers double vision over squinting. Otherwise, twoness will continue to set minorities off as misfits instead of setting them up as master players.[50] Du Bois himself leads in this divided direction of mutual irritations when he refuses to "bleach his Negro soul" (*Souls*, 215) in order to blend into white America. And Wittgenstein recommends a two-stage therapy for unhappy consciences: first get over your fixation with boring ideals, and then *train* your sensibility to maneuver among the endless and flexible games that humans play.[51]

Doubleness has not always been a losing proposition. A long history of some premodern societies is instructive. Consider medieval England, where Normans were wise enough to know that they ruled a country of foreigners. Jews, Germans, Danes, and others could not "speak the same language" in any literal way, but they were enjoined to deal fairly with one another. Prudent listening for the différend was a medieval practice, long before it became Lyotard's postmodern hope. A medieval mixed jury, which combined local subjects and foreigners as members of the same tribunal, would hear cases between culturally different litigants who could not be subject to one existing rule.[52] The mixed jury predates the contradiction between nation and republic that Lyotard locates at the inconsistent core of modern polities.[53] Now that our postmodern countries include mixed populations, we might take a lead from the Normans, and from the Moors in Spain, to cite one more example. They taxed thriving infidels rather than eliminating them as so much guano for conquest. More rational than Christian tradition has portrayed them, Muslim empires have traditionally been hosts to the cultural differences that Christendom does not abide.[54] Spanish modernity came with cultural and political coherence: the consolidation of reluctant and even embattled kingdoms, the expulsion of miscreants, and the continued surveillance of private devotions by public authority. Modernity also drove England to overcome internal differences; a uniform common law replaced the ad hoc mixed jury, and Jews were expelled (as elsewhere) because they preferred double consciousness over the coherence of one intolerant culture.

This is no time to lead the opposing drives of double consciousness in one direction, with Emerson's agile Anglo-Saxons who drive others aground, not the time to revive his easy and airless fit between Americans and America. Nor is this the time to follow Du Bois in vicious circles as race and nation dig each other into a ground that demands acculturation but doesn't allow it. Today we might notice that double consciousness is a normal condition. It is also, I have been saying, a structure of democratic feeling. Du Bois called it a curse, but he hinted that double consciousness could also be a double blessing, for minorities in particular and for America in general. Anything less impoverishes both: "In the merging he wants neither of the older selves to be lost. Both America and the Negro have much to teach the world" (*Souls*, 215).

The difference between acculturation and this syncretism may be lost on some American readers, since we have been trained to value assimilation as the process of becoming American. For many immigrants, the process begins with cutting loose, leaving a home culture to join the New World. Mary Antin's popular autobiography, *The Promised Land* (1912), opens with a tellingly clipped, "I was born, I have lived, and I have been made over. Is it not time to write my life's story? I am just as much out of the way as if I were dead, for I am absolutely other than the person whose story I have to tell."[55] Not everyone has been so categorical or sanguine about letting go. For others the Promised Land has meant a place to prosper, not to become extinct. Yet the standard meaning of acculturation demands taking sides, nurturing our common new culture and letting the others wither. Antin herself would recoil from the consequences, after the Great War aroused unfriendly passions in her German American husband. We hardly know how to name Du Bois's reluctance to cut and to choose when different cultures claim him. What does one call the game that bypasses amalgamation and practices o jogo de cintura between one culture and other?

Double consciousness may not yet sound enabling in the United States or any place where dreams of cultural coherence lull the senses. But doubleness is no longer a rush of mutually destructive forces. Let's admit that monocultural dreams are a greater threat to democracy than are the annoying interruptions.

Of course it is possible, and profitable, to mitigate cultural differences through easy-to-read translations from one language to another, in made-for-export editions. It may also be true, to hear host countries complain, that mass migrations overwhelm distinct national cultures to the point of threatening a home market for "authentic" stuff.[56] Add to these cultural concerns the anxiety about foreigners who fragment our societies and interrupt institutions, and the mix may look like a mess.

"Possible, but not interesting," says Borges's private detective when the monolingual police inspector solves a murder case at the beginning of "Death and the Compass" (1945). Solutions stop an investigation and the point of a (life) story is pursuit. Let's play games, is the message. Here's the set-up unabridged (abridge Borges?):

> "No need to look for a three-legged cat here," Treviranus was saying as he brandished an imperious cigar. "We all know that the Tetrarch of Galilee owns the finest sapphires in the world. Someone, intending to steal them, must have broken in here by mistake. Yarmolinsky got up; the robber had to kill him. How does it sound to you?
>
> "Possible, but not interesting," Lönnrot answered. "You'll reply that reality hasn't the least obligation to be interesting. And I'll answer you that reality may avoid that obligation but that hypotheses may not. In the hypothesis that you propose, chance intervenes copiously. Here we have a dead rabbi; I would prefer a purely rabbinical explanation, not the imaginary mischances of an imaginary robber."
>
> Treviranus replied ill-humoredly:
>
> "I'm not interested in rabbinical explanations. I am interested in capturing the man who stabbed this unknown person."

"Not so unknown," corrected Lönnrot. "Here are his complete works." He indicated in the wall-cupboard a row of tall books: a *Vindication of the Cabala*; *An Examination of the Philosophy of Robert Fludd*; a literal translation of the *Sepher Yezirah*; a *Biography of the Baal Shem*; a *History of the Hasidic Sect*; a monograph (in German) on the Tetragrammaton; another on the divine nomenclature of the Pentateuch. The inspector regarded them with dread, almost with repulsion. Then he began to laugh.

"I'm a poor Christian," he said. "Carry off those musty volumes if you want; I don't have any time to waste on Jewish superstitions."

"Maybe the crime belongs to the history of Jewish superstition," murmured Lönnrot.

"Like Christianity," the editor of the *Yidische Zaitung* ventured to add. He was myopic, an atheist and very shy.

No one answered him. One of the agents had found in the small typewriter a piece of paper on which was written the following unfinished sentence:

The first letter of the Name has been uttered

Lönnrot abstained from smiling. Suddenly become a bibliophile or Hebraist, he ordered a package made of the dead man's books and carried them off to his apartment.[57]

Delighted with the lead from a literally unspeakable foreign word, Lönnrot pursues his clever hypothesis and dismisses obvious meanings. Being right was not the point (the Witz) of a murder mystery, or of any game including this story. "Is there always winning and losing, or competition between players?" (*PI*, §66), Wittgenstein asks rhetorically. "Loser takes all," Pierre Bourdieu teased, is a principle of aesthetic accomplishment.[58] Losing can be an art so exquisite (think of books like *Manual de perdedores* and *Perder es un método*)[59] that playing to win will seem brutish and self-defeating for masters of the game. So Lönnrot overrides truth in favor of fun and heads for a sidetrack. He overreads and "loses" the game, but he plays brilliantly. The beginner Hebraist bears more than one resemblance to the proverbial rabbi who disdains obvious exegesis, "That's only one answer to the question," because right answers and real meanings overlook the inexhaustible mystery of sacred texts, including the Koran.[60] To follow rules means to play with them. Wittgenstein shows a rabbinical family resemblance too, when he describes "one interpretation after another, as if each one contented us at least for a moment, until we thought of yet another standing behind it. What this shews is that there is a way of grasping a rule which is *not* an *interpretation*, but which is exhibited in what we call 'obeying the rule' and 'going against it' in actual cases"(*PI*, §201). Plausible solutions to a murder mystery, or justified complaints against globalization, play boring matches with the challenges at hand.

If detective Lönnrot were at today's scene of violence against national languages, he might delay any conclusion about guilt or damage and offer questions instead: Does everyone suffer losses? When victims incur linguistic damage, is it a net loss, or are there mitigating factors including gains? Lönnrot might have observed, mischievously, that inside Argentina, and other Latin American countries where European and North American books have long been staples of education, strong national language traditions continue to thrive. Educated Argentines, who sometimes learn their first lessons in English, or French, or German, may be amused at the provincial anxiety over eroding linguistic coherence. Perhaps they feel the satisfaction of watching the whole literate world finally advance southward, where Argentines have often found their local frontier. (Paris is the other promised land.)[61] In Argentina and in Mexico, or Cuba, or anywhere in Latin America (especially in Brazil), patriots have long known that economics and education oblige them to cross national lines and languages. And the most "authentic" literature can be hilariously hybrid. Think of Guillermo Cabrera Infante's novel written in "Cuban," *Three Trapped Tigers*, where Sam Clemens follows San Anselmo in the list of Enlightened Philosophers and Menasha Twa is on the list of unnameables in France. The book opens with a very funny, imperfectly multilingual nightclub routine that could certainly have added a few ironic lines about a First World worried that creativity is lost in translation.

> *Showtime!* Señoras y señores. *Ladies and gentlemen. Muy buenas noches, damas y caballeros, tengan todos ustedes ... In the marvelous production of our Rodney the Great ...* En la gran, maravillosa producción de nuestro GRANDE, ¡Roderico Neyra! ... *"Going to Brazil"* ... Intitulada, *Me voy pal Brasil"* ... Taratará tarará, taratará tarará taratareo ... *Brazuil terra dye nostra felichidade ... That was Brezill for you, ladies and gentlemen. That is, my very very particular version of it!* ... en el idioma de *Chakespeare*, en *English*.[62]

You don't have to know a language well in order to play *with* it. In fact, it's probably more fun to let mistakes show while you take the risk of making contact. Is that precarious and imperfect competence also a philosophical advantage insofar as it recovers the "sensitivities we acquired as we mastered the language"?[63] The possibility means that winning can be losing, if the Witz of the game is to keep playing. Even after Lönnrot loses the match, as the killer's pistol rises to the height of his head, the loser's last words manage to adjust the rules of the game for a rematch in another life. Lönnrot could have closed the first homicide case in an endgame. Instead he opened it up with arcane gambits. Had the case been merely solved, it could not have been Borges's vehicle for one of his favorite themes, the codependence between law and crime, detectives and delinquents, signs and things. Detective Lönnrot was notorious in the underworld for his clever skirmishes with crime; this time, he is lured to engage through an exegetical sidetrack that the murderer developed for the exegete after Lönnrot himself showed the way. He had (mis)construed a piece of circumstantial evidence into an inviting signpost. He takes up the self-authored invitation, confident that he is smarter than his prey. The deadly game begins by spelling out God's unspeakably holy Hebrew name.

The story works along the fault lines of the common language, in the loose connections where restricted codes can play. Law (in Spanish, or in English translation) is a system that includes everyone. Law is clear, uniformly available, and therefore indifferent to foreign distractions. But some speakers, bored by the uniformity, prefer distractions. Why repeat the tedious game of being right, when you can be clever? So Lönnrot takes up the sacred language and communes with his counterpart. Their game may have little to do with the original texts that make it possible. Maybe the Hebrew language itself is vehicle enough for the special connection between the players. Not that the special vehicle leads to a conflict with the public language. Nothing here happens outside the law, nor despite it, and certainly not against it. Lönnrot, after all, has defended the law so effectively that criminals target him as enemy number one. But the inclusive code is thin in places; it is tedious or otherwise unimpressive when compared to the option of a particular language that the law finds irrelevant. Thanks to the very indifference or dismissal of foreign signs ("The inspector regarded them with dread, almost with repulsion."), players can sometimes revel unpoliced while staying inside a generally powerful system. Their games are collective, but restricted, hermeneutic adventures. And though the virtuosity seems pointless to the police and to the newspaperman, to the protagonists it is the medium of creative communication.

How strange that the shared language should be the mechanism of exclusion, and that minor characters are the ones who don't have a minor language. Yet the paradox can surprise only monolinguals. Those who hear nothing but the universal language in Borges's story (and in many others) actually miss the available fun. Specifically, his game depends on the option to spar in a difficult, privileged language. More generally, it depends on the simultaneous availability of universality and particularism. To stay inside only one is already to forfeit the possible games, or to be their target.[64]

I might have noticed the literary charms of code switching as long ago as my first reading of "Death and the Compass," or far earlier, in the multilingual games we immigrant children would play at the expense of competent English-only speakers, including our teachers. But theory can lag embarrassingly behind practice, and catching up now that the practice is so general, varied, and culturally significant is hardly an intellectual risk. It's a pedagogical obligation. We live inside dominant languages that often sparkle with the survivals of resistant speech, yet teachers either decline to notice or they feel beleaguered by the range of references that somehow, they feel, should be mastered. Otherwise, they worry, what could teaching add to reading? Readers of Cabrera Infante, happy to get a fraction of his jokes and jabs, cure themselves of demands for mastery.

Sometimes educators conclude, prematurely, that multicultural games are meant to enrich the dominant experience, so they complain if the material is hard to digest.[65] In fact, the appetite for enlarged and improved master codes misses the point of some double-dealing games. They are played at the center's expense. Self-authorized readers can be the targets of a minority text, not its coconspirators. Lönnrot confronted the difference at the end of his story when the Jewish crook, scoffing at goyim who dabble in Cabala, took aim at the hobbyhorse Hebraist and fired.

The point is that foreign disturbances can be flagrant, on purpose. They can be signatures of particular languages through a universal medium. In the asymmetry of reception that they impose, in the deferred stress or delayed apprehension of meaning, in the skipped beat of a conversation that achieves the rhythm of a joke, spaces open up to aesthetics in two different, but codependent moves. Double dealing is a corollary of the mixed blessing of double consciousness: One direction is toward the aesthetic effects that the formalists called "making the familiar strange," and the opposite direction notices that the "strange" or foreign is intimately familiar.

Double dealing, dual nationality, bicultural contradictions, all these pull the words *nation* and *state* in different directions today. Liberal states are forced to respond with a procedural lingua franca that can coordinate many national cultures. Perhaps we can learn from multilingual subjects that the cultural overload is not a psychological problem of fragmentation but an incomparable advantage for developing alternate perspectives, flexibility, and wisdom. Multilingual players handicap single-minded games and find unsettling twists. They interfere with any one culture, thank goodness, enough to refresh perception for our aesthetic pleasure, to keep us laughing at mistakes (yours and mine), to nudge politics toward procedural solutions, and to engage philosophy in its freshest games.

Let's play those games, inspired by Wittgenstein's lucid common sense. His therapy for the damage caused by rigid rules and restrictions was to respect the intricate and surprising functions of everyday creativity. Another way to describe that therapy is love for the contingent and changing world.

Notes

Invitation

1 See Lesley Milroy and Pieter Muysken, eds., "Introduction," *One Speaker, Two Languages: Cross-Disciplinary Perspectives on Code-Switching* (Cambridge: Cambridge University Press, 1995), 1: "In the last forty years or so, developments such as the expansion of educational provision to many more levels of society, massive population shifts through migration, and technological advances in mass communication have served to accentuate our sense of a visibly and audibly multilingual modern world. Other large-scale social changes have combined to lead to a considerable increase in bilingualism, not only as a European but as a world-wide phenomenon." They add that "the relatively recent phenomenon of large-scale language revival . . . has often led to the preservation, resuscitation and expansion in the use of minority languages which policy makers had already declared moribund and relegated to the scrapheap of history."

2 Víctor Hernández Cruz, "You Gotta Have Your Tips on Fire," *Mainland: Poems* (New York: Random House, 1973), 3–4.

3 This is Saul Bellow's frame for *Ravelstein* (New York: Penguin, 2000), 1: "Anyone who wants to govern the country has to entertain it. During the civil war people complained about Lincoln's funny stories. Perhaps he sensed that strict seriousness was far more dangerous than any joke." Robert R. Provine cites another model in *Laughter: A Scientific Investigation* (London: Faber and Faber, 2000), 32: "John F. Kennedy was unusual among U.S. presidents in having both a presence of command and an excellent sense of humor."

4   Michael Holquist, "Why We Should Remember Philology," *ADFL* 33.2 (2002): 19.

5   See José Esteban Muñoz's *Disidentifications: Queers of Color and the Performance of Politics* (Minneapolis: University of Minnesota Press, 1999).

6   Charles Taylor, "The Politics of Recognition," in *Multiculturalism: Examining the Politics of Recognition*, ed. Amy Gutmann (Princeton: Princeton University Press, 1994), 27.

7   These are register switches, as in "signifying": see Henry Louis Gates Jr., *The Signifying Monkey: A Theory of African-American Literary Criticism* (New York: Oxford University Press, 1988).

8   For a review of the skeptics, see Bee Gallegos, *English: Our Official Language?* (New York: H. W. Wilson, 1994).

9   See James Crawford, "Historical Roots of U.S. Language Policy," in *Language Loyalties: A Source Book on the Official English Controversy*, ed. James Crawford (Chicago: University of Chicago Press, 1992), 10. Crawford notes that in "1923 Washington J. McCormic, Congressman from Montana, introduced the first official language proposal ever considered at the federal level; a bill to enshrine 'American' in the place of English." For comparison, during the protofascist Getulio Vargas regime, the Brazilian government almost passed legislation to call the national language "Brazilian," still a popular usage.

10 Canadians target language diversity. See Albert Breton, ed., *Economic Approaches to Language and Bilingualism* (New Canadian Perspectives, Department of Public Works and Government Services, Canada, 1998), and Harold Chorney, "The Economic Benefits of Linguistic Duality and Bilingualism: A Political Economy Approach" (New Canadian Perspectives: Official Languages and the Economy, Department of Public Works and Government Services, Canada, 1997), 181. "The very act of acquiring knowledge and linguistic competence has a positive disproportional impact on the economic potential of an individual. Furthermore it contributes to the likelihood that the individual can make a greater contribution to society. Quite literally the capacity to participate in one's society is considerably enhanced. As central Europeans often say 'the more languages you speak the more times you are a human being.' " But the U.S. literature on diversity's advantages is vast. See, for example, the review article by Karin Price Mueller, "Diversity and the Bottom Line: Big Ideas," *Harvard Business Review* (1998): 3–4. Also Leigh L. Thompson's *Making the Team: A Guide for Managers* (Upper Saddle River, N.J.: Prentice Hall, 2003).

11 Objections to bilingual education are not new. See Crawford, *Language*

Loyalties; and Gallegos, *English: Our Official Language?* The current campaign to limit languages began in 1981 when Senator S. I. Hayakawa introduced legislation for an amendment to the U.S. Constitution that would declare English the official language of the country. It did not pass, but as leader of a lobby known as "U.S. English," Hayakawa continued to press for state constitutional amendments to restrict all official communication to English. Ron Unz, a California citizen, has promoted state referendum campaigns for English-only initiatives, and also led movements in other states, including Massachusetts, where bilingual education was defeated in the 2002 ballot. See his "California and the End of White America," *Commentary* 108.4 (1999): 17–28. See also the English Language Amendment's (ELA) chief sponsor Senator Steven D. Symms in the *Washington Post*, March 1985: "Unfortunately, our lavishly funded 'maintenance' style bilingual education program holds students prisoners in their native language."

12 In 1985, Secretary of Education William J. Bennett spoke in New York City against bilingual education and in favor of "sink-or-swim" programs. See Gallegos, *English: Our Official Language?*, 12.

13 Robert Bunge, "Language: The Psyche of a People," in Crawford, *Language Loyalties*, 378–79.

14 See Ludwig Wittgenstein, *Philosophical Investigations*, 3d ed., trans. G. E. M. Anscombe (New York: Macmillan, 1968): "*Essence* is expressed by grammar," §371; and "Grammar tells what kind of object anything is," §373. Hereafter referred to as *PI*.

15 See psychologist Richard Nisbett's *The Geography of Thought: How Asians and Westerners Think Differently . . . and Why* (New York: Free Press, 2003), and review by Hua Hsu, "Orienting the East," *Village Voice*, 22 April 2003: 16.

16 "For example, the word for 'school' in Welsh (*ysgol*) also means 'ladder,' while the English word has no such associations. Welsh bilinguals may have mental imagery connecting the concepts of 'school' and ladder', which allows them to create metaphorical links, e.g. the school is a ladder to knowledge." Reported in Suzanne Romaine, *Bilingualism*, 2d ed. (Oxford: Blackwell, 1995), 114–15. In the *New York Times*, Louise Erdrich wrote about her efforts to learn Ojibwah, a family language, mostly to get the inside jokes that leave white people outside. Also, Carrie Scheffield reminds me that Native American language arts offer expert bilingual games.

17 Zinik, "No Cause for Alarm," *Mind the Door: Long Short Stories* (New York: Context Books, 2001), 34–35.

18 Grammatically proper name, Bertrand Russell would call it, because unlike "logically proper names," these do not denote particulars but complex descriptions and have no meaning in isolation. "The Philosophy of Logical Atomism," reprinted in *Logic and Knowledge: Essays, 1901–1950*, ed. Robert Charles Marsh (London: George Allen and Unwin, 1956), 178–201. See also Ronald Suter, *Interpreting Wittgenstein: A Cloud of Philosophy, a Drop of Grammar* (Philadelphia: Temple University Press, 1989), 190–91.

19 Vladimir Nabokov, *Pnin* (New York: Vintage, 1989), 79.

20 Maya Slobin's inspiration, in conversations with Greta Slobin, author of *Remizov's Fictions* (DeKalb, Ill.: Northern Illinois University Press, 1992).

21 Bilingual programs do keep Latino students from dropping out. See *CQ Researcher*, 13 August 1993: 704–12, and Gallegos, *English: Our Official Language?*, 108. See also Gary Orfield and Nora Gordon on bilingual education in *Schools More Separate: Consequences of a Decade of Resegregation* (Cambridge: The Civil Rights Project, Harvard University, 2001).

22 Alejandro Portes and Lingxin Hao, "The Price of Uniformity: Language, Family and Personality Adjustment in the Immigrant Second Generation," *Ethnic and Racial Studies* 25.6 (2002): 889–912.

23 The classic study is by Elizabeth Peal and Wallace Lambert, *The Relation of Bilingualism to Intelligence* (Washington, D.C.: American Psychological Association, 1962). They found that bilingual children showed significant improvements in their cognitive performance. In a later study Lambert argued that "bilingual children, relative to monolingual controls, displayed greater cognitive flexibility, creativity and divergent thought." See Wallace Lambert, "Effects of Bilingualism on the Individual: Cognitive and Sociocultural Consequences," in *Bilingualism: Psychological, Social, and Educational Implications*, ed. Peter A. Hornby (New York: Academic Press, 1977), 16. See also Peter Homel et al., *Childhood Bilingualism: Aspects of Linguistic, Cognitive, and Social Development* (Hillsdale, N.J.: L. Erlbaum, 1987).

24 Tara Parker-Pope, "To Help Combat Senility, Learn a New Language or Read a Book," *Wall Street Journal*, 23 November 2001: "Doctors say new mental challenges—learning a second language . . .—help to map out new pathways in the brain. The affect is likened to a driver who knows only one route to work. If that road is damaged or filled with traffic, he's stuck. But if the driver learns several different routes [or different words for the same thing], he can still get where he wants to go even if certain paths becomes blocked."

25 John Rawls, for example, can simplify the terms of the "conflict in demo-
    cratic thought," by juxtaposing "the tradition associated with Locke,
    which gives greater weight to what Constant called 'the liberties of the
    moderns,' freedom of thought and conscience, certain basic rights of the
    person and of property, and the rule of law, and the tradition associated
    with Rousseau, which gives greater weight to what Constant called 'the
    liberties of ancients,' the equal political liberties and the values of pub-
    lic life." In Milton Fisk's "Justice as Fairness: Political Not Metaphysi-
    cal," *Justice, Key Concepts in Critical Theory* (Atlantic Highlands, N.J.:
    Humanities Press, 1993), 50.

26 Brian Barry, *Culture and Equality: An Egalitarian Critique of Multicul-
    turalism* (Cambridge: Harvard University Press, 2001), 133.

27 The Patriot Act of 2001 curbs a range of rights and obliges citizens to par-
    ticipate in surveillance. Among the many communities and institutions
    that have objected, the Stanford University Faculty Senate issued an ex-
    emplary statement on 9 January 2003. See Andrea M. Hamilton, "Faculty
    Senate Passes Resolution Warning against Anti-Terror Law's Unintended
    Effects," Stanford University News Service, 16 January 2003: 1. Two years
    ago, President Bush's order to create military tribunals, with jurisdic-
    tion over twenty million noncitizen residents, "was an act of executive
    fiat, imposed without even consulting Congress," Anthony Lewis empha-
    sizes in his warning, "Wake Up, America." *New York Times*, 30 November
    2001: A25.

28 Dennis Baron, "America Doesn't Know What the World Is Saying," *New
    York Times*, 27 October 2001: Op-Ed.

29 Doris Sommer, *Foundational Fictions: The National Romances of Latin
    America* (Berkeley: University of California Press, 1991).

1 Choose and Lose

1 Roberto G. Fernández, "Wrong Channel," in *Micro Fiction: An Anthology
   of Really Short Stories*, ed. Jerome Stern (New York: Norton, 1996).

2 Compare Robert G. Fernández, *Raining Backwards*, 2d ed. (Houston:
   Arte Publico Press, 1997), to Guillermo Cabrera Infante's books, espe-
   cially *Three Trapped Tigers*, trans. Donald Gardner and Suzanne Jill
   Levine (New York: Marlowe, 1997).

3 See Camille Forbes's "Performed Fictions: The Onstage and Offstage
   Lives of Bert Williams," Ph.D. diss., Harvard University, 2002. She cites
   Lawrence W. Levine's *Black Culture and Black Consciousness: Afro-
   American Folk Thought from Slavery to Freedom* (New York: Oxford Uni-

versity Press, 1977), 321, on black humor that is often directed at the joke teller and his immediate group.

4 Renato Rosaldo, "Politics, Patriarchs, and Laughter," *Cultural Critique* 6 (1987): 65–86.

5 Many commentators on bilingualism and intelligence testing point to the influential study by Peal and Lambert, *The Relation of Bilingualism to Intelligence*, that found superior performance of bilingual children on both verbal and nonverbal intelligence tests. See Romaine, *Bilingualism*, 133, where she summarizes research. On p. 118 she refers to Joshua Fishman, as well as Kenji Hakuta's *Mirror of Language: The Debate on Bilingualism* (New York: Basic Books, 1986), 43, regarding the inappropriateness of narrow intelligence testing for bilinguals. See also Josiane F. Hamers and Michel H. A. Blanc, *Bilinguality and Bilingualism*, 2d ed. (Cambridge: Cambridge University Press, 2000), 47–59.

6 Hakuta, *Mirror of Language*. Also, Ted Mouw and Yu Xie, "Bilingualism and the Academic Achievement of First and Second-Generation Asian Americans: Accommodation with or without Assimilation," *American Sociological Review* 64 (1999): 232–52.

7 Rhona S. Weinstein, *Reaching Higher: The Power of Expectations in Schooling* (Cambridge: Harvard University Press, 2002). See also Romaine, *Bilingualism*, 115. To summarize the difference between bilinguals from different socioeconomic backgrounds, Romaine refers to the "social context of acquisition": "migrant workers' children [are] brought up in a society where their parents' language is stigmatized."

8 Postcolonial positions are often ironic about these contrasts. Sophisticated by definition, they are heir both to an imposed culture and to a native one.

9 For the first half of the twentieth century, researchers almost always focused on the allegedly negative effects of bilingualism on intelligence. See Hakuta, *Mirror of Language*, 15.

10 Romaine, *Bilingualism*, xiv.

11 A recent exchange among scholars of code switching confronts the inevitable factor of "race" however questionable the term may be for science. Daniel Villa contributed the following to the listserv/newsgroup <code-switching@yahoogroups.com> on 15 February 2002: "In the southern part of New Mexico where I live, most Spanish speakers are dark complected—I am not. In any number of instances I've been in line in the grocery store with my sons, who are very fair. I speak only Spanish with them, and as often happens they want a last minute treat, so I'm carrying on (in Spanish) 'No, no, put that back, no I won't buy it for you it'll

rot your teeth, you can have an apple when you get home etc. etc.' and the checker and bagger will look at me with astonishment and ask 'es Ud. mexicano?' (are you Mexican?) to which I reply 'pos si que otra cosa voy a ser' (sure, what else would I be?) There is always a moment of disconnect, and then invariably one or the other will say 'oh, I have a cousin/uncle/father/brother/brother-in-law that looks just like you!' I should add here that I speak a local variety of Spanish, which is evidently being keyed on. I also drive a 1947 Chevy pickup, a popular 'fixer-upper' around here. Invariably, people who ask me what year it is, if I have an extra fender, bumper, door, whatever, will address me in Spanish, or codeswitch between Spanish and English, without asking me first if I know Spanish. Anybody know of any studies on the relationship between ethnic identity and pickup trucks?"

12 Romaine, *Bilingualism*, 118.

13 The "English Plus: Statement of Purpose" was published in *Epic Events* 2.4 (1989): 2, by the national Immigration, Refugee and Citizenship Forum, as a response to proposals at the federal level, by Senator S. I. Hayakawa, followed by statewide proposals, to legislate English as the official language. "The English Plus concept holds that the national interest can best be served when all members of our society have full access to effective opportunities to acquire strong English language proficiency plus mastery of a second or multiple languages . . . English Plus rejects the ideology and divisive character of the so-called English Only movement." See Gallegos, *English: Our Official Language?*, 24–25. By 1989, New Mexico, and then Washington and Oregon, declared an English Plus policy. Arizona followed just a year after passing an official English amendment (Gallegos, 14–15).

14 See Mary Louise Pratt, "Love, Tears, and Multilingualism: Toward a New Public Idea about Language" (forthcoming, *ADFL*). Also Carol L. Schmid, *The Politics of Language: Conflict, Identity, and Cultural Pluralism in Comparative Perspective* (Oxford: Oxford University Press, 2001), 168–70.

15 See, for example, Christina Bratt Paulston, *Linguistic Minorities in Multilingual Settings: Implications for Language Policies* (Amsterdam: J. Benjamins, 1994). She sees bilingualism as the "mechanism of language shift," where parents speak the original language with grandparents and the new language with the children. She predicts, then, that language loss occurs by the third generation. I thank Nicolás Fernández-Me for this reference.

16 Richard Weissbourd, who teaches education at Harvard University.

"Americanization erodes these critical aspects of parenting," he wrote recently in the *New Republic*. Quoted in Alan Elsner, "Immigrants to U.S. Often Depend on their Children," Reuters, 7 March 2002.

17 See Portes and Hau, "The Price of Uniformity." Also, Joshua Fishman, "What Do You Lose When You Lose Your Language?," in *Stabilizing Indigenous Languages*, ed. Gina Cantoni (Flagstaff: Northern Arizona University Press, 1996), 186–96.

18 See Guadalupe Valdes, *Expanding Definitions of Giftedness: Young Interpreters of Immigrant Background*, The Educational Psychology Series (Mahwah, N.J.: Lawrence Erlbaum, 2003).

19 Roberto Schwarz, "National by Subtraction," *Misplaced Ideas: Essays on Brazilian Culture* (New York: Verso, 1992).

20 Oswald de Andrade, "Manifesto Antropofagico," *Revista de Antropofagia* 1.1 (1928).

21 See Laura Ceia-Minjares's, Ph.D. diss. ms. "Tristan Tzara: Trapped between a Nostalgic History and an Urgent Revolution." Her references are to Tzara's *Oeuvres Complètes*. "In terms of critical bibliography, there isn't much, if anything at all," she writes in a note of 4 September 2002.
    In French, Tzara's Romanian past becomes a traumatic memory, one that cannot be accessed, that cannot be spoken of using a language that structures a different universe of symbols and experiences. Conversely, Romanian becomes the space that allows the experience of loss to be mourned via the poetic discourse and the longing to reconnect to a community of origin. Tzara's Romanian poetry was also directed to a different reader, the reader he had left behind. In this context, his verses sound almost like a desire to be understood and perhaps remembered as one who took risks in choosing to transgress a confining national universe and explore broader, more intricate worlds.
    There is a rift in experience that allows for Tzara's self to split into two forms of consciousness coexisting at once. One is linked to the explosive experience of the new (associated with French language); the other is constantly looking back, trying to reconnect to a nostalgic point of departure.

22 David Lloyd, "Keening," a paper presented at the Binghampton Conference, April 1999. See also his *Nationalism and Minor Literature: James Clarence Mangan and the Emergence of Irish Cultural Nationalism*, The New Historicism: Studies in Cultural Poetics (Berkeley: University of California Press, 1987).

23 Freud evidently appreciates that threshold as the stage for performing a minority identity, when he considers the inside-trading of witticisms be-

tween a teller and someone of his "nation." Surely bilingual jokes recon-
firm this collective identity more confidently than do the monolingual
culture clashes that he stages in his collection of jokes, simply because
outsiders don't easily cross the language divide.

24   Anne Anlin Cheng, *The Melancholy of Race: Psychoanalysis, Assimila-
      tion, and Hidden Grief* (Oxford: Oxford University Press, 2001).

25   Sigmund Freud, *Wit and Its Relation to the Unconscious* (1905), *The
      Basic Writings of Sigmund Freud*, trans. and ed. by Dr. A. A. Brill (New
      York: Modern Library, 1938), 633–803. At least this goes for the jokes
      he most enjoyed, like the one that introduces and recurs through the
      book: Heine's description of the Baron Rothschild, who treated the pau-
      per at his table just like family, forgotten family, very "famillionare." It
      will later inspire Lacan's extended riffs: 1."Le famillionnaire;" 2."Le fat-
      millonnaire," 3. "Le Miglionnaire" (see part 1: "Les structures freudi-
      ennes de l'ésprit," *Le seminaire de Jacques Lacan*, ed. Jacques-Alain
      Miller (Paris: Editions du Seuil, 1998), 9–64).   **201**

26   Sigmund Freud, "Humour" (1928), *Collected papers*, vol. 5, Essay 20
      (New York: Basic Books, 1959). See p. 220.

27   I learned this from Marcelo Suárez Orozco.

28   See R. C. Ainslie's "Cultural Mourning, Immigration, and Engagement:
      Vignettes from the Mexican Experience," *Crossings: Mexican Immigra-
      tion in Interdisciplinary Perspectives*, ed. Marcelo M. Suárez-Orozco
      (Cambridge: Harvard University, David Rockefeller Center for Latin
      American Studies; distributed by Harvard University Press, 1998), 283–
      300.

29   Ibid., 301–2.

30   A short reading list: Mary Patricia Brady, *Extinct Lands, Scarred Bodies:
      Chicana Literature and the Reinvention of Space*, Ph.D. diss., Univer-
      sity of California, Los Angeles, 1996; Margarita Theresa Barceló, *Geogra-
      phies of Struggle: Ideological Representations of Social Space in Four
      Chicana Writers*, Ph.D. diss., University of California, San Diego, 1995;
      Edward W. Soja, "The Socio-Spatial Dialectic," *Annals of the Associa-
      tion of American Geographers* 70.2 (1980): 207–25; Adrianne Estill, *Lyric
      Cartographies: Space, Body, and Subject in Contemporary Mexican and
      Chicano Poetry*, Ph.D. diss., Cornell University, 1997; David J. Langston,
      "Time and Space as the Lenses of Reading," *Journal of Aesthetics and
      Art Criticism* 40.4 (1982): 401–14.

31   See Arachu Castro, "Emigración y hábitos alimentarios," *Revista ROL
      de Enfermería* 151 (1991): 91–93.

32   Melancholia may have faded from a scientific vocabulary, but it remains

perversely radiant in literary criticism, a "black sun," in the metaphor Julia Kristeva borrows from Gerard de Nerval. It is a goad to creativity, as compensation and catharsis, therapies that alleviate sadness but don't cure it. Melancholia has also been the guide to philosophy. It "is not a philosopher's disease but his very nature, his *ethos* . . . With Aristotle, melancholia, counterbalanced by genius, is coextensive with man's anxiety in being. It could be seen as the forerunner of Heidegger's anguish as the *Stimmung* of thought. Schelling found in it, in similar fashion, the ' "essence of human freedom," an indication of man's affinity with nature. The philosopher would thus be 'melancholy on account of a surfeit of humanity.' " Julia Kristeva, *Black Sun: Depression and Melancholia*, trans. Leon S. Roudiez (New York: Columbia University Press, 1989), 7. Is there an analogous surfeit of cultures, identities, be-longings in bicultural subjects? Is the reluctance to streamline the surfeit into one clear cultural option a refusal of mourning as therapy?

202

33 Standard reviews of the research are in Romaine's *Bilingualism*, 107–99; and Hamers and Blanc, eds., *Bilinguality and Bilingualism*, 47–59.

34 Renzo Titone, "The Bilingual Personality as a Metasystem: The Case of Code-Switching," in Renzo Titone, ed., *On the Bilingual Person* (Ottawa: Canadian Society for Italian Studies, Biliblioteca di Quaderni d'italianistica, no. 7, 1989), 55–64, 63.

35 For example, the influential Otto Jespersen's *Language*; and Henry Herbert Goddard, *Feeble-Mindedness: Its Causes and Consequences* (New York: Macmillan, 1914), as well as his "Mental Tests and the Immigrant," *Journal of Delinquency* 2 (1917): 243–77. The literature is reviewed by Romaine, Hamers, and Hakuta.

36 See Titone, "Bilingual Personality" 63: "It is not facetious to add that this defense mechanism may pose an obstacle to psychotherapy or psychoanalysis, but that this problem is not so much the bilingual patient's as it is the psychiatrist's; . . . Moreover, if code-switching is the potentially adaptive device this author believes it to be, it might account for the further impression that there is a low incidence of reactive schizophrenia in bilingual populations, despite epidemiological studies."

37 See Anzaldúa's *Borderlands/La Frontera: The New Mestiza* (San Francisco: Spinsters/Aunt Lute, 1987). Also see Paula M. L. Moya's discussion, "Chicana Feminism and Postmodernist Theory," *Signs* 26.2: 469: "As a survival skill, *la facultad* allows such people to adjust quickly and gracefully to changing (and often threatening) circumstances. With origins in experiences of pain and trauma, *la facultad* involves a loss of innocence and an initiation into an awareness of discrimination, fear, depression, illness, and death."

38 Mary Louise Pratt, "Arts of the Contact Zone," in *Professing in the Contact Zone: Bringing Theory and Practice Together*, ed. Janice M. Wolff (Urbana: National Council of Teachers of English, 2002).

39 *Différence* is what Derrida calls this constitutive contamination of meaning by the alternatives it necessarily conjures. From another vantage point, Peter Elbow defends *error* in standard English to enable free writing for speakers of Ebonics, for example. See "Inviting the Mother Tongue: Beyond 'Mistakes,' 'Bad English,' and 'Wrong Language,'" *Everyone Can Write: Essays Toward a Hopeful Theory of Writing and Teaching Writing* (New York: Oxford University Press, 2000), 323–50.

40 Henry Louis Gates Jr., *The Signifying Monkey*; and Marcylina Morgan, "More than a Mood or an Attitude: Discourse and Verbal Genres in African-American Culture," in *African-American English: Structure, History and Use*, ed. Salikoko S. Mufwene, John R. Rickford, Guy Bailey, and John Baugh (New York: Routledge, 1998), 251–81.

41 Néstor García Canclini, *Consumers and Citizens: Globalization and Multicultural Conflicts*, trans. with an introduction by George Yúdice (Minneapolis: University of Minnesota Press, 2001), 71.

42 John Limon, *Stand-Up Comedy in Theory, or, Abjection in America* (Durham: Duke University Press, 2000), 4. Also see p. 74: "Maintained objectivity is funny when it 'sparks,' perhaps, because a joke is dreck enflamed by form, that is, by a standard it inhabits but to which it cannot aspire. Thus it becomes clear why laughter, disjoined from abjection generally, attaches to it when Kristeva comes to describe modernity: in our century, apocalyptic yet Godless, abjection is a psychopathology that happens to be realistic. When you cannot abject your abjection, according to Kristeva, as filth or sin (the God of the Jews and Christians alike being dead)—when objectivity lingers in the world only as a measure of abjectivity—you laugh."

43 Mel Watkins, *On the Real Side: Laughing, Lying, and Signifying: The Underground Tradition of African-American Humor that Transformed American Culture, from Slavery to Richard Pryor* (New York: Simon and Schuster, 1994), 17–18.

44 Ibid., 16.

45 Warren Goldfarb, Harvard University lecture, September 2001.

46 Lyotard, *Differend: Phrases in Dispute*, trans. George Van Den Abbeele (Minneapolis: University of Minnesota Press, 1988), 137. His section 185 refers to Wittgenstein, "Lectures on Ethics," *Philosophical Review* 74.1: 5.

47 Mikhail Bakhtin, "Discourse in the Novel."

48 Jan-Petter Blom and John J. Gumperz, "Social Meaning in Linguistic

Structures: Code-Switching in Norway," in *Directions in Sociolinguistics*, ed. John J. Gumperz and D. Hymes (New York: Holt, Rinehart and Winston, 1972), 407–34.

49 Peter Elbow argues for the "bilingual" double-take effect of etymology in a single language, in a letter to me dated 21 August 2002. I am grateful for the observation, but add that this particular aesthetic effect depends on privileged education, rather than on linguistic migrancy and unsettledness of everyday bilingualism.

50 Mikail Bakhtin, *Rabelais and His World*, trans. Hélène Isowolsky (Bloomington: Indiana University Press, 1984), 472: "The link of these forms with a multilingual world . . . seems to us extremely important . . . It is impossible to overcome through abstract thought alone, within the system of a unique language, that deep dogmatism hidden in all the forms of this system. The completely new, self-criticizing, absolutely sober, fearless, and gay life of the image can start only on linguistic borders."

51 W. E. B. Du Bois, *The Souls of Black Folk*, in *Three Negro Classics* (New York: Avon Books, 1965), 215.

52 For example, see the conservative arguments presented in Portes and Hau, "The Price of Uniformity."

53 Terry Eagleton, "Postcolonialism: The Case of Ireland," in *Multicultural States: Rethinking Difference and Identity*, ed. David Bennett (London: Routledge, 1998), 128–34.

54 Salman Rushdie, *Imaginary Homelands: Essays and Criticism, 1981–1991* (London: Granta Books, 1991), 15.

55 See Doris Sommer, *One Master for Another: Populism as Patriarchal Rhetoric in Dominican Novels* (Lanham, Md.: University Press of America, 1983), chapter 5, on *El Masacre se pasa a pie*, by Freddy Prestol Castillo, 161–96. See also, among many exposés, Jesús de Galíndez, in *The Era of Trujillo, Dominican Dictator*, ed. Russell H. Fitzgibbon (Tuscon: University of Arizona Press, 1973).

56 Michael Jones-Correa, "Under Two Flags: Dual Nationality in Latin America and Its Consequences for the United States," Harvard University, David Rockefeller Center for Latin American Studies, Working Papers on Latin America No. 99/00–3. "The bigamy analogy comes up a lot among critics of dual nationality" (19), which suggests the nineteenth-century "Foundational Fictions" motif of sliding from Eros to Polis that I considered in *Foundational Fictions*. Also see Jones-Correa's "Under Two Flags: Dual Nationality in Latin America and Its Consequences for the United States" printed in the *International Migration Review* 35.4 (2001): 997–1029.

57 Stanley Lieberson, *Language Diversity and Language Contact: Essays* (Stanford: Stanford University Press, 1981).

58 Portes and Hau, "The Price of Uniformity," 890. See also James Stalker, "Official English or English Only," *English Journal* 77 (1988): 18–23. In Gallegos, *English: Our Official Language?*, 48. A 1985 Rand Corporation study found that "more than 95 per cent of first-generation Mexican Americans born in the United States are proficient in English and that more than half the second generation speaks no Spanish at all." Another study found that "98 per cent of Hispanic parents in Miami felt it essential that their children read and write English perfectly." Gallegos also reports on continuing waiting lists for adult ESL classes: supply falls far short of demand (56).

59 François Grosjean, *Life with Two Languages: An Introduction to Bilingualism* (Cambridge: Harvard University Press, 1982), 11.

60 Johann Gottfried Herder, *Against Pure Reason: Writings on Religion, Language, and History*, trans. Marcia Bunge (Minneapolis: Fortress Press, 1993).

61 Taylor, "The Politics of Recognition," in *Multiculturalism*, ed. Gutmann.

62 Robert Greenberg, "Language, Nationalism, and the Yugoslav Successor States," *Language, Ethnicity, and the State, vol. 2: Minority Languages in Post-1989 Eastern Europe*, ed. Camille O'Reilly (New York: Palgrave, 2001), 17–43; and Ranko Bugarski, "Language, Nationalism, and War in Yugoslavia," *International Journal of the Sociology of Language* 151 (2001): 69–87.

63 I return to this point in chapter 3, in the "Juntos y Revueltos."

64 "Less is a bore" was Robert Venturi's response in *Complexity and Contradiction in Architecture* (New York: Museum of Modern Art, distributed by Doubleday, Garden City, N.Y., 1966), to modernist Mies van der Rohe's dictum "Less is more." See the web site for Venturi's Pritzker Prixe of 1991, <www.pritzkerprize.com/venturi.htm>.

65 Thomas Hobbes, *Human Nature* and *Leviathan* as cited in Provine, *Laughter: A Scientific Investigation*, 14. This is the only surviving theory of laughter for Charles R. Gruner, *The Game of Humor: A Comprehensive Theory of Why We Laugh* (New Brunswick, N.J.: Transaction Publishers, 1997).

66 As quoted in Watkins, *On the Real Side*, 39.

67 José María Arguedas, "El sueño del pongo," *Agua* (Lima: Universidad Nacional de San Marcos, Dirección Universitaria de Biblioteca y Publicaciones, 1974).

68 See David Suchoff's "Kafka's Languages," paper delivered at the MLA convention in December 2001.

69   I develop this observation in a paper delivered at the MLA convention in December 2000, where I attribute Mario Vargas Llosa's stylistic tic in *El hablador* (about jungle Indians) to Arguedas's experiments with Andean speech, specifically in the story "La agonía de Rasuñiti" in *Agua*.

70   Hemingway's pidginized English tries to sound "Spanish" in several major works, including *For Whom the Bell Tolls*.

71   Julio Marzán has this and other brilliant interpretations in *The Spanish American Roots of William Carlos Williams* (Austin: University of Texas Press, 1994).

72   Yunte Huang, *Transpacific Displacement: Ethnography, Translation, and Intertextual Travel in Twentieth-Century American Literature* (Berkeley: University of California Press, 2002).

73   See *Norton Anthology of Modern Poetry*, 2d ed. (New York: Norton, 1988), 375. The section on Pound details that while a student at Penn and Hamilton College "his interests were in Romance languages and literatures . . . Pound won a fellowship to go to Provence, Italy, and especially Spain, in preparation for a dissertation on Lope de Vega. This was never to be written."

74   Antje Wiener, "Crossing the Borders of Order: Democracy beyond the Nation-State?," in *Identities, Borders, Orders: Rethinking International Relations Theory*, ed. Mathias Albert, David Jacobson, Yosef Lapid (Minneapolis: University of Minnesota Press, 2001), 181–201. On p. 83 she describes a "shifting focus from (state-centric) models of democracy *toward practices and norms of democracy*. [my emphasis] While models are familiarly based on principles and procedures, practices and norms are assumed to be mutually constitutive of creating the *substance* of democracy."

75   The primacy of the political is a feature of the "war of position" that Gramsci named and that Laclau and Mouffe develop. And cultural overloads make necessary a meticulous methodology. See Ernesto Laclau and Chantal Mouffe, *Hegemony and Socialist Strategy: Towards a Radical Democratic Politics*, 2d ed. (London: Verso, 2001).

76   Nicholas Kulish, "Small Census Survey Finds Richer, More Educated, Multilingual Nation," *Wall Street Journal*, 6 August 2001: B1, B4. "California also leads the nation in residents who speak a language other than English at home. They make up 39.5% of the state's population, and 17.6% of the population nationally, an increase from 13.8% in 1990."

77   Don Feder, "Oakland Lays Foundation for Babel," *Boston Herald*, 2 May 2001.

78   The Association of Literary Scholars and Critics was founded in 1994 to

address "a deep and widespread concern about developments within the humanities that threatened to inhibit the freedom of the literary imagination. What was at stake for the founding members was—they said—the breadth and expanse of literature itself whose power to communicate to the human mind in its multifarious dimensions had been curtailed by a narrowing, often overtly political, within the discipline. Austin Quigley, ALSC President for 1998–99, put it this way: 'The goal of the association is to restore an intellectual terrain in which readers can exercise their capacity to think for themselves, rather than rely upon various kinds of theoretical/political machinery to do their thinking for them' (from flier for membership drive)." "I agree with Christopher Ricks," said fellow member David Bromwich, "the problem is not the presence of politics at the MLA, but the absence of nonpolitics." See William Grimes, *New York Times*, 7 December 1994: C15.

79 José Limón, for example, frames his *Mexican Ballads, Chicano Poems: History and Influence in Mexican-American Social Poetry* (Berkeley: University of California Press, 1992) with respectful debts to Harold Bloom, but also with an objection to his refusal of political responsibility. Bloom responded, deaf to Limón's acknowledged debts to him and unwilling to be upstaged. He edited a collection of critical essays, *Hispanic-American Writers* (Philadelphia: Chelsea House, 1998), perhaps only to exclude Limón, and to chastise him. In the petulant page and a half that serves as an "introduction," Bloom dismisses both the Chicano critic and his favorite subject.

80 Increasingly, students of "minority" literatures are exploring its rhetorical features, and "aesthetes" are acknowledging room for rapprochement. Robert Alter, for example, claimed dismay at "rumors and suspicions that we represent some sort of right-wing conspiracy" (*ALSC Newsletter* 3.3 [1997]: 2). And his successor as ALSC president insists that "literary scholars and critics know perfectly well that no work of art is isolated from its time and place." (Eleanor Cook, "Skills in Reading," *ALSC Newsletter* 4.4 [1998]: 1–4). I prefer to take them at their word, despite reliable counsel from David Suchoff.

81 See Carola Suárez-Orozco and Marcelo M. Suárez-Orozco, *Children of Immigration* (Cambridge: Harvard University Press, 2001).

82 See the much cited Hedley Bull, *The Anarchical Society: A Study of Order in World Politics* (London: Macmillan, 1977); Yale H. Ferguson, *Polities: Authority, Identities and Change* (Columbia: University of South Carolina Press, 1996), and "Democracy and Globalization," *Global Governance* 3 (1997): 251–67.

83   This is the recurrent theme in all the essays collected in *Identities, Borders, Orders*. See, for example, Martin O. Heisler, "Now and Then, Here and There: Migration and the Transformation of Identities, Borders, and Orders," 225–47.

2   Aesthetics Is a Joke

1   Victor Shklovsky, "Sterne's *Tristram Shandy*: Stylistic Commentary," in *Russian Formalist Criticism: Four Essays*, trans. Lee T. Lemon and Marion J. Reis (Lincoln: University of Nebraska Press, 1965), 25–57. Also, half of Shklovsky's "Art as Technique" (3–24) is given to erotic examples of defamiliarization.

2   Freud, *Wit*, 756.

3   See the *Encyclopedia of Aesthetics* (Oxford: Oxford University Press, 1998).

4   Shklovsky, "Art as Technique," 12: "And so life is reckoned as nothing. Habitualization devours works, clothes, furniture, one's wife, and the fear of war . . . And art exists that one may recover the sensation of life; it exists to make one feel things, to make the stony *stony*. The purpose of art is to impart the sensation of things as they are perceived and not as they are known. The technique of art is to make objects 'unfamiliar,' to make forms difficult, to increase the difficulty and length of perception because the process of perception is an aesthetic end in itself and must be prolonged. *Art is a way of experiencing the artfulness of an object; the object is not important.*"

5   From a worried Anglo-American tradition, Michael P. Clark conflates the two: "Literature as such simply disappears against a general background of material action or symbolic determination, and with the disappearance of literature—the possibility of productive independence, individual autonomy, effective resistance, and difference itself disappears as well." In *The Revenge of the Aesthetic: The Place of Literature in Theory Today*, ed. Michael P. Clark (Berkeley: University of California Press, 2000), 5–6.

6   Bakhtin, *The Dialogical Imagination*, 275.

7   The first two editions of "The Waste Land" were published in the *Criterion* (Eliot's own magazine) and the *Dial* in New York and did not have the conspicuous annotations "explaining the poem" that accompanied the first book edition of "The Waste Land" in 1922. These notes caused much regret to Eliot—"I have sometimes thought of getting rid of these notes; but now they can never be unstuck. They have had almost greater

popularity than the poem itself." As *The Norton Anthology* details, Eliot's notorious remark in an interview that "in 'The Waste Land' I wasn't even bothering whether I understood what I was saying" has been taken to mean that he was at odds with the explanatory notes that accompanied the text, that he viewed the poem as "just a piece of rhythmical grumbling." See *The Norton Anthology of English Poetry*, 2d ed., 491.

8 Freud, in chapter 6 of *Wit and Its Relation to the Unconscious*, 745–61.

9 When nonfamiliar material turns out to be familiar (through techniques of unification, similar sounds, manifold application, allusions, modification of familiar idioms), the mind saves the energy spent on separating them. Freud, *Wit*, 714.

10 Shklovsky, "Art as Technique," 9.

11 Freud explains that dreams are asocial, but wit is "the most social of all those psychic functions whose aim is to gain pleasure. It often requires three persons . . . At least one other person . . . No matter how concealed, the dream is still a wish, while wit is a developed play . . . Wit seeks to draw a small amount of pleasure from the free and unencumbered activities of our psychic apparatus, and later to seize this pleasure as an incidental gain." Freud, *Wit*, 760–61.

12 Paul Veyne, *Writing History*, trans. Mina Moore-Rinvolucri (Middletown, Conn.: Wesleyan University Press, 1984), 18.

13 Immanuel Kant, *The Critique of Judgement*, 1790; translated by James Creed, book 2, §54: When we laugh:

> This is because we keep for a time playing on our own mistake about an object otherwise indifferent to us, or rather on the idea we ourselves were following out, and, beating it to and fro, just as if it were a ball eluding our grasp, when all we intend to do is just to get it into our hands and hold it tight. Here our gratification is not excited by a knave or a fool getting a rebuff: for, even on its own account, the latter tale told with an air of seriousness would of itself be enough to set a whole table into roars of laughter; and the other matter would ordinarily not be worth a moment's thought.
>
> It is observable that in all such cases the joke must have something in it capable of momentarily deceiving us. Hence, when the semblance vanishes into nothing, the mind looks back in order to try it over again, and thus by a rapidly succeeding tension and relaxation it is jerked to and fro and put in oscillation. As the snapping of what was, as it were, tightening up the string takes place suddenly (not by a gradual loosening), the oscillation must bring about a mental movement and a sympathetic internal movement of the body. This continues involun-

tarily and produces fatigue, but in so doing it also affords recreation (the effects of a motion conducive to health).

14 For example, in Shklovsky's "Art as Technique," 24: "Attempts to systematize the irregularities have been made, and such attempts are part of the current problem in the theory of rhythm. It is obvious that the systematization will not work, for in reality the problem is not one of complicating the rhythm but of disordering the rhythm—a disordering which cannot be predicted. Should the disordering of rhythm become a convention, it would be ineffective as a device for the roughening of language."

15 Ted Cohen, *Jokes: Philosophical Thoughts on Joking Matters* (Chicago: University of Chicago Press, 1999), 11.

16 See Miguel Algarín's introduction to Nuyorican poetry in *Aloud: Voices from the Nuyorican Poets Café*, ed. Miguel Algarín and Bob Holman (New York: Owlet, 1994).

17 Julio Cortázar calls dictionaries the graveyards of words in *Rayuela*.

18 Celso Alvarez Cáccamo, <lxalvarz@udc.es>, founder of <code-switching @yahoogroups.com>, responded to questions about intentionality on 6 June 2003: "If the expected form is alternating languages (the 'unmarked choice,' Scotton), isn't then monolingualism a sort of code switching?" His general point is that intention, stylization, depends on surprise.

19 For a typical example, see Sheldon Pollock, "Cosmopolitan and Vernacular in History," *Public Culture* 12.3 (2001): 591–626.

20 Algarín, *Aloud*, 19.

21 For example, the work of Ilán Stavans, *Spanglish: The Making of a New American Language* (New York: HarperCollins, 2003).

22 Víctor Hernández Cruz, *Red Beans: Poems* (Minneapolis: Coffee House Press, 1991), 89.

23 Poaching amounts to resistance for Michel de Certeau in *The Practice of Everyday Life* (Berkeley: University of California Press, 1984), 174.

24 Jesuit, anthropologist, member of a bilingual commission in Paraguay, Bartolomeu Melia made this comment at the inaugural Cuzco Conference on Cultural Agency, January 2001. On Paraguay, see Clare Mar-Molinero, *The Politics of Language in the Spanish-Speaking World: From Colonisation to Globalization* (London: Routledge, 2000), 59–60: Guarani is "an exception to the rule. Whereas in all the former Spanish empire of Latin American indigenous languages and cultures have been marginalized, and in some cases have become extinct, Guarani in Paraguay has survived, and is an official language alongside Spanish . . . 90% speak some Guarani."

25   Zentella, *Growing Up Bilingual: Puerto Rican Children in New York* (Malden, Mass.: Blackwell, 1997), 3.

26   Edward Finegan, "Linguistics," in *Introduction to Scholarship in Modern Languages and Literatures*, 2d ed., ed. Joseph Gibaldi (New York: MLA, 1992), 6–8.

27   See Uriel Weinreich, *Languages in Contact: Findings and Problems* (The Hague: Mouton, 1974), 73.

28   See Milroy and Muysken, *One Speaker, Two Languages*.

29   Wittgenstein, *PI*, §§185–240.

30   I am grateful to Heidi Byrnes for the following references in a letter of 12 February 2002: "Systemic-functional linguistics departs from the syntagmatic and rule-based approach to language analysis and finds a paradigmatic approach that considers language use and choice in context to be considerably more insightful." See M. A. K. Halliday's *An Introduction to Functional Grammar*, 2d ed. (London: Edward Arnold, 1994). For consideration of classroom issues, consult Ann M. John's *Genre in the Classroom: Multiple Perspectives* (Mahwah, N.J.: Lawrence Erlbaum, 2002).

31   Kathryn A. Woolard, "Simultaneity and Bivalency as Strategies in Bilingualism," *Journal of Linguistic Anthropology* 8.1 (1998): 3. For a variety of perspectives, see *Code-Switching in Conversation: Language, Interaction, and Identity*, ed. Peter Auer (New York: Routledge, 1998), especially Auer's introduction, "Bilingual Conversation Revisited," 1–24.

32   Peter Auer, *Bilingual Conversation* (Philadelphia: John Benjamins, 1984), 105.

33   Robert Alan Dahl, *Dilemmas of Pluralist Democracy: Autonomy vs. Control* (New Haven: Yale University Press, 1982), 147. See all of chapter 7, "Changing Civic Orientations," 138–64.

34   Brian Barry, *Culture and Equality*, 104: "It goes without saying that speaking Spanish and maintaining Spanish culture . . . should not be a bar in itself to being enabled to enjoy rights and opportunities such as those listed by Young. The intention is, however, to suggest that one should be able to enjoy all these benefits without also having to be fluent in English. Whereas the first demand is completely unexceptionable, satisfying the second cannot reasonably be held to be a requirement of egalitarian liberal principles."

35   Woolard, "Changing Forms of Codeswitching in Catalan Comedy," *Catalan Review* 9.2 (1995): 223–52. For background on Spain's policies and language history, see Mar-Molinero, *The Politics of Language in the Spanish-Speaking World*.

36   See Robert Venuti, *The Scandals of Translation: Toward an Ethics of Difference* (New York: Routledge, 1998); see also Julio Marzán's *The Span-*

ish American Roots of William Carlos Williams, to read Williams with a depth that monolingual readings have missed.

37 Evangelina Vigil-Piñón, "Por la Calle Zarzamora," *Thirty an' Seen a Lot* (Houston: Arte Público, 1982), 20.

38 Fernández, "Boniato," *Raining Backwards*, 86.

39 See *The Essential Peirce: Selected Philosophical Writings*, ed. Nathan Houser and Christian J. W. Kloesel (Bloomington: Indiana University Press, 1998), 1:186–97; 2:226–41.

40 Limon, *Stand-Up Comedy in Theory*, 29–30: "I find myself pleased to register that 'just nice' replaces 'just right' in the evocation of 'Goldilocks.' 'Just nice' has the feel of off-English, the language of first-generation immigrants telling fables to their grandchildren."

41 Héctor Pérez offered this excellent reading at the School of Criticism and Theory (SCT) in 2002: "The local authority figures in *Raining Backwards* are the police captain James Carter, easily understood to refer to the former president who facilitated Cuban refugee migration to the U.S. The funnier joke is linguistic and has to do with Lieutenant Hodell, a perhaps well meaning yet bumbling sidekick to Carter. 'Hodell' sounds a lot like 'joder' meaning 'to fuck or screw' (the Mexican Spanish equivalent would be 'chingar'). The Caribbean pronunciation of the final 'r' typically glides into an 'l' sound. The references to a police lackey sticking his nose in people's business could easily be construed as someone who is there to 'joder' above all else. (Compare also the comic Tres Patines.)"

42 See Jan Ziolkowski, "Cultural Diglossia and the Nature of Medieval Latin Literature," *The Ballad and Oral Literature*, Harvard English Studies (Cambridge: Harvard University Press, 1991).

43 Zentella, "José Can You See: Latina Responses to Racist Discourse," in *Bilingual Games*, ed. Doris Sommer (New York: Palgrave, 2003).

44 Portes and Hau underline the economic and social benefits of competent bilingualism in the Children of Immigrants Longitudinal Study (CILS), Center for Migration and Development, Princeton University, quoted in their article. But the benefits of metaconsciousness attend to lower levels of expertise.

45 "On Elena Poniatowska," *Women Writers of Latin America: Intimate Histories, Interviews with Magdalena García Pinto*, trans. Trudy Balch and Magdalena García Pinto (Austin: University of Texas Press, 1991), 163. See also Beth E. Jörgensen, *The Writing of Elena Poniatowska* (Austin: University of Texas Press, 1994), 53. Sylvia Molloy's essay apears in *Bilingual Games*, ed. Doris Sommer (Palgrave, 2003).

46 To be fair to Herder's defense of particularity, against Enlightened trium-

phalism, see Juan Flores's subtle essay "Reclaiming Left Baggage: Some Early Sources for Minority Studies," forthcoming in *Cultural Critique*.

47 Herder, *Against Pure Reason*, 43: "The age that wanders toward the desires and hopes of foreign lands is already an age of disease, flatulence, unhealthy opulence, approaching death!"

48 I thank Raquel Araújo of Mérida for this translation at the Performance and Politics Conference, Monterrey, June 2001.

49 See Claudio Véliz on Spanglish and creativity in *The New World of the Gothic Fox: Culture and Economy in English and Spanish America* (Berkeley: University of California Press, 1994).

50 Derrida, *Monolingualism of the Other, or, The Prosthesis of Origin*, trans. Patrick Mensah (Stanford: Stanford University Press, 1998), 16.

51 Dominick La Capra's objections begin with the extreme case of Giorgio Agamben, specifically to his reading of Primo Levi, in Giorgio Agamben, *Remnants of Auschwitz: The Witness and the Archive*, trans. Daniel Heller-Roazen (New York: Zone Books, 1999).

52 Derrida, *Monolingualism of the Other*. See, among many examples, the slide from particular to universal on pp. 16–17. "I do not doubt either that such 'exclusions' come to leave their mark upon this belonging or non-belonging of language, this affiliation *to* language, this assignation to what is peacefully called a language. But who exactly posseses it? . . . What of this being-at-home in language toward which we never cease returning?"

53 Derrida, *Monolingualism of the Other*, 26, 60.

54 Ibid., 3–4.

55 Abdelkebir Khatibi, *Love in Two Languages*, trans. Richard Howard (Minneapolis: University of Minnesota Press, 1990), 4.

56 Ibid., 35.

57 Derrida, *Monolingualism of the Other*, 48, 54.

58 Ibid., 67.

59 Along with Renzo Titone, see Christine H. Rossell and Keith Baker, *Bilingual Educational Reform in Massachusetts: The Emperor Has No Clothes* (Boston: Pioneer Institute, 1996), especially chapter 1, "The Educational Effectiveness of Bilingual Education"; and Patrick Lee, "Cognitive Development in Bilingual Children: A Case for Bilingual Instruction in Early Childhood," *Bilingual Research Journal* 20.3–4 (1996): 499–522.

60 Brian Barry, *Culture and Equality*, 107: "No doubt every language has its own peculiar excellences, but any language will do as the medium of communication in a society as long as everybody speaks it. This is

one case involving cultural attributes in which 'This is how we do things here'—the appeal to local convention—is a self-sufficient response to pleas for the public recognition of diversity."

61 Sander L. Gilman, *Jewish Self-Hatred: Anti-Semitism and the Hidden Language of the Jews* (Baltimore: Johns Hopkins University Press, 1986).

62 See Slavoj Žižek's *Enjoy Your Symptom!: Jacques Lacan in Hollywood and Out* (New York: Routledge, 2001).

63 See Brian Barry, whose first section of *Culture and Equality* is called "Losing Our Way." "The spectre that now haunts Europe is one of strident nationalism, ethnic self-assertion and the exaltation of what divides people at the expense of that unites them . . . The views in question are known as the politics of difference, the politics of recognition or, most popularly, multiculturalism" (5). Later on, the relativists get scolded in chapter 4, 131–46.

64 See, for example, the respectable Bhikhu C. Parekh, *Rethinking Multiculturalism: Cultural Diversity and Political Theory* (Cambridge: Harvard University Press, 2000), 13: "Multiculturalism is about the proper terms of relationship between different cultural communities. The norms governing their respective claims, including the principles of justice, cannot be derived from one culture alone but through an open and equal dialogue between them."

65 See Emory Elliot, "Introduction," *Aesthetics in a Multicultural Age*, ed. Emory Elliot, Louis Freitas Caton, and Jeffrey Rhyne (Oxford: Oxford University Press, 2002): "The only way to approach this challenge with intellectual honesty and scholarly commitment is the same way that scholars of European Medieval and Renaissance literature have traditionally approached their subjects. By educating ourselves more fully and energetically in the languages and cultures of those parts of the world whose aesthetic contributions are now understood to be part of the culture of the United States, we will be much more competent to demonstrate to our students why texts by authors who are of African, Asian and Hispanic descent are as rich and aesthetically pleasing as they are. Scholarly competence in the rich and diverse literature of the United States requires larger, not downsized, literature programs."

66 Elaine Scarry's basic observation in *On Beauty and Being Just* (Princeton: Princeton University Press, 1999).

67 Gilles Deleuze and Félix Guattari, *A Thousand Plateaus: Capitalism and Schizophrenia*, trans. Brian Massumi (Minneapolis: University of Minnesota Press, 1987). Chapter 3 has the title "10,000 B.C.: The Geology of Morals (Who Does the Earth Think It Is?)," below which is a picture of a lobster with the caption: "Double Articulation" (39). On p. 40: "God is

a Lobster, or a double pincer, a double bind. Not only do strata come at least in pairs, but in a different way each stratum is double. Each stratum exhibits phenomena constitutive of a double articulation."

68   Marjorie Garber, "Prefiguring a Black Cultural Formation: The New Conditions of Black Cultural Formation," in *Between Law and Culture: Relocating Legal Studies*, ed. David Theo Goldberg, Michael C. Musheno, and Lisa C. Bower (Minneapolis: University of Minnesota Press, 2001), 50–73.

69   See Doris Sommer, *Proceed with Caution, When Engaged by Minority Writing in the Americas* (Cambridge: Harvard University Press, 1999).

70   Pierre Bourdieu's shorthand for the aesthetic effect is "Loser takes all," quoted in John Guillory, *Culture Capital: The Problem of Literary Canon Formation* (Chicago: University of Chicago Press, 1993), 21. This preference for failure as akin to aesthetic distance brings to mind titles of Latin American books, such as Juan Sasturian's *Manual de perdedores* and others interpreted by Ana Maria Amar Sanchez in *Juegos de seduccion y traicion: Literatura y cultura de masas* (Argentina: Beatriz Viterbo, 2000). Freud wonders about this too, repeatedly, when he considers the self-deprecating nature of Jewish humor.

71   Lyotard, *The Differend*, 137: section 185 is a reference to Wittgenstein, "Lectures on Ethics," *Philosophical Review* 74.1: 5.

72   Bhikhu Parekh is probably a back-door universalist, given his campaign for a "coherent conception of human beings, we need to subject each to a rigorous critique and break through their frozen polarity (between 'naturalists' and 'culturalists')" (Parekh, *Rethinking Multiculturalism*, 11).

73   Elaine Scarry, *On Beauty and Being Just*. See my chapter 4, "The Common Sense Sublime."

74   Benjamin, "Symbol and Allegory," *Origin of German Tragic Drama*, trans. John Osborne (New York: Verso, 1998).

75   Clark, *The Revenge of the Aesthetic*, 10, simplifies the point by reducing Benjamin's opposition to merely critique: "he described the strategic imposition of conventional formal attributes such as coherence and unity onto the world as a defining characteristic of fascist politics."

76   Again, Clark misses the charm of colliding systems as a goad to literary creativity. "Contradictions among the various symbolic systems operating at any moment allow for considerable variety in the dominant social forms, but those contradictions inevitably follow the lines of force characteristic of the system as a whole, rather than anything specific to the literary text" (5).

77   Freud, *Wit and Its Relation to the Unconscious*, 694–95.

78 Michael Ignatieff, "Human Rights as Idolatry," in *Human Rights as Politics and Idolatry*, ed. Amy Gutmann (Princeton: Princeton University Press, 2001), 74.

79 W. V. Quine, "Ontological Relativity," *Ontological Relativity and Other Essays* (New York: Columbia University Press, 1969), 26–68.

80 See Homi Bhabha, *The Location of Culture* (New York: Routledge, 1994); and Néstor García Canclini, *Hybrid Cultures: Strategies for Entering and Leaving Modernity* (Minneapolis: University of Minnesota Press, 1995), for the best formulations of hybridity as a dynamic rather than as a result.

81 Gilman, *Jewish Self-Hatred.*

82 Ernesto Laclau, *Emancipation(s)* (New York: Verso, 1996).

83 See David Harvey, chapter 8, "The Spaces of Utopia," in his book *Spaces of Hope* (Berkeley: University of California Press, 2000), 133–81. I am grateful to Jay Winter for defending this kind of utopian thinking.

84 Walter Benjamin, "Allegory and Symbol," *Origin of German Tragic Drama*. See also Doris Sommer, "Allegory and Dialectics: A Match Made in Romance," *Boundary 2* 18/1 (1991): 60–82.

85 Harvey, *Spaces of Hope*, 119–20.

86 Benedict Anderson, *Imagined Communities: Reflections on the Origins and Spread of Nationalism*, rev. and extended ed. (New York: Verso, 1991).

87 Literature includes lessons in writing as well as reading, Peter Elbow is wise to remind us, even if teachers themselves are not always necessary. See "The War Between Reading and Writing—and How to End It," *Everyone Can Write*, 281–99.

88 Responsibility is the keyword for goals now, not happiness. See the paper by Nicholas Emler and Roy Baumeister, inter alia, in review by Lauren Slater, "The Trouble with Self-Esteem," *New York Times Magazine*, 3 February 2002: 44–47. "Last year alone there were three withering studies of self-esteem released in the United States, all of which had the same central message: people with high self-esteem pose a greater threat to those around them than people with low self-esteem and feeling bad about yourself is not the cause of our country's biggest, most expensive social problems." Nevertheless, "'Research like that is seriously flawed,' says Stephen Keane, a therapist who practices in Newburyport, Mass. 'First, it's defining self-esteem according to very conventional and problematic masculine ideas. Second, it's clear to me that many violent men, in particular, have this inner shame; they find out early in life they're not going to measure up, and they compensate for it with fists.'"

89 Roland Barthes, *The Pleasure of the Text*, trans. Richard Miller (New York: Hill and Wang, 1975).

90 Friedrich von Schiller, *Naïve and Sentimental Poetry; and, On the Sublime: Two Essays*, trans. Julius A. Elias (New York: Frederick Ungar, 1966), 98.

91 Barbara Johnson, "Using People," in *The Turn to Ethics*, ed. Marjorie Garber, Beatrice Hanssen, Rebecca L. Walkowitz. Johnson's reference to Winnicott is to his concept of good enough mothering. See Winnicott's *Mother and Child: A Primer of First Relationships* (New York: Basic Books, 1957).

92 See my note 65.

93 See John M. Ellis, *Literature Lost: Social Agendas and the Corruption of the Humanities* (New Haven: Yale University Press, 1997); and Alan Bloom, *The Closing of the American Mind: How Higher Education Has Failed Democracy and Impoverished the Souls of Today's Students* (New York: Simon and Schuster, 1987); also Dinesh D'Souza, *Illiberal Education: The Politics of Race and Sex on Campus* (New York: Macmillan, 1991).

94 John Limon, *Stand-Up Comedy in Theory*, 12.

95 "Classical Concepts," *Encyclopedia of Aesthetics*, 248.

96 In Clark, *The Revenge of the Aesthetic*, distinguished essayists take up Murray Krieger's work to save aesthetics from politics.

97 John Brenkman, "Extreme Criticism," in *What's Left of Theory?: New Work on the Politics of Literary Theory*, ed. Judith Butler, John Guillory, and Kendall Thomas (New York: Routledge, 2000), 118.

98 See Stephen David Ross, "Beauty, a Conceptual Historical Overview," *Encyclopedia of Aesthetics*, 238–44; and "Classical Concepts," 244–50. Plato's "very willingness to think theoretically about beauty signals the distance that he will keep between it and art," 244. "The New Critics' model of literary form had been directly derived from what Coleridge had described as the organic symbol, and the autotelic model of the poem implied—and at times explicitly claimed—a unique status for literary language that was the aesthetic embodiment of the spiritual transcendence and ontic presence associated with the metaphysics of English Romanticism. To challenge the formal coherence of the poem and its discursive autonomy was therefore to challenge the philosophical foundation of Western humanism as it had been derived from the romantic preoccupation with the symbol and from a Kantian faith in the constitutive power of symbolic categories in general" (Ross, 2).

99 Scarry, *On Beauty and Being Just*. Beauty, she affirms, is inherent and

"clearly discernible" in the object. But then, she ushers in a dangerous supplement of interpretation, which can make "clearly discernible" beauty even more "clearly discernible" (5). Clearly, discernibility has a range. Nevertheless, Scarry doesn't pursue the logic of more or less visibility. For reasons of ethical outcomes, she prefers to argue that our responses to beauty are equal. Claiming the aesthetic equality of different objects, and valuing symmetry (Augustine) as both the essence of beautiful objects and as the lateral link among them, she levels differences. She worries, therefore, about the eighteenth-century excision of the sublime from the beautiful, because the break bleeds beauty of its former dignity (82–83).

100   Ana Celia Zentella, "José Can You See," in *Bilingual Games*, ed. Doris Sommer (New York: Palgrave, 2003).

101   Watkins, *On the Real Side*, 17–18.

102   Emory Elliot, quoting Eagleton: *Aesthetics in a Multicultural Age*, ed. Emory Elliott, Louis Freitas Caton, and Jeffrey Rhyne (Oxford: Oxford University Press, 2002).

103   See Ezra Pound, *The Literary Essays of Ezra Pound*, ed. Thomas Stearns Eliot (New York: New Directions, 1972).

104   Michael J. Dash, in *The Other America: Caribbean Literature in a New World Context* (Charlottesville: University Press of Virginia, 1998), reminds me that the surrealists, who sought strangeness, traveled the Caribbean. In the Dominican Republic, Andre Breton inspired "La poesía sorprendida," a local movement that managed to be political, under the Trujillo regime, by unhinging language from habitual meaning.

105   Gilman, *Jewish Self-Hatred*, 262.

106   "The ideal, as we think of it, is unshakable. You can never get outside it; you must always turn back. There is no outside; outside you cannot breathe.—Where does this idea come from? It is like a pair of glasses on our nose through which we see whatever we look at. It never occurs to us to take them off." Wittgenstein, *PI*, §103.

107   In Lacan, *Ecrits* (Paris: Editions du Seuil, 1966), 170.

108   The innovation, Lacan points out, is not about the "arbitrariness of the sign, as it has been elaborated since the earliest reflections of the ancients"; it is about "the illusion that the signifier answers to the function of representing the signified" (*Ecrits*, 149). To the disappointment of logical positivists, the signifier has a way of slipping into the signified. "We are forced, then, to accept the notion of an incessant sliding of the signified under the signifier—which Ferdinand de Saussure illustrates with

an image resembling the wavy lines of the upper and lower waters . . . a
double flux marked by fine streaks of rain" (154). Isn't this what happens
when "glance" slides into "Glanz"?

109   Limon, *Stand-Up Comedy in Theory*, 73.

3 Irritate the State

1   "Jihad" literally means "striving (in the path of God)," Bernard Lewis
writes in "Jihad vs. Crusade," *Wall Street Journal*, 27 September 2001:
A18. He adds that some modern Muslims interpret it as a spiritual and
moral duty, though most retain the military meaning too. What makes
Al Qaeda extremist beyond sanctions of Islamic law is the violation of
prohibitions against suicide and wanton slaughter. Stephen Zunes describes the U.S. pattern of promoting extremism. See "U.S. Policy toward
Political Islam," *Foreign Policy in Focus* 6.24 (2001): 1: "Washington has
used the threat of Islamic fundamentalism as a justification for keeping
a high military, economic, and political profile in the Middle East. Yet
it has often supported Muslim hard-liners when they were perceived to
enhance U.S. interests, as they did in Afghanistan, Pakistan, and Saudi
Arabia."

2   Just ten days after the attack against an apparently innocent country,
this obituary of a typical U.S. ally appeared with a photo reminiscent of
a Botero portrait: Larry Rohter, "Marcos Pérez Jiménez, 87, Venezuela
Ruler," *New York Times*, 22 September 2001: A12. "In the decade when
he dominated Venezuela, one of the world's largest producers of oil, General Pérez Jiménez was feared and hated inside his country and mocked
elsewhere as the prototype of the Latin American military despot. His
virulent anti-Communism and his tolerant attitude toward foreign oil
companies, however, gained him the backing of the United States. In
1954, nearly four years before his fall from power in a coup and uprising,
it even awarded him the Legion of Merit."

3   See the defensive response by the American Embassy in Tel Aviv, on
6 June 2003, "Wolfowitz Reasserts Iraq War Was Not about Oil," as an
indicator of the rash of accusations. Deputy Secretary of Defense Paul
Wolfowitz had commented at the Asian security summit in Singapore,
30 May 2003, that "we had virtually no economic options with Iraq because the country floats on a sea of oil." Defense Department transcript,
<http://www.defenselink.mil/transcripts/2003/tr20030531-depsecdef
0246.html>, updated 4 June 2003.

4   Bernard Lewis admits that President Bush's use of the word "was un-

fortunate, but excusable." In the West, crusade has "long since lost its original meaning of 'a war for the cross'; it "almost always means simply a vigorous campaign for a good cause . . . rarely, if ever, religious." But in the Middle East, the word refers to medieval precursors of European imperialism, a misleading association for Lewis, since the Crusades were a belated and rather ineffectual response to the jihad. See his "Jihad vs. Crusade," A18.

Nevertheless, some Western leaders are not shy or sorry to revive the original intent of crusade. For example, on 26 September 2001, Italian prime minister Silvio Berlusconi urged Europe to "reconstitute itself on the basis of its Christian roots," during a briefing in Berlin, where he met with Russian president Vladimir V. Putin and German chancellor Gerhard Schroeder to discuss international cooperation against terrorism. "We should be confident of the superiority of our civilization" against that of the Islamic world." Quoted by Steven Erlanger, "Italy's Premier Calls Western Civilization Superior to Islamic World," *New York Times*, 27 September 2001: A8.

5   Zunes begins his article "U.S. Policy Toward Political Islam" with a reminder that "ugly stereotypes of Muslims" don't take into account "the existence of moderate Islamic segments and secular movements that are at least as influential as radicals in the political life of Islamic countries," 1.

6   Theodor W. Adorno, *Negative Dialektik* (Frankfurt, A.M.: Surkamp, 1966), 172. The paradox of striving for complete understanding is that it misunderstands the particularity of its object. To understand is to establish identity; and this requires conceptualization that generalizes away otherness. Identifying, therefore, turns out to be a trap at two levels: empathic identification violates the other person; and ontological identification eliminates particularity for the sake of unity. The greedy subject, one who cannot abide lacking what belongs to the other, is Freud's formulation. See Diana Fuss, *Identity Papers* (New York: Routledge, 1996).

7   Israeli author David Grossman reckons the loss in "Terror's Long Shadow," *Guardian*, 20 September 2001: "Terror also sharpens one's awareness that a democratic, tranquil way of life requires a great deal of goodwill, the truly good will of a country's citizens. That is the amazing secret of democratic rule, and it is also its Achilles heel. All of us are, when it comes down to it, each other's hostages. Terrorists act on this potential, and so unstring the entire fabric of life."

8   Hua Hsu's review, "Orienting the East," *Village Voice*, 22 April 2003.

9   Robert Dahl's definition of polyarchy, a government of people so diverse they cannot know their neighbor's interests, and therefore depend on institutions. See "Changing Civic Orientations," in his *Dilemmas of Pluralist Democracy: Autonomy vs. Control* (New Haven: Yale University Press, 1982), 138–64. "To love a member of one's family or a friend is not at all like 'loving' abstract 'others' whom one does not know, never expects to know, and may not even want to know" (147).

10 See my *Proceed with Caution, When Engaged by Minority Writing in the Americas.*

11 See Niklas Luhmann, *Social Systems*, trans. John Bednarz Jr., with Dirk Baecker (Stanford: Stanford University Press, 1995); and also *Observations on Modernity*, trans. William Whobrey (Stanford: Stanford University Press, 1998). Irritation will be processed as information and keep what he calls autopoetic systems dynamic. Too much noise overwhelms systems.

12 Eleanor Roosevelt settled the debate between a Chinese Confucian and a Lebanese Thomist by suggesting they agree to disagree during the 1947 drafting of the Declaration of Human Rights. See Ignatieff, "Human Rights as Idolatry," 75–76. See also John Rawls, *The Law of Peoples*, and Charles Taylor, "A World Consensus on Human Rights?," *The Dissent* (summer 1996): 15–21, and "Two Theories of Modernity," *Public Culture* 11.1 (1999): 153–74.

13 See Martha Minow, *Making All the Difference: Inclusion, Exclusion, and American Law* (Ithaca: Cornell University Press, 1990). An argument for no-fault difference as the universal structure of participation.

14 Barry, *Culture and Equality*, 6. The reference is to Robert Hughes, but the attribution is evidently to Barry's own style in this book.

15 Glazer, *We Are All Multiculturalists Now.*

16 Barry, *Culture and Equality*, 132.

17 Taylor, "The Politics of Recognition," in *Multiculturalism*, 30–31. "Herder put forward the idea that each of us has an original way of being human . . . that is my way . . . Just like individuals, a *Volk* should be true to itself, that is, its own culture."

18 Ibid., 30.

19 For example: Aimé Césaire, *A Tempest*, trans. Richard Miller (New York: Ubu Repertory Theater Publications, 1992); Roberto Fernandez Retamar, *Caliban and Other*, trans. Edward Baker (Minneapolis: University of Minnesota Press, 1989); E. K Brathwaite, "Letter Sycora X," *Middle Passages*; *Daughters of Caliban: Caribbean Women in the Twentieth Century*, ed. Consuelo López Springfield (Bloomington: Indiana Uni-

versity Press, 1997); Paget Henry, *Caliban's Reason: Introducing Afro-Caribbean* (New York: Routledge, 2000).

20 Authenticity is a name for egotism in a society that values comfort over responsibility, according to G. Lipovetsky, *Le crépuscule du devoir: L'éthique indolore des nouveaux temps démocratiques* (Paris: Gallimard, 1992), 13–14. In the name of unmasking the repressive institutions of church, union, family, schools, "authenticity" has a devastating effect on democracy. See Xavier Rubert de Ventós, *Etica sin atributos* (Barcelona: Anagrama, 1996), 179. Both are quoted in Jesús Martín Barbero, "Desencantos de la socialidad y reencantamientos de la identidad," a paper delivered at the Cultural Agency: Rhetorics of Identity, Representation, and Participation Conference, New York University, 3 October 2000, 4.

21 Michael Walzer overrides the rights of subnational groups in his defense of (Herderian) national autonomy. See *Spheres of Justice: A Defense of Pluralism and Equality* (New York: Basic Books, 1983). John Rawls adapts this respect for sovereignty in *The Law of Peoples*.

22 Recent work in political economy revives its dependence on sentiment. See Emma Rothschild, *Economic Sentiments: Adam Smith, Condorcet, and the Enlightenment* (Cambridge: Harvard University Press, 2001).

23 Simone Chambers and Will Kymlicka, *Alternative Conceptions of Civil Society* (Princeton: Princeton University Press, 2002), 20.

24 Charles L. Griswold, Jr., *Adam Smith and the Virtues of Enlightenment* (New York: Cambridge University Press, 1999), 110. In fact, Smith proposes a dialectic between the "longing for symmetry" and the "fear of measurelessness." See also Kant, *Anthropology from a Pragmatic Point of View*, ed. Hans H. Rudnick, trans. Victor Lyle Dowdell (Carbondale: Southern Illinois University Press, 1996).

25 John H. Zammito, *The Genesis of Kant's* Critique of Judgement (Chicago: University of Chicago Press, 1992), also his *Kant, Herder, and the Birth of Anthropology* (Chicago: University of Chicago Press, 2002).

26 Taylor, "The Politics of Recognition," in *Multiculturalism*, 33.

27 Bakhtin, *Problems of Dostoevsky's Poetics*, trans. R. W. Rotsel (Ann Arbor, Mich.: Ardis, 1973), 6, 4. Bakhtin's emphasis.

28 Homi K. Bhabha, for example, comments on Taylor's reluctance to budge from the position of Ideal Observer in a reading that parallels my own. See his "Culture's in Between," Bennett, *Multicultural States*, 29–36.

29 Brian Barry, *Culture and Equality*, 266: We should "'accord equal respect to all actually evolved cultures.'"

30 Susan Moller Okin, *Is Multiculturalism Bad for Women?* (Princeton: Princeton University Press, 1999).

31   This is a perhaps unfair way to summarize Will Kymlicka's position, be-
     cause cultural rights should not trump liberal principles for him.

32   See Barry, *Culture and Equality*, 141.

33   Jürgen Habermas, *Between Facts and Norms: Contributions to a Dis-
     course Theory of Law and Democracy*, trans. William Rehg (Cambridge:
     MIT Press, 1996), 156. See also Thomas McCarthy's defense, "Alter/Native
     Modernities—On Reconciling Cosmopolitan Unity and National Diver-
     sity," *Public Culture: Bulletin of the Project for Transnational Cultural
     Studies* 11.1 (1999): 175–208.

34   Michael Ignatieff, "Human Rights as Idolatry," *Human Rights as Politics
     and Idolatry*, 57.

35   John Trumpbour and Elaine Bernard, "Unions and Latinos: Mutual
     Transformation," in *Latinos: Remaking America*, ed. Marcelo M. Suarez-
     Orozco and Mariela M. Paez (Berkeley: University of California Press,
     2002), 126–45.

36   Hannah Arendt, *Origins of Totalitarianism*, rev. ed. (New York: Har-
     court Brace Jovanovich, 1973). The nation overtook the state in Germany
     (274). "Linguistic distinctiveness" is good, she argues, because "forceful
     assimilation" can cause a decline in the strength of the nation state (273).

37   Jürgen Habermas, "Struggles for Recognition in the Democratic Con-
     stitutional State," in *Multiculturalism*, 129: "Multiculturalism does not
     require special justification or an alternative principle. For from a nor-
     mative point of view, the integrity of the individual legal person cannot
     be guaranteed without protecting the intersubjectively shared experi-
     ences and life contexts in which the person has been socialized and has
     formed his or her identity . . . Hence the individual remains the bearer
     of 'rights to cultural membership,' in Will Kymlicka's phrase. But as the
     dialectic of legal and actual equality plays itself out, this gives rise to ex-
     tensive guarantees of status, rights to self-administration, infrastructural
     benefits, subsidies, and so on." "A democratic constitutional state that is
     serious about uncoupling these two levels of integration can require of
     immigrants only the political socialization" (139). See also Drucilla Cor-
     nell and William W. Bratton, "Deadweight Costs and Intrinsic Wrongs
     of Nativism: Economics, Freedom, and Legal Suppression of Spanish,"
     Cornell Law Review 84.3 (1999): 595–695.

38   Bilingualism promotes Habermas's recommendations for increased com-
     municative competence, writes Harold Chorney in "The Economic
     Benefits of Linguistic Duality and Bilingualism," 181. "Quite literally the
     capacity to participate in one's society is considerably enhanced. As cen-
     tral Europeans often say 'the more languages you speak the more times
     you are a human being.' "

39 Anne Phillips, "Does Feminism Need a Conception of Civil Society?" in Chambers and Kymlicka, *Alternative Conceptions of Civil Society*, 78.

40 Okin, *Is Multiculturalism Bad for Women?* Okin asserts that women suffer when group rights have priority over individual rights. Many respondents (whose essays are included in the book) differ, including Bonnie Honig, Homi Bhabha, Azizah Y. al-Hibri, and Will Kymlicka.

41 *The Forward*, a Jewish weekly, regularly runs articles about the expanding role of women in orthodox practices. See, for example, Ami Eden, "Gender Taboos Fall at New Orthodox Prayer Services," *The Forward*, September 2002.

42 See Leila Ahmed, *Women and Gender in Islam: Historical Roots of a Modern Debate* (New Haven: Yale University Press, 1992).

43 When it is self-conscious, traditionalism "is itself a thoroughly modern movement of renewal." See Habermas, "Struggles for Recognition in the Democratic Constitutional State," in *Multiculturalism*, 132.

44 Limon, *Stand-Up Comedy in Theory*, 22.

45 Will Kymlicka considers the case of two Hutterites, expelled for apostasy. But it is not clear if his objection is to the expulsion or to the failure to compensate the long-term contributors to the collective property. See *Multicultural Citizenship: A Liberal Theory of Minority Rights* (New York: Clarendon Press, 1995), 161.

46 Cass R. Sunstein, "Should Sex Equality Law Apply to Religious Institutions?," in Susan Moller Okin, *Is Multiculturalism Bad for Women?*, 85–94.

47 See Yúdice's *The Expediency of Culture* (Durham: Duke University Press, 2003).

48 Michael Warner, *The Trouble With Normal: Sex, Politics, and the Ethics of Queer Life* (Cambridge: Harvard University Press, 2000).

49 See Santiago's protagonist in *Stella Manhattan*, trans. George Yúdice (Durham: Duke University Press, 1994).

50 See also Michael Sandel, Chandran Kukathas, and Bhikhu Parekh in J. A. Laponce, *Languages and Their Territories* (Toronto: University of Toronto Press, 1987), who develops the linguistic argument. I thank Silvana Seabra for this reading.

51 Bonnie Honig, *Democracy and the Foreigner* (Princeton: Princeton University Press, 2001), 72.

52 Ibid., chapter 5.

53 Chava Alberstein, title and only English song from *Foreign Letters* (Rounder Records, Cambridge, Mass. 11661 195–2 C2001), song #12 (lyrics on p. 14 of CD booklet).

54 Honig, *Democracy and the Foreigner*, 39: "Democracy is always about living with strangers under a law that is therefore alien (because it is the mongrel product of political action—often gone awry—taken with and among strangers). Even at its very best, or especially so, democracy is about being mobilized into action periodically with and on behalf of people who are surely opaque to us and often unknown to us."

55 Ibid., 106.

56 See also David Jacobson, "The Global Political Culture," in *Identities, Borders, Orders: Rethinking International Relations Theory*, 161–79. "Social solidarity can take many forms—it does not have to be the *Volksgemeinschaft* or other territorially defined forms of nationality, or the state" (162). "We are seeing the disaggregation of the nation-state. The political, communal, and territorial components of the nation-state, once thought so intertwined as to be unremarkable, are being unbundled" (164).

57 Honig, *Democracy and the Foreigner*, 108.

58 Seyla Benhabib, *Claims of Culture: Equality and Diversity in the Global Era* (Princeton: Princeton University Press, 2002).

59 Honig, *Democracy and the Foreigner*, 67.

60 Crawford, "Editor's Introduction," *Language Loyalties*, 3–4. See also Gallegos, *English: Our Official Language?*, 14. In 1988, "a memo written by John Tanton surfaces during the campaign to have English declared the official language of Arizona. The memo speculates on the negative effects of continued Hispanic immigration, including 'the tradition of the *mordida*' (bribe), 'low educability,' and high birth rates. Further investigations reveal funding for U.S. English comes from questionable sources. Linda Chavez and John Tanton resign from U.S. English and Walter Cronkite steps down from its Board of Directors." And, further, see Schmid, *The Politics of Language*, especially the reviews of recent color-coded language politics and practices. "As of 2000, twenty-five states and forty cities had passed some form of law declaring English the official language . . . as English is indisputably the primary language of the United States, declaring English the official language appears harmless. However benign the declaration of an 'official' language seems, such laws may have severe discriminatory repercussions" (57).

61 *Hernández v. New York* (1991) Supreme Court case no. 89–7645; argued 25 February 1991, decided 28 May 1991. Crawford, *Language Loyalties*, 302.

62 Crawford, *Language Loyalties*, 301. (*U.S. v. Perez*, case 658 F2nd 654 [9th circuit] 1981.)

63 Paul Zielbauer, "UConn Officials Consider Dismissing Physics Professor," *New York Times*, 12 January 2002: A15.

64 Mari Matsuda, "Voices of America: Accent, Antidiscrimination Law, and a Jurisprudence for the Last Reconstruction," *Yale Law Journal* 100.5 (March 1991): 1329–407.

65 For a good summary, see Susan Miner, "Legal Implications of the Official English Declaration," in *Language and Politics in the United States and Canada: Myths and Realities*, ed. Thomas Ricento and Barbara Burnaby (Mahwah, N.J.: Lawrence Erlbaum, 1998), 171–84. Here, however, the same case of Filipino Manuel Fragante that Matsuda investigates is reported without criticism (176). I am indebted to Carrie Sheffield for this source.

66 Mignolo, *The Darker Side of the Renaissance*.

67 John Rawls, *The Law of Peoples*, and *Political Liberalism* (New York: Columbia University Press, 1993).

68 McCarthy's summary in "Alter/Native Modernities," *Public Culture*, 195.

69 William Connolly thinks this distinction too artificial and impractical. See "Refashioning the Secular," in *What's Left of Theory?*, where the case for "pluralizing" participation in the public sphere includes admitting religious voices.

70 McCarthy, "Alter/Native Modernities," *Public Culture*, 205.

71 Taylor, "A World Consensus," 20.

72 See *Federalist* 51; also Jack N. Rakove, "Once More into the Breach: Reflections on Jefferson, Madison, and the Religion Problem," in *Making Good Citizens: Education and Civil Society*, ed. Diane Ravitch and Joseph P. Viteritti (New Haven: Yale University Press, 2001), 253:

> Here it was Madison I think, who better grasped the unique implications and consequences that the commitment to disestablishment would have for the constitution of American civil society. In part, this was because he predicated his general solution to the overarching problem of "curing the mischief of faction" on the empirical evidence that the existing multiplicity of sects had already promoted the general security of religious liberty that he now hoped to advance in an even more principled and consistent way. As the classic formulation of *Federalist* 51 asserts: "In a free government, the security for civil rights must be the same as that for religious rights. It consists in the one case in the multiplicity of interests, and in the other, in the multiplicity of sects."

73 Today, though, Brian Barry is sure that anarchism would prevail. See his *Culture and Equality*, 133.

74 See, for example, John Rawls, "The Idea of Public Reason Revisited," *The Law of Peoples*, 166. n.75: "While most of the American colonies had known establishments of some kind (Congregationalist in New England, Episcopalian in the South), the United States, *thanks to the plurality of its religious sects* and the First Amendment which they endorsed, never did. A persecuting zeal has been the great curse of the Christian religion" (my emphasis).

75 Bennett, introduction, *Multicultural States*, 7.

76 Glazer, *We Are All Multiculturalists*, 159: "Let us agree that ethnic and racial affiliation should be as voluntary as religious affiliation, and of as little concern to the state and public authority."

77 In Grosjean, *Life with Two Languages: An Introduction to Bilingualism*, 20.

78 The section "India: An Improbable Democracy," in *On Democracy* (New Haven: Yale University Press, 1999), explains on p. 162: "India's widespread poverty combined with its acute multicultural divisions would appear to be fertile grounds for the rampant growth of antidemocratic movements . . . Why has this not happened?

227

First, every Indian is a member of a cultural minority so tiny that its members cannot possibly govern India alone. The sheer number of cultural fragments into which India is divided means that each is small, not only far short of a majority but far too small to rule over that vast and varied subcontinent. No Indian minority could rule without employing overwhelming coercion by military and police forces. But the military and police are not available for that purpose."

79 Thomas L. Friedman, "Where Freedom Reigns," *New York Times*, 14 August 2002: "The more time you spend in India the more you realize that this teeming, multiethnic, multireligious, multilingual country is one of the world's great wonders—a miracle with a message. And the message is that democracy matters . . . for all these reasons that the U.S. is so wrong not to press for democratization in the Arab and Muslim worlds. Is it an accident that India has the largest Muslim minority in the world, with plenty of economic grievances, yet not a single Indian Muslim was found in Al Qaeda?"

80 See Selma K. Sonntag, "Ideology and Policy in the Politics of the English Language in North India," in *Ideology, Politics and Language Policies: Focus on English*, ed. Thomas Ricento (Philadelphia: John Benjamins, 2000), 133–50. Nehru found English necessary for "co-opting the South to participate in the new national project," since Tamil speakers resented the hegemony of Hindustani (137). "The right's agenda of propagating

a Hindu imagining of the nation contains an elitist component; hence the right sometimes finds itself defending the elite language of English, sometimes promoting a chaste Hindi over English" (134).

81 P. Dasgupta, *The Otherness of English: India's Auntie Tongue Syndrome* (New Delhi: Sage, 1993), 99. Of course Gandhi resented English, and in his wake, Rammanohar Lohia went so far as to ally with the elite defenders of Sanskritized Hindi against using English. See Sonntag, "Ideology and Policy," 138.

82 Paul R. Brass, *Language, Religion and Politics in North India* (New York: Cambridge University Press, 1974). I am grateful to Amrita Basu for the reference. She commented that today the conflicts around Kashmir could be negotiated as territorial, but when religion is the issue, difference becomes intractable.

83 Avi Shlaim, *War and Peace in the Middle East: A Concise History* (New York: Penguin Books, 1995). "During World War I Britain and its allies destroyed the old order without considering the long-term consequences . . . But most of the new states were weak and unstable, the rulers lacked legitimacy, and the frontiers were arbitrary, illogical, and unjust, giving rise to powerful irredentist tendencies" (5, 16–17).

84 James Brooke, "Fujimori, the Exile, Repackages His Peruvian Past," *New York Times*, 11 January 2002: Arts and Leisure, 1: "What does a former president do after he has led his country for 10 years, crushed two guerrilla insurgencies, gone into exile and dodged an international warrant for his arrest?

   If you are Alberto K. Fujimori of Peru, you repackage yourself as an expert on terrorism with an eye toward a political comeback . . . Mr. Fujimori . . . has reportedly consulted leaders of the ruling Liberal Democratic Party about running for a seat in Japan's Parliament."

85 During the late 1990s, Professor Juan Carlos Godenzzi was able to establish a new bilingual educational program in Peru on a national scale by the creation of a *dirección Nacional* within the Secretary of Education in Peru. Also see Virginia Zavala's *Desencuentros con la Escritura: Escuela y comunidad en los andes peruanos* (Lima: PUCP, 2002).

86 See Werner Sollors, *Neither White nor Black but Both: Thematic Explorations of Interracial Literature* (Cambridge: Harvard University Press, 1999).

87 José Vasconcelos, *The Cosmic Race (The Mission of the Ibero American Race)*, trans. Didier T. Jaén (Los Angeles: California State University Press, 1979), 15.

88 Fernando Ortiz, *Cuban Counterpoint, Tobacco and Sugar*, trans. Harriet de Onís (Durham: Duke University Press, 1995), 98.

89 See *Rethinking Literary History*, ed. Linda Hutcheon and Mario J. Valdés (Oxford: Oxford University Press, 2002), and in the *The Oxford Comparative History of Latin American Literary Cultures*, ed. Mario J. Valdés and Djelal Kadir, 3 vols. (Oxford: Oxford University Press, 2003).

90 Ortiz, *Cuban Counterpoint, Tobacco and Sugar*, 103.

91 Cornel West, in *The Future of the Race*, by Henry Louis Gates Jr. and Cornel West (New York: Knopf, 1996).

92 See José Vasconcelos, *La Raza cósmica*, as paradigm for many projects.

93 See William E. Connolly, *Why I Am Not a Secularist* (Minneapolis: University of Minnesota Press, 2000).

94 See Wittgenstein, *PI*, §6, on the necessity for more than ostensive teaching. Training is needed as well. In addition, see also Raymond Williams, "Patterns of Life," on training that changes the structures of feeling.

95 See Leonardo Paggi, "Gramsci's General Theory of Marxism," in *Gramsci and Marxist Theory*, ed. Chantal Mouffe (London: Routledge and Kegan Paul, 1979), 113–67, 131. Also, Antonio Labriola, Gramsci's teacher, *Socialism and Philosophy*, trans. Ernest Untermann (Chicago: Charles Kerr, 1907).

229

96 Gramsci's critique of economism was not abstract; it responded to the Second International, where the working class in Germany and Italy suffered defeats. Spokespersons such as Karl Kautsky considered the proletarian revolution inevitable, and so adopted a "wait and see" attitude. See Chantal Mouffe, "Hegemony and Ideology in Gramsci," in *Gramsci and Marxist Theory*, ed. Mouffe, 168–204, esp. 172, 176.

97 See Norberto Bobbio, "Gramsci and the Conception of Civil Society," in *Gramsci and Marxist Theory*, ed. Mouffe, 21–47, 39. To Lenin's "political leadership" Gramsci adds "cultural leadership."

98 In 1918 Gramsci wrote it is "not only by economic facts that the history of a people can be documented. It is a complex and confusing task to unravel its causes and in order to do so, a deep and widely diffused study of all spiritual and practical activities is needed." *Studi Gramsciani* (Rome: Editori Riuniti, 1958), 280–81. Quoted in Bobbio, "Gramsci and the Conception of Civil Society," 33. Bobbio concludes that Gramsci inverted Marxism, favoring the determinance of superstructure (including civil society for Gramsci) over structure, and within the superstructure, claiming that ideologies are the primary moment of history and institutions secondary (35). This is a scandal for Jacques Texier, in "Gramsci, Theoretician of the Superstructures: On the Concept of Civil Society," in Mouffe, 48–79. The only difference between Marx and Gramsci is emphasis. Otherwise you could misread him to say that the working class will "turn the revolutionary party into a House of Culture!" (52). Mouffe

and Paggi underline the young Marx's emphasis on expressive culture. See their essays in Mouffe, *Gramsci and Marxist Theory*.

99   Antonio Gramsci, *Selections from the Prison Notebooks*, trans. Quintin Hoare and Geoffrey Nowell-Smith (London: Lawrence and Wishart, 1973), 437: "The historical dialectic is replaced by the law of causality and the search for regularity, normality, and uniformity. But how can one derive from this way of seeing things the overcoming, the 'overthrow' of praxis?" See Prison Notebook #4 and Mouffe, "Hegemony and Ideology," 181.

100   Gramsci, *Prison Notebooks*, 3–43. See also Nicola Badaloni, "Gramsci and the Problem of the Revolution," in Mouffe, 80–109.

101   Gramsci, *Prison Notebooks*, 328.

102   "What was previously secondary and subordinate, or even incidental, is now taken to be primary—becomes the nucleus of a new ideological and theoretical complex" (Gramsci, *Prison Notebooks*, 195).

103   See Nicola Badaloni, "Gramsci and the Problem of the Revolution," 85. "The extraneity [*estraneita*] of consciousness of the producers was affirmed historically with a suddenness which imposed on the new political groups tasks of political leadership." Later Gramsci abandoned extraneity, which seemed too pure and simple an opposition, adopting an articulation based on antithesis (88). Badaloni cites Gramsci, *Political Writings*, 36, 48. Can we speculate that this movement from strangeness to articulation is parallel to the shocking surprise of the sublime, followed by the satisfaction of recovering balance through reason?

104   Laclau and Mouffe, *Hegemony and Socialist Strategy*, 65–71.

105   Or, the "political, intellectual and moral leadership over allied groups." *Prison Notebooks*, 161.

106   Mouffe, "Hegemony and Ideology," 194, cites *Quaderni del carcere*, ed. V. Gerratana (Turin: Einaudi, 1975), vol. 2, 1084, also vol. 3, 1724; *Prison Notebooks*, 241.

107   Gramsci, *Quaderni*, vol. 3, 1729. Mouffe, "Introduction," *Gramsci and Marxist Theory*, ed. Mouffe, 10–11.

108   In Gramsci's sense of including ideological practices (schools, etc). See *Prison Notebooks*, 12, 60–61.

109   Ibid., 114.

110   Laclau and Mouffe, *Hegemony and Socialist Strategy*, 69–70.

111   Laclau, *Emancipation(s)*, 2, 8.

112   Charles R. Hale articulated these differences in a brilliant reflection written after the January 2001 "Cuzco Conference on Cultural Agency."

113   See Jesús Martín Barbero, "Desencantos de la socialidad y reencanta-

mientos de la identidad," paper delivered at NYU conference "Cultural Agency: Rhetorics of Identity, Representation, and Participation," 3 October 2001 (9).

114 Ernesto Laclau, "Universalism, Particularism, and the Question of Identity," in *The Identity in Question*, ed. John Rajchman (New York: Routledge, 1995), 107. Judith Butler cautiously agrees that universality can be a site of translation: in *Feminist Contentions: A Philosophical Exchange*, ed. Seyla Benhabib (New York: Routledge, 1995), 130: "the universal is always culturally articulated, and that the complex process of learning how to read that claim is not something any of us can do outside of the difficult process of cultural translation . . . the terms made to stand for one another are transformed in the process, and where the movement of that unanticipated transformation establishes the universal as that which is yet to be achieved and which, in order to resist domestication, may never be fully or finally achievable."

115 Lyotard, *The Differend*.

116 Judith Butler, *The Psychic Life of Power: Theories in Subjection* (Stanford: Stanford University Press, 1997).

117 For example, the congressmen involved in the English-Plus initiative, including the honorable José Serrano from New York.

118 See Benhabib, *The Claims of Culture*, for a review of the debates.

119 See Mathias Albert, David Jacobson, and Josef Lapid, eds., *Identities, Borders, Orders: Rethinking International Relations Theory* (Minneapolis: University of Minnesota Press, 2001).

120 From Hobbes on, liberalism understands that conflicting interests and values demand the institutions of government. One way to pose the dynamic is to appreciate and even promote conflicts (economics calls it competition) as stimuli to insure the vitality of those institutions. This is the twist William H. Riker puts on his defense in *Liberalism against Populism: A Confrontation between the Theory of Democracy and the Theory of Social Choice* (San Francisco: W. H. Freeman, 1982).

121 Dahl, *On Democracy*.

122 James C. Scott, *Domination and the Arts of Resistance: Hidden Transcripts* (New Haven: Yale University Press, 1990), 31: "In the past, the polite and familiar forms of the second person pronoun (*vous* and *tu* in French, respectively) were used asymmetrically in a semantic of power. The dominant class used tu when addressing commoners, servants, peasants and received back the more polite, dignified vous . . . Inasmuch as there was a determined effort by the revolutionaries in France immediately after 1789 to ban the use of vous, we can take it for granted that

this semantic of power was not a matter of popular indifference. To this day, at socialist and communist gatherings, Europeans who are strangers will use the familiar form with one another to express equality and comradeship. In ordinary usage vous is now used *reciprocally* to express not status, but lack of close acquaintance." There is no hint in Scott that the third person can continue to show respect, even affectionately, while it marks asymmetry. Even when it's used reciprocally, it can perform the necessary distancing that safeguards against intimate overlapping and the danger of *fungibility*.

123 This is the recurrent theme in all the essays collected in Albert et al., eds., *Identities, Borders, Orders*. See, for example, chapter 10, "Now and Then, Here and There: Migration and the Transformation of Identities, Border, and Orders," by Martin O. Heisler, who refers to earlier work by Jacobson (1996) and Sassen (1996).

124 Alexis de Tocqueville's *Democracy in America* (1835) is one of the inspirations for Jean Bethke Elshtain's defense of religious institutions in "Civil Society, Religion, and the Formation of Citizens," in Ravitch and Viteritti, eds., *Making Good Citizens*, 263–78. On p. 267: "According to Tocqueville, democracy requires laws, constitutions, and authoritative institutions. But it also depends on what he called 'habits of the heart' forged within the framework such institutions provided."

125 Connolly, "Refashioning the Secular," in *What's Left of Theory?*, ed. Judith Butler, John Guillory, Kendall Thomas (New York: Routledge, 2000), 163.

126 Chambers and Kymlicka, *Alternative Conceptions of Civil Society*. See especially chapter 4 by Anne Phillips, "Does Feminism Need a Conception of Civil Society?," 71–89; and chapter 5 by Simone Chambers, "A Critical Theory of Civil Society," 90–110.

127 George Steiner's version of Western history, through Pascal, Kierkegaard, Dostoevsky, for whom skepticism corrodes all value once faith fails. *In Bluebeard's Castle: Some Notes toward the Redefinition of Culture* (New Haven: Yale University Press, 1971).

128 Barbero, "Desencantos de la socialidad y reencantamientos de la identidad," 6.

129 Part of Puerto Rico's nonaggressive heroism is the refusal to give up Spanish, despite half a century of "English-only" restrictions in education and politics. And on the mainland, Latinos continue to speak both. "One in four New Yorkers is Latino, and most speak both English and Spanish." Curiously, as if the either/or language logic of U.S. assimilation cancelled the news she reports, the title of Mireya Navarro's article

is "Redefining 'Latino,' This Time in English," *New York Times*, 8 August 2003: "New York Report," 30.

130 Identity affirmation is, of course, not only a tactic for the poor and excluded, but also a reaction to them by nativists, not only in the United States. In *Relatos de la diferencia y la igualdad: Los bolivianos en Buenos Aires*, ed. Alejandro Grimson (Buenos Aires: EUDEBA: Federacíon Latinoamericana de Facultades de Comunicación Social, 1995), Martín Barbero mentions "la intolerancia con la que en Argentina o Chile son excluidos, por los propios sectores obreros, los migrantes provenientes de Bolivia o Paraguay," 10. Russell Hardin gives this useful formulation of democratic life as belonging to more than one community: "Unless a community is merely one of many to which I belong, none of which makes very great demands on my life, there cannot be genuine communities in the modern world." *One for All: The Logic of Group Conflict* (Princeton: Princeton University Press, 1995), 25.

131 Immigrants and internal migrants also watch TV and listen to the radio in particular circuits that can strain against the national networks (Quechua radio plays in Lima; Aymara in Bolivia). Barbero reports some worries about the loss of collective values in segmented audiences that no longer amount to a public which can take to the streets or even meet at the movies. But he hears heartening responses to the fragmentation from feminists who admit their fissured subjectivity, between the identity politics of gender and general goals of emancipation. A politics of recognition also sounds promising to him, but I'm not sure why, since it hopes to heal the fissures by closing the ranks of community.

132 See Stuart Hall for his widely cited formulation of cultural identity in postmodernity. See also his essays in *Critical Dialogues in Cultural Studies*, ed. David Morley and Kuan-Hsing Chen (New York: Routledge, 1996).

133 On "alternative modernities," see *Public Culture*'s Alter/Native Modernities issue 27 (1999), ed. Dilip Parameshwar Gaonkar.

134 No doubt our love of freedom cringes at the prospect of endless antagonism that breeds fear and care. (*Sorge* is the ambivalent word that captures both meanings, between the High German that Heidegger used and the middle German Yiddish where it still means *worry*.)

4 The Common Sense Sublime

1 The distinction between interest or need and disinterested pleasure defines aesthetic experience for Kant and his followers. Lyotard insists on

the difference between interested and noninterested pleasure as a problem for the sublime. Insofar as it generates respect, it locates the good. To that degree, it also loses freedom of choice and troubles aesthetic purposelessness. See Lyotard, "The Interest of the Sublime," *Of the Sublime: Presence in Question*, trans. Jeffrey S. Librett (Albany: State University of New York Press, 1993), 109–32. See also Lyotard, *Lessons on the Analytic of the Sublime*, trans. Elizabeth Rottenberg (Stanford: Stanford University Press, 1994), although the lessons begin with a deliberate confusion between sensation and reflection: "For 'logically' reflection is called judgment, but 'psychologically,' if we may be permitted the improper use of this term from a moment, it is nothing but the feeling of pleasure and displeasure" (4).

2   Grace is Friedrich Schiller's code-word for the harmony humans can achieve between opposing drives of dignity (a tragic view of life) and genius. See his *Anmut und Würde* (Grace and Dignity); also Julius Elias's introduction to Schiller's *Naïve and Sentimental Poetry; and, On the Sublime*, esp. 4–5.

3   The full passage: "Therefore the feeling of the sublime in nature is respect for our own vocation which we attribute to an object of nature by a certain subreption (substitution of a respect for the object in place of one for the idea of humanity in our own self—the subject); and this feeling renders, as it were, intuitable the supremacy of our cognitive faculties on the rational side over the greatest faculty of sensibility. The feeling of the sublime is, therefore, at once a feeling of displeasure, arising from the inadequacy of imagination in the aesthetic estimation of magnitude to attain to its estimation by reason, and a simultaneously awakened pleasure, arising from this very judgement of the inadequacy of the greatest faculty of sense being in accord with ideas of reason, so far as the effort to attain to these is for us a law. It is, in other words, for us a law (of reason) which goes to make us what we are." Immanuel Kant, *The Critique of Judgement*, 1790; translated by James Creed, §27. Hereafter referred to as *CJ*.

4   Paul Guyer, *Kant and the Claims of Taste*, 2d ed. (Cambridge: Cambridge University Press, 1997), 238.

5   Eva Schaper, "Taste, Sublimity, and Genius: The Aesthetics of Nature and Art," in *The Cambridge Companion to Kant*, ed. Paul Guyer (Cambridge: Cambridge University Press, 1992), 383.

6   Schiller, *Naïve and Sentimental Poetry; and, On the Sublime*, 201.

7   Claudio Lomnitz, "Fissures in Mexican Nationalism," *Public Culture* 9 (1996): 55–68.

8 From Dominick La Capra, public talk at SCT, 2002.

9 "For just as we taunt a man who is quite inappreciative when forming an estimate of an object of nature in which we see beauty, with want of taste, so we say of a man who remains unaffected in the presence of what we consider sublime, that he has no feeling. But we demand both taste and feeling of every man, and, granted some degree of culture, we give him credit for both. Still, we do so with this difference: that, in the case of the former, since judgement there refers the imagination merely to the understanding, as a faculty of concepts, we make the requirement as a matter of course, whereas in the case of the latter, since here the judgement refers the imagination to reason, as a faculty of ideas, we do so only under a subjective presupposition (which, however, we believe we are warranted in making), namely, that of the moral feeling in man," *CJ*, §29.

10 See Schaper, "Taste, Sublimity, and Genius," *The Cambridge Companion to Kant*, 384.

11 Kant, *Analytic of the Beautiful*, from *The Critique of Judgement*, trans. Walter Cerf (Indianapolis: Bobbs-Merrill, 1963), §§20, 47.

12 Hannah Arendt, *Lectures on Kant's Political Philosophy*, ed. Ronald Beiner (Chicago: University of Chicago Press, 1982), 38; reference to Kant, *Critique of Pure Reason*, §B884.

13 Ibid., 64, 71.

14 Ibid., 7. Kant, she quips, didn't take his political writings seriously. Even "Perpetual Peace" is ironic in tone.

15 Ibid., 4.

16 See Lyotard, *Lessons*, 51.

17 Arendt, *Lectures on Kant's Political Philosophy*, 67.

18 Ibid., 4.

19 Hannah Arendt, "The Crisis in Culture: Its Social and Its Political Significance," *Between Past and Future: Eight Exercises in Political Thought.* (New York: Viking, 1968), 219.

20 Schiller, *Naïve and Sentimental Poetry; and, On the Sublime*, 198.

21 Paul Guyer, *Kant and the Claims of Taste*, 236.

22 Kant apparently wavered on the one-step or two-step rhythm of the sublime; see Paul Guyer, *Kant and the Experience of Freedom: Essays on Aesthetics and Morality* (New York: Cambridge University Press, 1993), 204.

23 Schiller, *Naïve and Sentimental Poetry; and, On the Sublime*, 211.

24 Kirk Pillow, *Sublime Understanding: Aesthetic Reflection in Kant and Hegel* (Cambridge: MIT Press, 2000).

25 Kant, from §12 of the *Analytic*: (p. 27) "We *dwell* upon the contemplation of the beautiful because this contemplation strengthens and reproduces itself. This is analogous to, but not at all identical with, the way we dwell upon an object when some attractive element in its representation captivates attention repeatedly, whereby the mind remains, however, passive."

26 Schiller, *Naïve and Sentimental Poetry; and, On the Sublime*, 89.

27 Ibid., 91.

28 Elaine Scarry, *On Beauty and Being Just*, 5. Dispensing with the sometimes perverse charm of baroque excess, and collapsing the disturbing category of the sublime back into a preromantic category of the beautiful, Scarry purges the term of cultural overloads. Multiculturalism becomes a series of translatable equivalences, not a field of resistant differends.

29 On the ethical dangers of empathy, see my *Proceed with Caution, When Engaged by Minority Writing in the Americas*.

30 That gap is where Spivak stakes out her position in *A Critique of Postcolonial Reason: Toward a History of the Vanishing Present* (Cambridge: Harvard University Press, 1999). Like a scar, it records the anthropological moment that both interfered with philosophy and grounded it — when Kant distinguished between raw fearful humanity and cultured peoples who can appreciate awesome nature as sublime (3). *Kultur*, not *Bildung*, Spivak insists. Europeans have it; others do not. Nor do they have the potential *Anlage*, "the structure of feeling for the moral" (14). The great Western philosophers (Kant, Hegel, Marx) all needed a "native informant" to set off civilized subjects. But they also needed to foreclose that informant, lest she dare to speak intelligently and thereby derail philosophy toward anthropology. Spivak taunts Kant as his improper "mistaken" reader, the subaltern whom the critique would exclude from philosophy (9), and who dares to play informant too fully and freely.

31 David Carrasco on the growing variety of Latino religious practices and organizations.

32 Moni Basu, "Citizens of Two Worlds: Dual Citizens Fight Doubts over Loyalty," *Atlanta Journal-Constitution*, 3 July 2002, <http://www.access atlanta.com/ajc/news/atlanta_world/0702/03dual.html>: "As many as 40 million Americans — one in seven of the population — could be dual citizens. They include those born in the United States as well as immigrants who have become naturalized."

33 John Tierney, "The Big City: Polyglot City Raises a Cry for English," *New York Times*, 16 August 1999: "After leading the revolt against bilingual education in California, Ron Unz would like to see one in New York City." The most recent battleground is Boston, a center for higher education.

See also Scott Greengerber, "Bilingual Ed Law Gets a New Foe," *Boston Globe*, 31 July 2001: "The Silicon Valley millionaire whose money helped demolish bilingual education in California and Arizona is bringing his crusade to Massachusetts."

34   Ron Unz, *Wall Street Journal*, 24 May 2001: Op-Ed.

35   See David Harvey, "Cosmopolitanism and the Banality of Geographical Evils," *Public Culture* 12.2 (2000): 529–64, for a summary of many contemporary calls to pedagogical action based on (Kantian) appeals to knowledge and understanding, to which Harvey counterpoises an equally misleading (Foucauldian) taste for heterotopia and misunderstanding.

36   Antonio Cornejo Polar, "Condición migrante e intertextualidad multicultural: El caso de Arguedas," *Revista de Critica Literaria Latinoamericana* 21.42 (1995):101–09.

37   Stephen Greenblatt, "Racial Memory and Literary History," *PMLA* 116.1 (2001): 48–63.

38   Ana Celia Zentella, "José Can You See," in *Bilingual Games*, ed. Doris Sommer (New York: Palgrave, 2003).

39   Milroy and Muysken, *One Speaker, Two Languages*, 2–3. "The historical roots of European linguistics can be located in the Romanticism of von Humboldt and Grimm, and the discipline flourished with particular vigour in officially monolingual nation states with powerful standard languages. The assumption dominating linguistics continues to be one which views as the normal or unmarked case the monolingual speaker in a homogeneous speech community. Academic linguists trained in this tradition have sometimes assumed that speakers who mix languages know neither language adequately. Particularly well-known is L. Bloomfield, 1927. 'Literate and illiterate speech.' American Speech, 2: 432–9. Reprinted in D. Hymes ed. *Language in culture and society*. (New York: Harper and Row, 1964) 391–6."

"Noam Chomsky's meta-theoretical focus on the ideal native speaker" promotes this tradition; and even William Labov limited his research on nonstandard English to native-born New Yorkers (3). Most research, after Wallace E. Lambert's *Language, Psychology, and Culture* (Stanford: Stanford University Press, 1972), finds more cognitive advantages than disadvantages in bilingualism.

40   Don Feder, *Boston Herald*, 2 May 2001.

41   See Mari J. Matsuda, "Voices of America." She accounts for cases of cultural intolerance as the obstacle to justice despite perfectly reasonable laws, and celebrates cultural difference beyond the tolerance that liberals

like Richard Rorty defend. Difference is a value in itself, a negativity that requires toleration and keeps democratic process lively.

42   Greg Toppo, "House Bill to Limit Bilingual Education," Associated Press, 19 May 2001. "Schools could teach non-English-speaking students in their native tongue for only three years before moving them into regular classrooms under legislation being considered by the House. The measure closely resembles a proposal in President Bush's education plan."

43   Jacques Steinberg, *New York Times*, 20 August 2000.

44   Terry Eagleton, "Postcolonialism: The Case of Ireland," 128.

45   Sander L. Gilman asks these questions too in "Learning a Foreign Language in a Monolingual World," *PMLA* 115.5 (2000): 1032–40.

46   Patricia Gándara, State Education Commission's recommendation to the State of California, 8 May 2002. In a note of 21 May 2002 she wrote to me: "Recommendation 12.4 . . . got to the language and changed it before it got to type!! We just discovered this and I have been assured that the following language, which I provided and which is what the committee had agreed to, is being inserted in the next draft: 'The State should ensure that all schools provide all students with curriculum and coursework that include the knowledge, skills, and experiences that enable them to attain mastery of oral and written expression AND COMPREHENSION OF AT LEAST TWO LANGUAGES, AND THAT ONE OF THESE BE English. A foundation for mastery of a second language SHOULD BE LAID by the end of elementary school, and STUDENTS SHOULD BE PROVIDED THE OPPORTUNITY TO ATTAIN oral proficiency and full literacy in both English and at least one other language by the end of secondary school.' (The caps represent the newly inserted words to change 12.4 to conform with the committee's intent.)"

47   Jim Boulet Jr., *National Review*, 7 May 2001.

48   Martin Barbero, "Desencantos de la socialidad y reencantamientos de la identidad."

49   Iain Chambers also proposes a recovery of baroque taste, in *Border Dialogues, Journeys in Postmodernity* (New York: Routledge, 1990). See especially chapter 1, "The Double Solution," 1–13.

50   As cited in Neil Herz, *The End of the Line: Essays on Psychoanalysis and the Sublime* (New York: Columbia University Press, 1985), 49.

51   Herz, *The End of the Line*, 46.

52   Examples appear every day. Here is today's: "Divided by a Call for a Common Language: As Immigration Rises, a Wisconsin County Makes English Official" (Jodi Wilgoren, *New York Times*, 19 July 2002: A10). Thanks to Bonnie Wasserman for bringing it to my attention.

53   Immanuel Kant, "An Answer to the Question: What Is Enlightenment?"

54   See Pheng Cheah and Bruce Robbins, eds., *Cosmopolitics: Thinking and Feeling Beyond the Nation* (Minneapolis: University of Minnesota Press, 1998).

55   See Guyer, *Kant and the Experience of Freedom*.

56   See John Brenkman's cagey reading of Kant "against the grain of his own search for intrinsic mental structures": "Extreme Criticism," in *What's Left of Theory?* ed. Butler et al., 114–36.

57   I am grateful to Paola Gambarota, and to her excellent essay, presented at MLA, in 2000, "Vico, the Syntax of Passions": "The modern controversy about these questions goes back to the Port-Royal Grammar of 1660 and lasts then throughout the first half of the 18th century. It engages philosophers such as Diderot, Condillac, Du Marsais, Cesarotti, Leopardi, Herder and culminates in two positions mirroring each other. In the articles *Langage* and *Inversion*, the *Encyclopedie* (1765) condemns the use of inversions as 'contre nature' but J. G. Herder reclaims 'Inversionen' as quintessential to 'nature' and in particular to the 'nature' of the German language and people. *Inversionen* express an original and uniquely German individuality (*Fragmenten ueber die neuere deutsche Literatur* (probably written around 1764)" (2).

58   Hazard Adams dates Longinus in the first century A.D. in *Critical Theory since Plato*, ed. Hazard Adams (New York: Harcourt Brace Jovanovich, 1971).

59   Longinus, *On the Sublime*, *Critical Theory since Plato*, 90.

60   Ibid., 89.

61   Herz, *The End of the Line*, 6–7.

62   On the Longinian tradition in England, including Burke, David Hume, Lord Kames, Joseph Priestly, and others, see Samuel Holt Monk, *The Sublime: A Study of Critical Theories in Eighteenth-Century England* (Ann Arbor: University of Michigan Press, 1960).

63   See Andrew Ashfield and Peter de Bolla, *The Sublime: A Reader in British Eighteenth-Century Aesthetic Theory* (Cambridge: Cambridge University Press, 1996). Also *Hybridity and Postcolonialism: Twentieth-Century Indian Literature*, ed. Monika Fludernik (Tübingen: Stauffenburg, 1998); Sara Suleri's *The Rhetoric of English India* (Chicago: University of Chicago Press, 1992); and Frances Ferguson, "The Sublime of Edmund Burke, or the Bathos of Experience," *Glyph* 8 (1981): 62–78.

64   See chapter 3 of Limon's *Stand-Up Comedy in Theory*, "Analytic of the Ridiculous: Mike Nichols and Elaine May," 50–67, esp. 51. Reference to Kant's *Observations on the Feeling of the Beautiful and Sublime*, trans.

239

John T. Goldthwait (Berkeley: University of California Press, 1965), 83. In a less technical, stand-up tone, Stanley Myron Handelman writes "From the Sublime to the Ridiculous," *Handbook of Humor Research*, vol. 2, ed. Paul E. McGhee and Jeffrey H. Goldstein (New York: Springer-Verlag, 1983), 23–31.

65   Limon, *Stand-Up Comedy in Theory*, 4.

66   Clement Greenberg, "The Jewishness of Franz Kafka: Some Sources of His Particular Vision," *The Collected Essays and Criticism*, ed. John O'Brian, vol. 3: *Affirmations and Refusals, 1950–1956* (Chicago: University of Chicago Press, 1986), 202–9. The essay was originally published in the April 1955 issue of *Commentary*.

67   David Suchoff's essay "Kafka's Canon: Hebrew and Yiddish in *The Trial* and *Amerika*" in *Bilingual Games*, ed. Doris Sommer (New York: Palgrave, 2003).

68   Clement Greenberg, "The Jewish Joke: Review of *Royte Pomerantzen*, edited by Imanuel Olsvanger," *The Collected Essays and Criticism*, vol. 1: *Perceptions and Judgements, 1938–1944*, 184. The essay was originally published in the December 1947 issue of *Commentary*.

69   Limon, "Inrage: A Lenny Bruce Joke and the Topography of Stand-Up," *Stand-Up Comedy in Theory*, 11–27.

70   Even Kant accounted for some cultural differences, for example in the evaluation of physical beauty. See Kant, *CJ*, §17.

71   See, for example, Schiller's *Naïve and Sentimental Poetry*, 96.

72   Ibid., 212. Also see 206: "Freedom makes him a citizen and co-regent of a higher system in which it is incomparably more honorable to occcupy the lowest rank than to lead the procession of the physical order."

73   Friedrich Schiller, *On the Aesthetic Education of Man*, ed. and trans. Elizabeth M. Wilkinson and L. A. Willoughby (Oxford: Oxford University Press, 1967), Ninth Letter, points 1, 2, and 3, p. 55.

74   Wilkinson and Willoughby "Introduction," xi–cxcvi, xxv, Schiller, *On the Aesthetic Education of Man*.

75   See the introduction to Schiller's *Naïve and Sentimental Poetry* by Julius A. Elias, 1–79.

76   Ibid., 98.

77   Wilkinson and Willoughby, "Introduction," xxiv.

78   Ibid., xxv.

79   Schiller, *Aesthetic Education*, Fourteenth Letter, points 3, 4, and 5, p. 97.

80   Wilkinson and Willoughby, "Introduction," xxxiii.

81   From a conversation with Paul Guyer, 21 February 2002.

82   See "Kant and Schiller" from Paul de Man's *Aesthetic Ideology*, ed.

Andrzej Warminski (Minneapolis: University of Minnesota Press, 1996), 129–62.

83 Wilkinson and Willoughby, "Introduction," xxix.

84 De Man, *Aesthetic Ideology*, 154. Aside from the elitism, the reference is also unfair. Quoting from the introduction by Schiller's translators and editors, de Man blames Schiller for Goebbels's program, but he cuts the editors short. They had continued the passage about the several ironies of reception with this example: before the Nazis used him, Schiller was condemned by both left and right as essentially apolitical. See Wilkinson and Willoughby, "Introduction," cxliii.

85 Wilkinson and Willoughby, "Introduction," ci.

86 Clark, *The Revenge of the Aesthetic*, 5–6: "The rhetoric of argument at this level is usually that of the jeremiad, and the professed stakes are nothing less than a defense of human rights or of the fate of civilization as we know it." Also see John M. Ellis, *Literature Lost*; Bloom, *The Closing of the American Mind*; and D'Souza, *Illiberal Education*.

87 This is the theme of several essays in Albert et al., *Identities, Borders, Orders: Rethinking International Relations Theory*.

88 Schiller, *Aesthetic Education*, Eighth Letter, point 5, p. 51. See also the Seventh Letter, point 1, where he says that political reform is untimely, because both the State and our current level of humanity are the problem (45).

89 Simone Chambers, "A Critical Theory of Civil Society," *Alternative Conceptions of Civil Society*, 90–110, 102.

90 De Man, *Aesthetic Ideology*, 141.

5 Let's Play Games

1 Warren Goldfarb was kind enough to corroborate this impression. At its most flexible stretch, through Quine, philosophy considers the residue of opacity of one language for another. A measure of failure is constitutive of translation. See one of W. V. Quine's last books, *Theories and Things* (Cambridge: Harvard University Press, 1981), 54. "I have been concerned in all these remarks with monoglot semantics, not polyglot; not translation. Criteria are harder to come by in the polyglot domain."

2 Eugene Gendlin has rescued me from at least some boorish mistakes, during a conversation on 31 August 2002. The errors that may remain show my continuing dependence on patient teachers.

3 The edition I cite of the *Philosophical Investigation* is the one translated by G. E. Anscombe (Oxford: Blackwell, 1995). From here onward, and if

not indicated otherwise, the bibliographical reference of this text refers to the section of it and not to a specific page number (*PI*, number of section).

4 Eugene Gendlin's letter to me, 19 August 1998: "I recall my teacher saying, 'Don't first say the German word to yourself and then translate it. Let the English word go directly with the thing.' I made a great discovery! *I knew everything without words!* I could attach either language words not just to objects, but to anything I knew, or wanted to say. Doesn't every bilingual person notice this? This means we exist daily and ordinarily in the space into which poets listen for new sayings, the space where we are human not before but beyond (each) culture. It's not an accident that foreigners often sound poetic. They have to speak from the before-phrased situation."

I am generally grateful for his lessons on Wittgenstein, especially the appreciation of a world that exists before words and comes into focus in the space between one language and another. I also thank Peter Elbow for reminding me of Gendlin's attention to this "felt sense." See Eugene T. Gendlin, "What Happens When Wittgenstein Asks 'What Happens When'?" *Philosophical Forum* 28.3 (spring 1997). E. T. Gendlin, *Experiencing and the Creation of Meaning: A Philosophical and Psychological Approach to the Subjective* (Evanston: Northwestern University Press, 1997), xi–xxiii. Also, Gendlin, "Thinking beyond Patterns: Body, Language and Situations," in B. den Ouden and M. Moen, eds., *The Presence of Feeling in Thought* (New York: Peter Lang, 1991), 25–151.

5 Professor Warren Goldfarb lecture, class handout (22 October 2001): "Wittgenstein's grammatical investigation is meant to accomplish two things: first, to diagnose what leads us to think of understanding as a hidden state or process (arising from dissatisfaction with variegation); and second, to lead us to see how poor that model is. To give the diagnosis some force, we must see what motivates the idea that there must be the thing ascribed. Part of the motivation is unhappiness with the non-uniform, unsharp character of our ascriptions of understanding. We seem *driven* to talk of something underlying correct use. We make the lack of uniformity accidental, arising from merely practical features. The feeling is that there must be some final item grounding the ascription, which is what the ascription ascribes; and that without such an item the ascriptions are arbitrary. That is what the Interlocutor expresses in talk of the source of the correct use. The question is: What goes lacking if we do not have this final item? It is hard to pin down. There is a feeling that at any particular point, there is always some conceivable thing that is still

missing; so that there is always more in the understanding than what we already had to go on."

6   I am grateful to Professors Hilary Putnam and Stanley Cavell for their Wittgenstein seminar, spring 1996, Harvard University, particularly here for Putnam's focus on Wittgenstein's tolerance for indefinition.

7   Wittgenstein disagreed with Bertrand Russell's distinction in *The Philosophy of Logical Atomism* between logical particulars (that give proper nouns meaning) and the "grammatically proper nouns" that often refer to people, which cannot be understood out of context. For Wittgenstein, context determines the meaning-use of words in general (see *PI*, §§79, 40–42). See also chapter 11 of Suter's *Interpreting Wittgenstein*.

8   See Kant's *Critique of Pure Reason*, §B823, also quoted in Arendt, *Lectures on Kant*, 35.

9   A trainer for this posture was probably Fritz Mauthner, a Viennese journalist who wrote philosophy too. His *Dictionary of Philosophy* demonstrates that metaphysics is based on an illicit assertion that there are "objects" which correspond to properties that we perceive. Also, the contingent nature of senses makes eternal Truth impossible. But Wittgenstein would counter that despite skepticism, "representational" language was possible. See Allan Janik and Stephen Edelston Toulmin, *Wittgenstein's Vienna* (New York: Simon and Schuster, 1973), 179.

10   Alice Crary's conclusion, after counterpoising political interpretations of Wittgenstein. Alice Crary, "Wittgenstein's Philosophy in Relation to Political Thought," *The New Wittgenstein*, ed. Alice Marguerite Crary and Rupert J. Read (New York: Routledge, 2000), 118–45. Most of the essay takes issue with Richard Rorty for collapsing contingent realism back into metaphysics and thereby missing, Crary says, the politically promising feature of intrinsic judgment.

11   Unwilling to free philosophy from the responsibility they assign it, Habermas and Lyotard, for all their differences, take issue with Wittgenstein's "positivism." Habermas, in *The Philosophical Discourse*, writes, "It is not habitual linguistic practice that determines just what meaning is attributed to a text or an utterance. Rather, language games only work because they presuppose idealizations that transcend any particular language game; as a necessary condition of possibility reaching understanding, these idealizations give rise to the perspective of an agreement that is open to criticism on the basis of validity claims" (198). And Lyotard, in *The Differend*, #122, 76, calls Wittgenstein's exclusive attention to "use" "anthropological empiricism."

12   Janik and Toulmin, *Wittgenstein's Vienna*, 244.

13   Crary and Read, *The New Wittgenstein*, 133, and Wittgenstein, *PI*, §§562–64.

14   Romaine, *Bilingualism*, 114–15.

15   " 'But still, it isn't a game, if there is some *vagueness in the rules*'.—But *does* this prevent its being a game?—'Perhaps you'll call it a game, but at any rate it certainly isn't a perfect game.' This means: it has impurities, and what I am interested in at present is the pure article.—But I want to say: we misunderstand the role of the ideal in our language. That is to say: we too should call it a game, only we are dazzled by the ideal and therefore fail to see the actual use of the word 'game' clearly" (*PI*, §100).

16   "And I have admitted that the foreigner will probably pronounce a sentence differently if he conceives it differently; but what we call his wrong conception need not lie in anything that accompanies the utterance of the command" (*PI*, §20).

17   Crary and Read, *The New Wittgenstein*, 140–41, my emphasis.

18   Goldfarb, class lecture notes: he is going directly at a traditional picture that you have a sentence that has a meaning and that you use in certain ways (as a command, question, assertion, etc.). Wittgenstein is trying to urge, instead, the "spread effect": surroundings enter into the determination of how a sentence is meant—not (merely) grammatical forms or mental acts. This is an attack on a picture of language according to which a sentence's job is to present a possible situation: a "proposition-radical," as Wittgenstein sometimes calls it.

19   Wittgenstein, *Remarks on the Foundations of Mathematics*, VI §31, as quoted in Crary and Read, *The New Wittgenstein*, 130.

20   Rush Rhees, lecture note in Ludwig Wittgenstein, *Lectures and Conversations on Aesthetics, Psychology and Religious Belief*, ed. Cyril Barrett (Oxford: Blackwell, 1966), 41.

21   Ibid., 42–44.

22   The extended image belongs to Henry Staten, *Wittgenstein and Derrida* (Lincoln: University of Nebraska Press, 1984), 107: "Now in this essay I have woven together portions of Wittgenstein's text and portions of that of Derrida. Most of the words have been Wittgenstein's, but I have been continually guided by the patterns of Derrida's text. I have tried to show how such a weaving is done, how one must feel for the material of the fibers and threads. When doing philosophy, Wittgenstein writes, we feel as though we are pursuing the most extreme subtleties, as though we were trying to repair a torn spider's web (*Spinnenetz*) with our fingers. The web of language is not subtle beyond experience, but it is as subtle as experience. And we are not called upon to repair it, but only to continue to weave it—which always means to reweave it."

23   Language troubles philosophy when it idles, says Wittgenstein, that is, when it appears as a whole, with myriad potentials (*PI*, §132.) For different evaluations of the parallels between Wittgenstein and Saussure, see Staten, *Wittgenstein and Derrida*, 79; Roy Harris's *Language, Saussure, and Wittgenstein: How to Play Games with Words* (New York: Routledge, 1988); and Suter, *Interpreting Wittgenstein*.

24   Milroy and Muysken, "Introduction," *One Speaker, Two Languages*: "Taken together, the developments set out above lead to a widespread bilingualism as a pervasive phenomenon in the modern world, which seems set to increase in the future. European linguistics (and indeed Western linguistics generally) has been slow to catch up with this contemporary situation" (2).

25   Staten, *Wittgenstein and Derrida*, 106.

26   Wittgenstein, *Wiener Ausgabe* (Vienna: Springer, 1993).

27   Janik and Toulmin, "Wittgenstein the Man, and His Second Thoughts," *Wittgenstein's Vienna*, 202–38.

28   Staten brings out the slapstick quality of this primal scene of philosophy, *Wittgenstein and Derrida*, 66–67.

29   "Augustine describes the learning of human language as if the child came into a strange country and did not understand the language of the country; that is, as if it already had a language, only not this one" (*PI*, §32).

30   "Both Russell's 'individuals' and my 'objects' (*Tractatus Logico-Philosophicus*) were such primary elements" (*PI*, §46).

31   Janik and Toulmin, *Wittgenstein's Vienna*, 217.

32   Ibid., 230.

33   Suzanne Oboler calls them strategically ambivalent; that is, ironic, subtle. See her *Ethnic Labels, Latino Lives: Identity and the Politics of (Re)Presentation in the United States* (Minneapolis: University of Minnessota Press, 1995). For examples, see 11–12, 93–98, 145–50, 161–62.

34   Consider the complicated California case of telemarketing employees, hired for their Mexican American bilingualism and repeatedly censured for gossiping about Anglo coworkers in Spanish. Management's exasperated response was to forbid casual conversation in Spanish. The workers brought suit and the boss relocated. National Public Radio report of 19 February 1998. See also Mar-Molinero's summaries of related cases in part 2 of her *Politics of Language*.

35   Nevertheless, what Wallace Lambert coined "subtractive bilingualism," to describe French Canadian immigrant children, prevails for recent immigrant children generally. They are apparently losing their native languages more quickly than did earlier groups. "The only difference is that the process appears to be taking place much more rapidly today. Few

among us realize what is really happening. Quite the contrary. Over the past several years, there has been an increasing concern among educators, policymakers, and members of the public that the new immigrants are not assimilating fast enough." Quoted in Lily Wong Fillmore, "When Learning a Second Language Means Losing the First," *Early Childhood Research Quarterly* 6 (1991): 324.

36 "One particular advantage that bilingual children have is in the area of metalinguistic awareness—the ability to analyze the form as well as the content of language, knowledge of how to talk about language, and control over nonliteral uses of language, like puns, irony, and figures of speech. Certain kinds of metalinguistic skills—such as recognizing that words have no intrinsic connection to the objects they refer to—typically emerge several years earlier in bilingual than in monolingual children. Nor is it surprising that the process of learning a second language or of switching back and forth between two languages would heighten one's likelihood of becoming aware of the formal aspects of the linguistic system and one's understanding of the arbitrariness of the linguistic code." Catherine Snow, "Rationales for Native Language Instruction: Evidence from Research," in *Bilingual Education: Issues and Strategies*, ed. Amado M. Padilla, Halford H. Fairchild, and Concepción M. Valadez (Newbury Park, Cal.: Sage, 1990), 65.

37 Henry A. Giroux also argues against the "politics of clarity . . . becomes a code word for an approach to writing that is profoundly Eurocentric in both context and content." See his "Language, Power, and Clarity, or Does Plain Prose Cheat?," in *Living Dangerously: Multiculturalism and the Politics of Difference*, Counterpoints: Studies in the Postmodern Theory of Education (New York: Peter Lang, 1993), 166. Della Pollock glosses his argument against flattening the relationship between language and audience, dismissing subaltern claims on language use: "Claims for such writing assume a correspondence theory of language that effaces questions of voice, style and difference." See "Performing Writing," in *The Ends of Performance*, ed. Peggy Phelan and Jill Lane (New York: New York University Press, 1998), 73–103.

38 Edouard Glissant, *Le discours antillais* (Paris: Editions du Seuil, 1981), 11. "Nous réclamons le droit à l'opacité."

39 On the creativity of error, see George Lipsitz, " 'It's All Wrong, but It's All Right': Creative Misunderstandings in Intercultural Communication," in *Mapping Multiculturalism*, ed. Avery F. Gordon and Chirstopher Newfield (Minneapolis: University of Minnesota Press, 1996), 403–12.

40 Néstor García Canclini develops similar observations in everyday arti-

sanal productions among working-class and rural populations in Mexico. See *Hybrid Cultures*.

41 This is a commonplace of political philosophy. See John Rawls, "Justice as Fairness: Political Not Metaphysical," *Philosophy and Public Affairs* 14 (1985): 223–51. "Liberalism as a political doctrine supposes that there are many conflicting and incommensurable conceptions of the good, each compatible with the full rationality of human persons" (248); Dahl, *Dilemmas of Pluralist Democracy*; and Milton Fisk, "Introduction: The Problem of Justice," *Justice*, 1–8. "There has to be at least a conflict based on an actual lack of homogeneity for what is distinctive about justice to become relevant" (1).

42 In Crary's refocusing of his imaginative work of interpretation, *The New Wittgenstein*, 141.

43 Eric Stener calls this "signification trauma." See Honig, *Democracy and the Foreigner*.

44 Ibid., 71.

45 I thank Werner Sollors for pointing out helpful recent explorations of the philosophical origins of the term *double consciousness* and of its meanings in contemporary America. See Shamoon Zamir, *Dark Voices: W. E. B. Du Bois and American Thought, 1888–1903* (Chicago: University of Chicago Press, 1995); Gerald Early, ed., *Lure and Loathing: Essays on Race, Identity, and the Ambivalence of Assimilation* (New York: Allen Lane, Penguin, 1993); and *W. E. B. Du Bois: Of Cultural and Racial Identity*, a special issue of the *Massachusetts Review* 35.2 (1994), ed. Robert Gooding-Williams.

46 From Ralph Waldo Emerson's "Fate," originally published in *The Conduct of Life* (1860) (though a version did appear in 1851, when it was delivered as a lecture). Quoted here from *The Norton Anthology of American Literature*, ed. Ronald Gottesman (New York: Norton, 1979), 808.

47 Ibid., 816.

48 Ibid., 801. No wonder Emerson welcomed Whitman, who dared to speak for the master and for the slave, for the hunter and the hunted, husband and the wife. No wonder both live on in Jorge Luis Borges's version of Schopenhauerean fate, "La nadería de la personalidad," which expounds the emptiness of personal identities. They are mere masks that cover the "nothingness" of roles such as victim or murderer. Borges, like most of Whitman's fans, loved the jumbled catalogues that joined unlikely neighbors and flattened dramatic differences into more of the same familiar rhythm during the drone of long lists. (Emerson's "Fate" shows some of the same love of lists, the lushness of more than enough ex-

amples that train us in familiar expectations as much as they convince readers through argument.) The down-to-earth equality of Whitman's *Leaves* is also worth mentioning, with Emerson's bias toward material history in mind. Not even Nietzsche promised as much relief from dualism as did Whitman, say Deleuze and Guattari, because he respatialized our political imagination from thinking in terms of circles, or poles, or dialectical spirals, to thinking in terms of the rhizome. The figure is "an underground stem" that proliferates laterally without any center or goal, so that each growth is equal to and connects with all others. This radically American image allegedly sets the model for the "successive lateral shoots" that can loosen Europe's fixation on deep roots. (They might also have gone back to Jefferson's ideally repeatable Cartesian plots of land, and to Emerson's repeatable self-reliant citizen.) The problem with *proliferation* (as opposed to the heterogeneous game of shoots and ladders) is that it assumes a model that is endlessly repeated. Who establishes that representative, the commonest and cheapest, man? And how can endless repetition accommodate the different styles, interests, desires that Deleuze and Guattari defend?

49   Gilman, *Jewish Self-Hatred.*

50   Watkins, *On the Real Side*, 38.

51   The sections between 140 and 150 of the *Philosophical Investigations* are dedicated to what learning and teaching mean. The answer is more training than explaining. See also *PI*, §206, about an explorer training in a new language.

52   See Marianne Constable, *The Law of the Other: The Mixed Jury and Changing Conceptions of Citizenship, Law, and Knowledge* (Chicago: University of Chicago Press, 1994).

53   Jean-François Lyotard, "The Other's Rights," in *On Human Rights: The Oxford Amnesty Lectures*, ed. Stephen Shute and S. L. Hurley (New York: Basic Books, 1993), 139.

54   See Maria Rosa Menocal, *Shards of Love: Exile and the Origins of the Lyric* (Durham: Duke University Press, 1994).

55   Mary Antin, *The Promised Land* (New York: Penguin, 1997), 1.

56   See Doris Sommer, "Our AmeRíca," in *Field Work: Sites in Literary and Cultural Studies*, ed. Marjorie Garber, Rebecca L. Walkowitz, and Paul B. Franklin (New York: Routledge, 1996), 77–86.

57   Jorge Luis Borges, "Death and the Compass," *Labyrinths, Selected Stories and Other Writings*, (New York: New Directions, 1962), 77–78.

58   Pierre Bourdieu, *The Rules of Art: Genesis and Structure of the Literary Field*, trans. Susan Emanuel (Stanford: Stanford University Press, 1996), 21.

248

59 See Ana Maria Amar Sanchez, *Juegos de seduccion y traición* (Rosario: Beatriz Viterbo Editores, 2000).

60 Alexander Stille, "Scholars Are Quietly Offering New Theories of the Koran," *New York Times*, 2 March 2002: A1: "A handful of experts have been quietly investigating the origins of the Koran, offering radically new theories about the text's meaning and the rise of Islam. Christoph Luxenberg, a scholar of ancient Semitic languages in Germany, argues that the Koran has been misread and mistranslated for centuries. His work, based on the earliest copies of the Koran, maintains that parts of Islam's holy book are derived from pre-existing Christian Aramaic texts that were misinterpreted by later Islamic scholars who prepared the editions of the Koran commonly read today.

So, for example, the virgins who are supposedly awaiting good Islamic martyrs as their reward in paradise are in reality "white raisins" of crystal clarity rather than fair maidens." Thanks to Peter Kahn for this reference.

61 I thank Diana Sorensen for reminding me about bifurcated attitudes about foreignness in Argentina.

62 Guillermo Cabrera Infante, *Tres tristes tigres*, 4th ed. (Barcelona: Seix Barral, 1967), 15.

63 Crary's formulation of Wittgenstein, *The New Wittgenstein*, 140.

64 Ahora con todo lo que se habla de Borges cuando recordamos 100 años de su nacimiento encontré esta apreciación del maestro: La entrevista es Ramón Chao e Ignacio Ramonet, fue publicada en la revista *Triunfo* y *Le Monde* y reproducida por el Magazín dominical de *El Espectador*, el 7 de agosto de 1994.

PREGUNTA: ¿Usted piensa que efectivamente el porvenir de América Latina es constituir un solo país?

RESPUESTA: Diría que el porvenir del mundo está en un solo país. Después podríamos unirnos con la otra América, hablar en dos idiomas: castellano e inglés. El ruso es muy difícil. El chino hablado por millones de millones de hombres es tan difícil, que chinos de diversas regiones sólo pueden entenderse por escrito. Creo que si en las escuelas primarias se enseñaran los dos idiomas tendríamos una humanidad bilingüe. El castellano y el inglés son idiomas fáciles porque la gran dificultad del inglés está en la ortografía. Fuera de ello es un idioma sencillo. No hay géneros gramaticales, usted tiene the, en cambio en español tenemos él, la, los, las y en alemán es peor todavía, porque hay tres géneros. El español es de más fácil pronunciación. Me parece un idioma de vocales abiertas. El inglés es más difícil porque casi no se oyen las vocales, es un idioma de consonantes.

Es una lástima porque hasta el siglo XVII el inglés fue un idioma vocal.

65 Enrichment is what Bill Buford hastily celebrated when he praised contemporary Indian authors for refreshing the English language. They responded, however, that English enrichment was neither the goal nor the most significant effect of their writing. Bill Buford, "Declarations of Independence: Why are There Suddenly So Many Indian Novelists?" *New Yorker* 73.17 (1997): 6–11. See responses in same issue by Salman Rushdie, G. V. Desani, Abraham Verghese, and Amit Chaudhuri. I thank Greta Slobin for this reference.

Index

253

254

Doris Sommer is a Professor of Romance Languages and
Literature and the Director of Graduate Studies in Spanish
at Harvard University.

Library of Congress Cataloging-in-Publication Data
Sommer, Doris
Bilingual aesthetics : a new sentimental education /
Doris Sommer.
p. cm. — (Public planet)
Includes index.
ISBN 0-8223-3332-5 (alk. paper) —
ISBN 0-8223-3344-9 (pbk. : alk. paper)
1. Bilingualism—Social aspects.   2. Aesthetics.   I. Title.
II. Public planet books
P115.45.s66 2004   306.44'6—dc22   2003022713